WHY COMMUNISM FAILED

JASPER BECKER

Why Communism Failed

HURST & COMPANY, LONDON

First published in the United Kingdom in 2022 by
C. Hurst & Co. (Publishers) Ltd.,
New Wing, Somerset House, Strand, London, WC2R 1LA

Distributed in the United States, Canada and Latin America by
Oxford University Press, 198 Madison Avenue,
New York, NY 10016, United States of America.

A Cataloguing-in-Publication data record for this book
is available from the British Library.

ISBN: 9781787388062

www.hurstpublishers.com

Printed in Great Britain by Bell and Bain Ltd, Glasgow

CONTENTS

INTRODUCTION

On Christmas Day, 1991, the hammer and sickle flag was finally lowered from a cupola on the Kremlin. Mikhail Gorbachev, the last Soviet leader, gave a farewell address on television announcing the end of the Soviet Union. The red, white and blue flag of Russia went up on the roof, and soon after Gorbachev left the building. After seventy-four years, the Soviet Union was no longer a state.

Barely a shot had been fired. The Soviet military was undefeated. When the Berlin Wall fell in 1989, the Soviet Union still commanded 59,000 tanks and 30,000 nuclear warheads—the largest force in the world. It faced virtually no organized internal opposition.[1]

The USSR vanished from the maps because its own rulers had tired of a project that they concluded was an irredeemable failure. Yet at the time, nearly everyone outside the USSR, including the lavishly funded Central Intelligence Agency (CIA), still believed it was destined to remain a permanent part of the world order.

The CIA had been founded after the Second World War explicitly to study the Soviet Union. By 1989, it employed 30,000 people and had a vast budget, but its analysts were caught completely by surprise. Daniel Moynihan, the US senator who had long served on the Senate Select Intelligence Committee, declared that this was the costliest intelligence-gathering effort in history—and it had failed. Moynihan indignantly—and unsuccessfully—called for the CIA to be abolished because it had proved so utterly useless. 'For a quarter century,' he declared, 'the C.I.A. has been repeatedly wrong

1

about the major political and economic questions entrusted to its analysis…' For thirty years, according to Moynihan, 'the intelligence community systematically misinformed successive Presidents as to the size and growth of the Soviet economy'. It had portrayed the USSR 'as a maturing industrial society with a faster growth rate than the United States', a country 'destined, if the growth rates held, to surpass us in time, and in the interval well able to sustain its domestic military and its foreign adventures'. The Soviet economy, he said, was thought to be roughly 'three times as large as it turned out to be'. That 'was the conventional wisdom among economists', but the fact that economists had taken that view was scarcely an excuse, since 'the C.I.A. was meant to do better'.[2] Until the last moment, leading Western economists wrote textbooks claiming that the Soviet Union was operating a planned economic system that was inherently superior to anything in the West. The USSR was going to overtake the United States in fifteen years.

America's NATO allies were equally mistaken. During the Cold War, they relied almost entirely on the judgement of the CIA and other American intelligence agencies because no other Western power could match the resources that America threw into its intelligence gathering.

The breadth of CIA ignorance about many communist countries was sometimes truly astonishing. When Henry Kissinger set out on the secret negotiations that led to President Nixon's surprise visit to China in 1972, Chairman Mao was seriously ill, suffering from Parkinson's disease, and his economic policies had caused over 30 million deaths by starvation and split the ruling Party. Yet CIA analysts doubted that a famine had taken place. They described a successful economy with double-digit industrial growth rates.

In fact, the Chinese communists had struggled to institute a working planned economy. Under Chairman Mao Zedong, they only ever carried out one five-year plan—no plans were followed either during the Great Leap Forward or during the Cultural Revolution. They didn't gather any meaningful statistics between 1958 and 1980,[3] so nobody, even those in the Chinese Politburo, could know how big the population was, or their health or their education level, or how much grain was harvested or how much steel was forged. Yet the

Americans still believed that Mao was negotiating from a position of strength. Within a few years, Mao was dead and embalmed, and his successors quickly overturned his disastrous policies. The Chinese Communist Party is still very much in power but only by abandoning its founding ideology.

The CIA applied the same methodology it used for the Soviet Union to study East Germany. Shortly before the German Democratic Republic (GDR) disappeared as a state, the CIA claimed it was doing better than West Germany. In the mid-1980s, the CIA thought that the GDR's per capita Gross National Product (GNP) was as large, if not larger, than that of West Germany. The same insight was applied to the Korean Peninsula. For many years, it believed that North Korea would overtake South Korea. These misconceptions had huge strategic consequences. The Cold War is a misnomer—it may have been cold in the European theatre, but large-scale wars were fought in Korea, Vietnam, Cambodia and elsewhere in Asia, and there were numerous insurgencies and civil wars across Africa, the Middle East and Latin America. From 1917 onwards, communist revolutions and wars killed over 100 million people across the world. Vast numbers fled their homes or were enslaved in labour camps.

By the mid-1970s, communist parties ruled over thirty countries. Even where they did not win power, communist parties played a major role. The communist movement seemed unstoppable. Even in Western Europe, large and influential communist parties seemed poised to win power through the ballot box. Communism's relentless march across the world—and the single-minded fanaticism of its followers, the secrecy, cruelty and ruthlessness of its leaders—posed a terrifying threat.

Many countries that did not formally declare themselves communist nevertheless copied the Soviet model by building a one-party state, a powerful military and a huge domestic system of surveillance and repression, all under a revered absolute ruler. These one-party states operated centrally planned economies with state controls over prices and wages. They all tended towards autarky, and what foreign trade there was, was often conducted on a state-to-state basis, usually in the form of barter deals.

Yet suddenly, almost miraculously, the threat evaporated. Not just across the Soviet Union and Eastern Europe but everywhere. Its ideas lost their popular appeal, and so countries' communist parties often shrank to just small fringe groups. Only a handful of countries like North Korea and Cuba continued as communist states.

Thirty years on, students in the UK studying the history of the twentieth century are not taught why any of this happened. On the contrary, the information provided makes communism's failure all the more puzzling. Take the BBC's website catering for sixteen-year-olds studying for their GCSE history exam. It offers the following bite-size information under the heading: 'How Successful was Collectivisation?'

- Grain production rose to nearly 100 million tonnes in 1937, although the numbers of animals *never* recovered.
- Russia sold large quantities of grain to other countries.

The improvements in production between 1928 and 1937 were phenomenal:

- Coal—from 36 million tonnes to 130 million tonnes.
- Iron—from 3 million tonnes to 15 million tonnes.
- Oil—from 2 million tonnes to 29 million tonnes.
- Electricity—from 5,000 million to 36,000 million kilowatts.

The other key achievements it tells children about include:

- The Turkestan–Siberian Railroad.
- The Dnieper Dam.
- The Belomor Canal.

These figures allegedly show that Stalin achieved most of his aims and that his five-year plans were 'phenomenally successful'.

The GCSE textbook *Modern World History*, which covers Mao's China, is also a paean to the virtues of five-year plans and the crushing of the market economy:

> The five-year plan achieved astonishing results. The highly motivated Chinese workers surpassed all the targets for the five-year plan. In five years, China was criss-crossed with railways which moved vital goods and materials across vast distances. The

population of China's towns and cities soared as peasants moved to the jobs created in the new industries.

After this passage of breathless enthusiasm comes a bar chart showing immense increases in electricity output, steel, coal and so on; although it admits that some experts now question the veracity of these figures, it says they were still impressive. Further, a chart shows that grain production virtually doubled from 1949 to 1958. The text claims that by fixing wages and prices, and tackling black-marketeers, Mao crushed inflation and stabilized the currency by taking over the banks.[4]

It claims that before 1949, Mao had worked closely with peasants, understood them, had 'worked wonders' with them during the civil war and was determined to keep their loyalty. It follows the Chinese Communist Party propaganda line that it was principally the communists who fought the Japanese and not the Kuomintang armies. But the Chinese communists played a minor role in only one engagement, and its guerrilla actions were insignificant, while the Kuomintang fought twenty-two major battles, notably the 1937 Battle of Shanghai and lost millions of troops.[5] The text also says that the murder of millions of 'landlords' in arbitrary 'trials' was carried out by peasants, and this increased support for Mao. In fact, it was a deliberate campaign to sow terror in the villages and strengthen Party control. During the Great Leap Forward, the text repeats the lie that a man-made famine was partly caused by floods, drought and other unusual weather.

On the AQA 'Cold War History' A-Level course, students learn that Stalin turned Russia into a mighty industrial power in just ten years, building an industrial base beyond the reach of the German invaders.[6] In other words, students are taught that collectivization, costly though it was, was justified because this industrialization drive enabled Stalin to defeat Hitler.

Students are also left with other debatable notions, such as that Lenin never got a chance to try out his communist programme after 1917 and had to settle for 'war communism'; that Stalin's absurd statistics showing massive economic gains in the 1930s are credible; that Russia was not really a military state but was forced into high

5

defence spending by its rivalry with the United States; and that the Soviet Union only fell behind in the late 1970s with the rise of modern electronics and computers.

They learn that after 1945, two superpowers with different ideologies recklessly competed for global hegemony. Students learn therefore that 'capitalism' is an 'ideology' comparable to Marxism–Leninism. They are then told that one of these powers unexpectedly, indeed mysteriously, dissolved itself. Revision notes for the Oxford *AQA History of the Cold War* primer explains the Soviet Union's demise by saying that the USSR was falling behind technologically, spent excessively on the military and was struggling to feed a growing population addicted to drinking too much vodka.[7]

Sometimes the information proved by these history courses is there out of a laudable aim of presenting students with different sources: to encourage them to explore different interpretations and then to weigh them up. They are encouraged to assess both sides. This means that UK history school textbooks present positive aspects of communism. It means that students are encouraged to consider that while communist governments brought famine, purges, totalitarian dictatorship and labour camps, they also introduced female emancipation, low-cost childcare, universal public health services and compulsory education.

Yet this all too easily leads to nonsense that would be ridiculed if applied to Nazi Germany. Children in Mao's China mostly didn't attend school and indeed were encouraged to kill and eat their teachers; their mothers did not enjoy free childcare but were forced to do manual labour in military-style labour gangs. Almost all the elements on the plus side are wrong or at best misleading because they invoke questionable statistics such as those showing the fantastical economic gains achieved by Stalin's first five-year plan in the 1930s or Mao's first five-year plan in the 1950s, or achievements in healthcare or education that cannot be verified. After all, Mao's China didn't produce any statistics about anything for twenty-five years.

It is also essentially the line put out by unrepentant apologists for the Soviet Union like Seumas Milne, the Labour Party's director of strategy and communications under the party's former leader Jeremy Corbyn:

> For all its brutalities and failures, communism in the Soviet Union, eastern Europe and elsewhere delivered rapid industrialisation, mass education, job security and huge advances in social and gender equality. It encompassed genuine idealism and commitment ... Its existence helped to drive up welfare standards in the west, boosted the anticolonial movement and provided a powerful counterweight to western global domination.[8]

Socialism's grip on the Western intelligentsia should have ended with the dissolution of the Soviet Union. Yet thirty years after the collapse of the Soviet Union, surveys of academics and university administrators in both British and American universities reveal that the majority identify as left-wing and indeed more identify as left-wing than ever before. A Gallup poll released in 2018 revealed that over 51 per cent of young people in America hold a favourable view of socialism. A report by the Adam Smith Institute in 2018 said that the number of British academics who are liberal or left-wing has been steadily on the rise since the 1960s and that eight in ten university lecturers are 'left-wing'.

Although communism is responsible for a death toll that far exceeds that of the Holocaust, children are not taken to museums to learn about the 80 million people made to work as slaves, the tens of millions forced to flee their countries or homes or the over 50 million who perished from hunger in man-made famines. There are no such museums in Western countries.

Films and dramas exploring the history of communism are largely absent from popular culture. There's almost nothing between *Dr Zhivago* (1965) and *The Death of Stalin* (2017). The Nazis, who were only in power for twelve years, feature in innumerable films, but for Hollywood, communists are almost invisible.

British universities offer undergraduates plenty of courses on imperialism, feminism or colonialism but none on the history of communism. Few study it at university level. Students are therefore unable to understand exactly why socialism did not work no matter in which country it was tried. They don't get to learn the nuts and bolts of why, as a system of economic management, it failed. The lessons of that failure are poorly addressed in the history courses or in the economics curriculum taught in schools or universities. Nor are students encouraged to investigate just why it proved to be so inhumane or why it cost so many human lives.

Instead, school history serves up a succession of wars, crises, summits and treaties. China's modern history becomes a series of unfortunate events, a confusing kaleidoscope of purges, wars, slogans and propaganda campaigns in which the Chinese Communist Party's own propaganda talking points are used as a credible explanation for what was going on. The real explanation—that Mao's policies were a huge and avoidable failure—is absent.

The overarching narrative boils down to a description of China—or Russia, or Vietnam or wherever—as a terrible backward place that a group of revolutionaries, driven by the noblest ideals, attempts to modernize but somehow it all goes horribly wrong. The communist victory in Vietnam is given enormous prominence in a way that suggests it was foolish to fight the communists, who were on the right side of history.

The pretension that the Chinese (or Russian, Vietnamese, etc.) communists were simply nationalists opposed to foreign interference in their countries or idealists driven to help the poorest classes in society, redistribute land and promote egalitarianism is not scrutinized. If Mao really wanted to help Chinese peasants prosper, why did he force them to give up all their tools, land and livestock knowing that this might cause a famine as it already had in the Soviet Union?

How words are used is vitally important. Collective farms—or communes in China—are not accurately presented for what they are. Our textbooks subscribe to the terminology used in communist propaganda. Such collectives or communes are like the Roman Empire's *latifundium* with a few tractors thrown in. In Roman times, soldiers and officers were given huge agricultural estates formed out of the land confiscated from conquered peoples who were made to work them as slaves.

The collective farms Stalin established in the early 1930s like those in Ukraine were much the same. Whether in the Soviet Union or China, the people in charge were usually former officers drawn from the ranks of the secret police or military. As in a *latifundium*, the labourers were not allowed to leave without permission, nor could they possess any private property. They were not paid anything apart from basic rations, or at best some kind of notional work points.

The Europeans later took this *latifundia* system to the New World, where the agricultural plantations were called *haciendas* in the Spanish-speaking world—*estancia* or *fazenda* in the Portuguese New World—and were worked either by the indigenous population or by imported African slaves. In the English-speaking world, they were called plantations. Only in a few colonies did colonists succeed as small farmers.

A *hacienda* can also refer to a mine. Was the Spanish Empire's famous Potosí mine, where 60 per cent of the world's silver was once extracted by a huge workforce of local labourers or African slaves, operated differently from Stalin's Dalstroy gold mines in the Russian Far East, where vast numbers of Gulag prisoners were worked to death? There was the same reckless cost in human life. The silver funded the Spanish Empire's wars in Europe just as the Dalstroy gold funded the expansion of the Soviet military machine.

British school history textbooks are a distillation of the accepted version of events presented by academic historians. However, for decades many leading academics had done a poor job of understanding the USSR, China and other communist states. There may be a reluctance to acknowledge past errors or a fear of being targeted by the 'anti-anti-communism' movement to which so many powerful intellectuals like Jean-Paul Sartre lent their weight.[9]

A lot of the confusion in British school textbooks can be traced back to American economists and academics who occupied leading posts in America's top universities. From the 1950s onwards, Americans came to dominate the fields of Sinology, Sovietology and above all economics. Every American economics student since 1948 studied from economics textbooks that claimed that the Soviet economy was half the size of the United States' and that it was growing so fast that it would inevitably overtake it. And that its defence spending was 5 per cent of GNP.

In fact, the USSR was more like one-sixth the size of the US economy, and its defence spending consumed at least a third of its economic activity. As for China, America's leading China expert, John K. Fairbank, taught generations of students that Mao Zedong's victory was the best thing that happened to Chinese peasants when in fact his rule killed around 50 million of them and left the rest in grinding poverty. The American textbooks had an unshakeable confidence in the Soviet economy as a model for the modernization of the backward developing country. This meant that the economic success of Japan, South Korea, Singapore, Taiwan and Hong Kong was downplayed or ignored.

The persistent belief in the economic success of the Soviet Union, which is explained in detail later in this book, was based on misunderstandings of the value of Soviet statistics. With the benefit of new research into the archives, we can finally grasp how falsified and manipulated statistics blindfolded communist governments and confused Western leaders. The impossibility of gathering reliable statistics in a communist economy made rational planning impossible. Top Western experts and the analysts in the CIA made huge errors of judgement by imagining that they could glean some meaningful statistics from countries where there was only a stream of falsified data.

Often, the rulers of such states, despite the despotic power they commanded, were unable to see the extent of this economic planning failure. Sometimes, the consequences of malinvestment took a long time to manifest. Everything was always hidden by the fog created by pervasive secrecy, propaganda and bogus statistics. Even if the data was not being deliberately manipulated or falsified, leaders would still have no ability to make rational decisions. There was no way to replace the constant and helpful feedback that markets offer. To put it crudely—in a planned economy everyone was cheating, and while there may also be cheats in market economies, market prices give everyone a corrective dose of reality.

The other phenomenon that is underplayed in school histories of the Soviet Union and other communist states is the hidden black-market economy. Arguably, it was this 'criminal' economic activity that stopped the various 'socialist' experiments from immediately falling apart. The Bolsheviks briefly allowed private trading and markets after 1924, and in later years the underground market became so important the system could hardly function without it. Much of the activity that went on was obviously not recorded in statistics other than as crimes such as 'speculation'. Traders were criminals who belonged to a Russian 'Mafia'. Much the same happened in China, and in the 1970s private markets and even enterprises began to secretly flourish.

Further, apart from the first five-year plan in the USSR and the same in China, many of these states soon stopped publishing plans or indeed any useful statistics. The respective leaders simply ruled by diktat through a bureaucratic-administrative state. Although this is noted by some historians, how and why this came to be the case has not really been explained.

How were so many experts taken in? And for so long? The misreporting started back in the 1920s and '30s. The Soviet Union was a closed society where most categories of information were treated as state secrets. Even facts about everyday life were shrouded in a fog of secrecy. Very few people had the opportunity to visit the Soviet Union and see for themselves what life was like. Even fewer Soviet citizens were permitted to leave.

Despite the dearth of reliable information, whole libraries of books came to be written about these countries. A tiny handful of authors had the chance to actually live in the USSR, and they often proved to be wrong on a fabulous scale. One was *New York Times* correspondent Walter Duranty, who arrived in Moscow in 1921 and spent the next twelve years covering Russia yet saw only what Russian leaders wanted him to see. Up to 7 million people died in Ukraine (and elsewhere in the USSR) from Stalin's man-made famine, but in September 1933, after Duranty returned from a trip through the heart of Ukraine, he reported that 'the harvest is splendid and all talk of famine now is ridiculous'. He won a Pulitzer Prize for his reporting.[1011]

Rereading these books with the benefit of hindsight is amusing in a cruel sort of way. One volume on my bookshelf, *The Unloved Country*, was written about East Germany, by *Guardian* journalist Michael Simmons. Although it was published in 1989, the year the Berlin Wall came down, the author betrays not the faintest inkling that such an event was even possible. In the mid-1980s, the CIA was also certain that East Germany was going to last. It reckoned that its per capita GNP was as large, if not larger, than that of West Germany, and that since the 1970s it had counted as the world's tenth largest economy.[12]

A very strange set of assumptions underpinned Western thinking. It was taken for granted that the Stalinist economic system worked well, but it was admitted that it was not always properly implemented—either because of the shortcomings of the people, or because of the personal failings of this or that leader. So, the thinking went, the Russians had created a brilliant new planning system, but it didn't work perfectly because sadly the Russian people—or the Chinese, Germans, Koreans or whoever—had been corrupted by centuries of feudalism into lethargic and apathetic creatures. Hence, it all made sense when the Soviet and later the Chinese communists wanted a 'Cultural Revolution' to wipe the state clean so that its leaders could work with a blank sheet of paper.

Blaming the past is an all too easy game to play. In *Russia Reported*, Duranty explained that centuries of oppression and serfdom had given the Russian masses a 'servile mentality'. They were a rootless, fatalistic people who needed to be educated, drilled and disciplined. They needed a strong leader like Stalin, and the Russians welcomed the absolute authority of the state and lusted after a communal life on collective farms. Duranty used his authority to convince Western readers that communism suited the Russian soul.

When Aleksandr Solzhenitsyn's *The Gulag Archipelago* became a best-seller in the West in 1974, Soviet apologists stopped denying the Soviet Union's appalling human rights record. With détente in full swing, experts were called upon to explain why a country that had raised living standards so dramatically and had enlightened policies on women's rights, universal education and public health also suffered from monstrous tyranny. Yet the answer was the same.

New York Times correspondent Hedrick Smith tackled the issue in *The Russians*, published in 1976. The book was soon hailed as 'the defining exploration of the Russian soul', and it became a best-seller. Hedrick also won a Pulitzer. The burden of centuries under the Tatar yoke, followed by more centuries of tsarist autocracy and serfdom, Smith argued, explained both the cruelty of the state and the apathetic resignation of the populace. And this listlessness had little to do with the economic system.

Books about other communist states generally followed this tack. Simmons suggested that East Germany's cold bureaucracy was an imprint of Prussian military authoritarianism. Philip Short's work *Pol Pot: Anatomy of a Nightmare*, about Pol Pot's Cambodia, stated that whatever happened was 'rooted in history' and consistent with Khmer culture and traditions. Others like Australian academic Ben Kiernan considered the genocidal massacres to be related to a legacy of racism. When it came to developing countries like Cambodia, scholars could blame a long legacy of colonial oppression. In *The Quality of Mercy: Cambodia, Holocaust and Modern Conscience*, William Shawcross speculated that the Khmer Rouge behaved so murderously because the Cambodians had been brutalized by years of American bombing.

For forty years, the Chinese communists and their apologists got away with the argument that their wonderful theories never worked out because the Chinese people had let them down. Taiwanese writers like Bo Yang made similar arguments, describing the Chinese as stuck at the bottom of a 'putrid stinking soya vat' created by 5,000 years of Chinese culture, including 2,000 years of Confucianism and feudalism.[13] Funnily enough, not long after market reforms began powering strong economic growth, many scholars—often the same ones—started declaring that economic growth was all due to China's Confucian culture.

Some writers also argued that the personalities of Stalin, Mao or Pol Pot were key to understanding what happened. Duranty wrote that Lenin's 'special genius' and Stalin's 'unrivalled genius for political management' had changed the direction of the revolution at critical moments.

Mao too was hailed as a genius, as was Ho Chi Minh and many others. A great deal of time was spent trying to piece together fragmentary information about their lives and then connect their biographies to their politics. Yet because these communist leaders were almost without exception unbending ideologues, it was often an unenlightening task. Other analysts became fascinated by Kremlinology, who stood where on some podium, the meaning and motives behind purges, or the Politburo rivalries and bureaucratic machinations, or they tried to spin some meaning from the arcane study of communist hierarchies and organizations.

Yet it was odd and really quite startling for anyone travelling from one communist country to another to see that no matter what the country's history and culture might be, one encountered the same queues, the same shabby apartment blocks, the same shoddy goods, the same cruelty, the same vast armies and slave labour camps. Whether they were Germans, Russians, Chinese, Vietnamese or Koreans, they all seemed to be just as apathetic, passive and cynical. Of course, no one in China is going to admit that under communism Chinese people behaved just like Russians—and the other way round. That would be to admit that history, culture or ethnicity are less significant than an economic system.

University- and school-level history textbooks largely accept this fiction by assuming that history should best be studied on a country-by-country basis. What was actually done to crush so many people in so many different cultures is curiously absent from the school textbooks on twentieth-century history. Even when it is mentioned, it is stripped of context and significance.

Two key aspects of communism are minimized by these textbooks—class warfare and world revolution. Starting in early 1918, the state in Russia (and later China and elsewhere) declared war on at least a third of its own citizens. Huge numbers were murdered or persecuted solely on account of their hereditary class background. And sometimes their religion or race.

Since large groups of people were condemned by their class or race, the world faced recurrent waves of refugees desperately fleeing for their lives. Huge groups fled or tried to flee from Russia, Ukraine, Latvia, Lithuania, Mongolia, Poland, Hungary, China, North Korea, Tibet, Cambodia, East Germany, Czechoslovakia, Cambodia, Laos, Afghanistan, Angola, Mozambique, Somalia, Ethiopia, Syria, Venezuela, Cuba, El Salvador, Nicaragua and so on. Many nationalities—Finns, Poles, Ukrainians, Kalmyks, Mongols, Cossacks, Tatars, Koreans, Kazakhs, Jews, Old Believers, Muslims and of course ethnic Russians of all kinds—were also displaced within the USSR, effectively becoming internal refugees.

The leaders of all communist states believed that world revolution was essential to establishing their utopia and devoted huge resources to training and funding revolutionaries anywhere and everywhere. These communist insurgencies displaced millions as they tried to escape violent civil wars. The list of countries—Vietnam, Laos, Philippines, Greece, Nepal, Malaya, Peru, Thailand, Sri Lanka, India, Mexico, Burma, Indonesia and Colombia to name just some—is a very long one indeed.

Communism was the cause of the greatest population movement in world history. It affected more people than the First or Second World Wars, or the losses inflicted by natural disasters. In order to prevent large numbers of their residents from fleeing, communist regimes introduced internal passport security systems and erected physical barriers, the most famous of which were the Berlin Wall and the Iron Curtain. At no point has there ever been a mass migration *into* any of these communist states.

Some people continue to believe that Hitler's socialism was based on racism and hence morally inferior to the ideology of the communist leaders who sought to create multi-ethnic states. But this is not true. Stalin launched genocidal campaigns against whole nationalities quite early on: Poles, Finns, Chechens, Tatars, Koreans, Ukrainians, Cossacks, ethnic Germans, and Mao did the same, wreaking collective punishments on Manchus, Mongolians, Uyghurs, Tibetans and many other ethnic groups.

In 1917, Lenin and the Bolsheviks jettisoned 'capitalism' in order to re-introduce a primitive barter economy to Russia. Without private property, they believed that greed and war would disappear. Man would return to the life of leisure that he once enjoyed in the Stone Age. Russian men and women would become 'new people', freer, more altruistic, nobler, better educated, more honest and more sexually liberated and equal, as they returned to humanity's natural state of primitive communism. The Bolsheviks aimed to return to a barter society without money, private property or the specialization of labour because they believed this was what man in his natural state enjoyed 10,000 years ago. They believed that 'capitalism' started with the spread of farming and private property.

Those who joined Marxist or socialist or anarchist parties were convinced a more productive economy and a fairer society could be created by abolishing money and markets. People instead of profits would be put first.

The narrative presented to students is therefore that the terrors of communist revolution and the horrors of communist rule were an unforeseen and unexpected aberration. The systemic and persistent abuse of human rights was not directly related to the economic system but could be excused by references to the history of the Russians (or whoever) or the psychological failings of the leadership, or just the exigencies of the circumstances at the time.

None of the above is of much use when it comes to explaining the unexpected demise of the USSR and the collapse of the communist movement across the world. In 1991, the Soviet communists weren't defeated by some richer and more ruthless foreign power, nor by drinking too much vodka. The Russians had been drinking too much for a long time. The USSR had spent excessively on its military right from the start. None of this was critical.

Communism was destroyed from within by a persistent failure to make its economic theories work in practice. Even its leaders recognized that they didn't want to carry on any longer because they felt it was beyond any kind of reform. In Beijing, Deng Xiaoping and other aged leaders of the Chinese Communist Party watched with disbelief. They had no hesitation in crushing opposition and carrying on. But what exactly did go wrong with central planning? What was its fatal flaw? To start to investigate the answer, one must journey back to the coffee houses of Vienna in the final decades of the Habsburg Empire.

1

VIENNA 1914
TWO MEN WHO CHANGED HISTORY

Before the guns of August 1914 brought the old order to an end, Vienna nurtured many great minds. Men whose thinking shaped the modern world, transforming the fields of psychiatry, architecture, music, painting, literature, philosophy and economics. Sigmund Freud, Adolf Loos, Gustav Mahler, Gustav Klimt, Stefan Zweig, Oskar Kokoschka—any of these could be seen in one of the fancy cafés on the Ringstrasse sipping a strong coffee topped with whipped cream. And then there was a bunch of obscure ne'er do wells who turned up in Vienna too, drawn to its free spirit of intellectual enquiry—Hitler, Stalin, Tito, Leon Trotsky and Nikolai Bukharin.

Bukharin would soon be in Moscow along with Stalin and Trotsky, helping to implement Marx's vision of a communist society. After the October Revolution, Lenin charged Bukharin with implementing his economic programme. Bukharin went on to write the standard primer on Marxism–Leninist economics—*The ABC of Communism*— which every communist around the world would study, for at least the next thirty years. After five years working in the Bolshevik underground, Bukharin left Russia in 1911. For three years, he travelled around the world, apparently without the need to earn a living, often hosted by European social democratic parties.

In 1914, Bukharin was just twenty-six, and people said he looked like a saint in a Russian icon. He was a slightly built man, just over 5 feet tall, with a boyish face and blue-grey eyes, a prominent forehead, red hair and a thin beard.[1]

He turned up in Vienna 'like a holy avenger' determined to confront the Austrian economists who were attacking Marx's labour theory of value.[2] His particular enemy was a very grand figure— Professor Eugen von Böhm-Bawerk, president of the Austrian Academy of Sciences, a former minister of finance and elder statesman in the upper house of the Austrian Parliament. When Bukharin arrived, Professor Böhm-Bawerk's main academic responsibility was delivering a course on advanced economic theory at the University of Vienna, which he gave during the winter semester. These lectures were almost certainly attended by Bukharin, who spent two years hanging around the university and the coffee houses before being expelled as a foreigner at the outbreak of the war.

In *Karl Marx and the Close of His System* (1896), Professor Böhm-Bawerk examined Marx's theory of labour value and pointed out a basic error in Marx's system. The rate of profit and the prices of production described in the third volume of Marx's *Das Kapital* contradicted Marx's own theory of value in the first volume. Marx argued that one could only measure the value of a product or a commodity on the basis of the number of manhours it took to make something. This was the labour theory of value. It was not money but human capital that should be the starting point to calculate for everything. In the third volume, Marx contradicts this by saying that 'individual commodities do and must exchange with each other in a proportion different from that of the labour incorporated in them, and this not accidentally and temporarily, but of necessity and permanently'.

As Marx believed that labour is the source of all wealth, money is therefore commoditized labour, so he called it 'dead labour' or 'congealed labour'. Markets are consequently neither important nor necessary since market prices just reflect the labour expended in making something. Money, said Marx, 'is the alienated essence of man's labour and his being'. This alien being had come to possess him, so in a communist society there would be no need for money, which both he and Engels considered inherently evil. The Marxist assigned value to labour and argued that as the capitalist system cheated the worker out of his rightful due, the proletariat should rise up.

Marx lived in a period when many writers in the German-speaking world had become fascinated by the role of money. Others argued that money was not evil but on the contrary a great facilitator of human happiness. For example, in 1900 Georg Simmel published a massive tome, *The Philosophy of Money*, in which he said money played a very positive role because it facilitated cooperation between people, which is essential for creating a peaceful and civilized society. He pointed out that the development of ancient Greece's marvellous civilization was closely tied to the growing use of money.

Marxists generally believe that money, capitalism and private property started to come into being some 10,000 years ago with the invention of farming. Simmel and others like Carl Menger thought its origins might be much older, well before any known civilization. Professor Menger was another grand figure, a professor at the University of Vienna—the oldest university in the German-speaking world—and one-time tutor to Archduke Rudolf von Habsburg— the crown prince who died in a suicide pact with his mistress in 1889. Among his works, Menger wrote a whole book simply called *On the Origins of Money*.

A long, long time ago, people started using a common currency such as gold to facilitate trade. Menger said it was a spontaneous event that in turn led to prices. The Austrians were following the tradition that included Scottish philosopher Adam Smith. He wrote that we are all born to 'higgle, haggle, swop and dicker'. In other words, they all believed that trading is an innate part of our make up as Homo sapiens.

The Marxists believed that before the invention of money people lived in a barter society. No one has ever found evidence of any barter society existing anywhere or at any time, but it's equally hard to show how or when trading with money started. The Bolsheviks' real ambition was not a Stone Age hunter-gatherer economy but a planned collectivized economy commanded by an all-powerful state that fixed prices and wages and controlled every individual's life from cradle to grave.

Menger also wrote the *Principles of Economics*, in which he explained that the value of any good or service entailed a subjective judgement of the buyer and seller. He argued that things only have value insofar as such people want such goods. Böhm-Bawerk explained it like this:

> A pioneer farmer had five sacks of grain, with no way of selling them or buying more. He had five possible uses—as basic feed for himself, food to build strength, food for his chickens for dietary variation, an ingredient for making whisky and feed for his parrots to amuse him. Then the farmer lost one sack of grain. Instead of reducing every activity by a fifth, the farmer simply starved the parrots as they were of less utility than the other four uses; in other words, they were on the margin. And it is on the margin, and not with a view to the big picture, that we make economic decisions.[3]

The Vienna school therefore developed a theory of marginal utility according to which value is determined not by the amount of labour incorporated in a product but by its utility to individual buyers.

Böhm-Bawerk said that the whole value of a product is not produced by the worker's labour, and that labour can only be paid according to the current value of any foreseeable output. He argued that capitalists do not exploit their workers but rather help their employees by providing them with an income well in advance of the revenue from the goods they produce. He asserted that 'labour cannot increase its share at the expense of capital' and that a redistribution of profits from capitalist industries would undermine the usefulness of interest rates as a vital tool for monetary policy.

He attacked Marx for downplaying the influence of supply and demand in determining prices. Another of his works, *Positive Theory of Capital* (1889), developed the ideas on marginal utility.

This school of thinking became known as the Austrian school and later as the monetarist school. Not everyone who attended the lectures before the outbreak of the Great War was convinced. In the summer semesters, Bukharin attended the weekly graduate seminar led by Böhm-Bawerk along with the Austrian Marxists Rudolf Hilferding, Otto Neurath and Otto Bauer, people who would be at the forefront of post-war left-wing parties in Austria after the dissolution of the Austro-Hungarian Empire.

After war broke out, Bukharin was arrested and expelled to Switzerland. There, he wrote several books in quick succession that earned him a reputation as the leading Bolshevik economics theorist, second only to Lenin.

In 1915, he published *Imperialism and World Economy*, in 1918 *The Economics of the Transition Period*, and in 1920 *The ABC of Communism* (with Evgenii Preobrazhensky), followed by *Historical Materialism* (1921) and *Economic Theory of the Leisure Class* (first published in 1919), a direct attack on the Austrian theory of marginal utility. In Soviet Russia, this became the definitive refutation of the Austrian school, a basic textbook in educational institutions.

Bukharin's *ABC of Communism* was even more influential. It went through eighteen Russian editions and twenty foreign translations, making it one of the most important books of communist propaganda. No one reads his works now or regards them as significant contributions to economics, but at the time little else had been written to guide the Bolshevik government after 1917. Everybody studied it, making its author almost as famous as Lenin and Trotsky. It was widely studied by the future Chinese communist leaders and by Pol Pot and his fellow Khmer Rouge leaders.

The economic programme Bukharin developed for revolutionary Russia was based on the pamphlet *Critique of the Gotha Programme*, which Marx wrote in 1875 for the United Workers' Party of Germany. Marx explains how money will be replaced by labour certificates:

> The laborer gives his 'quantum of labor'. He receives a certificate from society that he has finished such and such an amount of labor (after deducting his labor for the common funds), and with this certificate he draws from the social stock of means of consumption as much as costs the same amount of labor. The same amount of labor which he has given to society in one form he receives back in another.

This, Marx explained, meant that a given amount of labour in one form is exchanged for an equal amount of labour in another form.

21

The idea of labour notes or certificates had been tried in America and elsewhere. Josiah Warren created an experimental 'labour for labour store'—the Cincinnati Time Store—which lasted for three years, until 1830. The idea was that no one should profit from the labour of another. Customers bought goods with notes promising to perform a certain amount of labour. For instance, a standard exchange was 12 pounds of corn for one hour of labour. If the work was difficult or unpleasant, then the labourer could get more. Warren put up a board on the wall of his store where anyone could request or offer services so there could also be a kind of trade in certificates. The goods in the store were initially marked up 7 per cent to account for the labour required to bring them to market. The price went up if a customer spent more time with a shopkeeper, which was measured by a timer dial.[4]

In Marx's scheme, the labourer paid part of his income into a fund that invested in upgrading or replacing worn-out machinery. Another part was taxed to cover administrative expenses. Then it was taxed to pay for social care like schools, hospitals, old people's homes and so on.

So who would be keeping accounts of the labour done, and the deductions? What about difficult and arduous labour, and mental and physical labour?

Engels wrote that once society had taken over the 'means of production', everyone's labour would be counted as useful social labour. Assessing its value would be very simple:

> From the moment when society enters into possession of the means of production and uses them in direct association for production, the labour of each individual, however varied its specifically useful character may be, becomes at the start and directly social labour. The quantity of social labour contained in a product need not then be established in a roundabout way; daily experience shows in a direct way how much of it is required on the average. Society can simply calculate how many hours of labour are contained in a steam-engine, a bushel of wheat of the last harvest, or a hundred square yards of cloth of a certain quality.[5]

When it came to weighing up the utility of the different objects of consumption against the labour necessary for their production, there was no need to put a monetary value because Engels said that '[t]he people will decide everything quite easily without the intervention of the much-vaunted value'.[6]

When in 1917 Lenin wrote *The State and Revolution*, he recognized that 'accounting and control is the main thing required to bring about the smooth working, the correct functioning of the first phase of communist society'.

In the first phase, some people would be better off than others, but Marx said in the second phase the difference between mental and physical labour would disappear. Thus, everyone would be given according to his needs, and goods would be freely available.

In the meantime, Lenin was absolutely convinced that 'bookkeeping and control' were within the reach of 'anyone who can read and write and knows the first four arithmetical rules'. It was all so simple that any cook could be taught how to administer a planned economy.

In *Principles of Communism*, Engels had already explained that industry would be operated according to a plan. 'Education will enable young people quickly to familiarize themselves with the whole system of production and to pass from one branch of production to another', he said. And he predicted that the division of labour would disappear, thanks to machinery, so anyone could do anyone else's job. 'The form of the division of labor which makes one a peasant, another a cobbler, a third a factory worker, a fourth a stock-market operator, has already been undermined by machinery and will completely disappear.'[7]

Lenin is very clear that keeping accounts is really a very simple matter. Everyone would learn to 'administer and really independently administer social production, independently keep accounts'.

He believed that 'accounting and control ... have been simplified by capitalism to the extreme and reduced to the extraordinarily simple operations—which any literate person can perform—of supervising and recording, of knowing the basic rules of arithmetic and of issuing the appropriate receipts'.

Later, Lenin explains how the next, higher stage of communism would be reached: 'From the moment when all members of society, or even only the vast majority, have learned to administer the state themselves, ... the need for administration of any kind begins to disappear altogether.'[8]

In this planned economy, Lenin first thought that what he called 'bourgeois experts' would be immediately replaced but later conceded it might take as long as a year to replace them. The whole of society, he predicted, will become 'a single office and a single factory' with 'equality of labour and equality of pay'.

Bukharin believed that such a system already existed in large vertically integrated American corporations like the Ford Motor Company as well as those monopolists operating big steel companies, coal mines, iron mines and steamships. In these advanced American capitalist corporations, everything is distributed on the orders of a central head office because one branch does not sell its components to another section according to its market price.[9]

In the same way, he envisaged that an entire industrial economy could be run like this once it was brought under the ownership of the workers. That is how he foresaw the use of money and markets dying away.

The Bolsheviks were very confident that an economy like this would run like clockwork with just the help of various kinds of book-keeping offices or statistical bureaus.

So instead of traders in a market, there would be a statistical bureau that would keep daily accounts of 'production and all its needs'. It would decide 'whither workers must be sent, whence they must be taken, and how much work there is to be done'.

Everyone would be transformed into hired employees of the state working for a single all-people state 'syndicate'. Then, 'when the social order is like a well-oiled machine, all will work in accordance with the indications of these statistical bureaux':

> There will be no need for special ministers of State, for police and prisons, for laws and decrees—nothing of the sort. Just as in an orchestra all the performers watch the conductor's baton and act accordingly, so here all will consult the statistical reports and will direct their work accordingly. The State, therefore, has ceased to exist.

Bukharin and Preobrazhensky, his co-author of the *ABC*, even doubted whether it was necessary to have a permanent civil service of trained experts:

> In these statistical bureaux one person will work today, another tomorrow. The bureaucracy, the permanent officialdom, will disappear ... The most forcible blow to the monetary system will be delivered by the introduction of budget-books and by the payment of workers in kind. In the work book will be entered how much the holder has done, and this will mean how much the State owes him.[10]

Bukharin envisaged the abolition of money in stages: first between nationalized enterprises, then in the accounting between state and workers, then between state and small producers like farmers.

As for small-scale industry, he envisaged that barter would soon replace the use of money, although he added that money would not completely disappear until small-scale industry itself disappeared.

To this programme, the Bolsheviks added other measures: the compulsory deposit of money into the People's Bank; the introduction of budget or ration books; the replacement of money by written or printed tokens, that is, by tickets giving the right to the receipt of goods but available only for short periods. 'Communist society will know nothing of money', Bukharin predicted in *The ABC of Communism*.

In his *ABC of Communism*, Bukharin said the economy would be turned into 'a gigantic cooperative' that would churn out products that would be stored in 'communal warehouses' and then delivered to those who need them: 'In such conditions, money will no longer be required', he said.

'At first, doubtless, and perhaps for twenty or thirty years, it will be necessary to have various regulations', he wrote. 'Maybe certain products will only be supplied to those persons who have a special entry in their workbook or on their work card.'

But later, when a communist society had been fully established, there would be no such regulations because a person will take from the communal storehouse 'precisely as much as he needs, no more'.

'No one will have any interest in taking more than he wants in order to sell the surplus to others, since all these others can satisfy their needs whenever they please. Money will then have no value', he predicted.

After the storming of the Winter Palace in Petrograd (St Petersburg), Lenin and Bukharin had a chance to put their plans into practice. All over the world, a new order was beginning. Revolution followed on the heels of defeat. Across the defeated empires of Russia, Germany and Austria–Hungary, new states emerged and communist parties were waiting in the wings, impatient to start their economic experiment.

The Russian tsar had abdicated, ending five generations of unbroken Romanov power. In November 1918, the German kaiser was forced into exile. Within days, the last Habsburg emperor, Charles I, left the Schönbrunn Palace in Vienna and effectively abdicated, bringing down the curtain on a 500-year-old dynasty. The Habsburg Empire of over 50 million fell apart. Hungary set up its own republic and so did other nationalities. This left a small rump state of Austria of just 6 million.

Over the border in Bavaria, Ludwig III left the palace of the Wittelsbach family who had ruled much of Europe for over 700 years. He went into exile, reportedly carrying nothing but a box of cigars under his arm. On the other side of the world, the Manchu family who had ruled China for over 270 years abdicated, too.

The German Bolsheviks—the Spartacists—took to the streets of Berlin to seize power. In Munich, the communists declared a Soviet republic. In Hungary, Béla Kun arrived from Moscow and by March 1918 had established the Hungarian Soviet Republic. In 'Red Vienna', Otto Bauer and Victor Adler, the leaders of the Social Democratic Party, were proposing to impose full-scale Bolshevism. But soon, things began to go very, very wrong, and not just in Austria. Russia would soon be on its knees.

2

VIENNA AND THE SOCIALIST
CALCULATION PROBLEM

In 1918, a wounded artillery officer, Ludwig von Mises, was discharged from an army that had fought for an empire that no longer existed. On 11 November, he became the citizen of a new state, the Republic of German-Austria. It was 'a grey, lifeless shadow of the old Austro-Hungarian Monarchy ... a mutilated torso bleeding from all its arteries ... a country which did not want to exist', as Viennese writer Stefan Zweig put it.[1]

Vienna, once called the gayest city in Europe and famed for its coffeehouses, grand balls, opera houses and waltzes, was a dying city. By 1918, the Austrian economy had shrunk by 40 per cent. One in ten was dying from starvation and a third were starving. It was now a country of 6 million people of which a third crowded into Vienna. Every day, more and more people—soldiers, prisoners of war, displaced people, refugees—arrived seeking food and shelter.

'Bread was nothing but black crumbs tasting of pitch and glue, coffee was a decoction of roasted barley, beer was yellow water, chocolate a sandy substance coloured brown. The potatoes were frozen. Most people trapped rabbits so as not to forget the taste of meat entirely.'[2]

'You often saw trousers made of old sacks. Every step you took along the streets, where the shop windows were as empty as if they had been looted, mortar was crumbling away like scabs from the ruinous buildings, and obviously malnourished people dragged themselves to work with difficulty', Zweig observed.

Until 1914, the 50 million-strong Austro-Hungarian Empire had been largely self-sufficient in food. Decades of growth had left a strong industrial base—iron and steel works, textile and paper mills, armaments factories and much else. Until the war started, the Austrian krone like the German mark and the Russian imperial rouble had been backed by gold. Then the central banks started printing money in ever larger quantities, and now the paper money was no longer redeemable with gold. The result, even before the war's end, was massive inflation—a rate of 1,226 per cent per year.

In 1917, when Mises returned from active duty to join the military command HQ to help with its economic planning, the starving workforce was on strike. From 1914 to 1917, the empire was ruled by emergency decrees, a quasi-military dictatorship that had sweeping powers to manage every aspect of the economy.

By now, rations had been cut and cut until no one could work and survive. The ration cards were useless. By 1917, there were 700,000 workers in Vienna on strike simply demanding more food. Theatres and cinemas closed, trains and trams stopped running, factories and power stations shut down because there was no coal or oil. Spanish flu claimed thousands of victims, and Viennese children were dying in large numbers from malnutrition and infectious disease. From the end of October 1918 to June 1919, Vienna was the scene of bloody demonstrations and clashes.

Mises now feared that worse would follow. The Marxists tried to start a revolution and take power in a putsch. Instead, the Social Democrats (Social Democratic Workers' Party or SDAPÖ) took power in Vienna through the ballot box and sought to impose a full Bolshevik programme, just like that being enacted in Moscow. Throughout Vienna, workers and residents organized councils modelled on the Russian Revolution and the Council Republics in Germany and Hungary. Their opponents, the Christian Democrats, who held sway in the rest of the largely Catholic and conservative country, were no economic liberals either, as they too distrusted market forces. The country was run by a coalition of the two parties.

After 1918, Mises worked for a while on the League of Nations' Reparations Commission and then joined the Austrian Chamber of Commerce, an important body representing all the country's commercial, manufacturing and banking enterprises. It gave him a platform to write opinion pieces in the press and to meet the socialist politicians running the country. He tried to persuade them to think more clearly. In the eyes of the Austrian school of which Mises was now a leading light, state control of the economy during the war with its price and wage controls, rationing, money printing, black markets and rent controls had proved a disaster that contributed to defeat. Now the socialists wanted to impose even more control over the economy and promised low rents and high wages.

'It was a daily fight against ignorance', as Mises later put it. Mises credits his persuasive powers for dissuading the leaders of what was dubbed 'Red Vienna' from replicating a full-scale Bolshevik programme in the city. Mises warned that the result would be starvation and collapse. 'I was the economic conscience of post-war Austria', he wrote in *Notes and Recollections*, his memoir later published in America. 'Only a few helped me and all political parties distrusted me.'[3]

Compared to Russia or indeed neighbouring Hungary where opponents were simply shot, the Viennese kept things relatively civilized in keeping with the Viennese spirit. As the saying went: 'In Berlin the situation is serious but not hopeless—in Vienna, the situation is hopeless but never serious.' One of the leading lights of the Austrian socialists was Karl Polanyi, and in the pages of the highbrow publication *Österreichische Volkswirt* Mises and Polanyi debated whether a socialist economy was capable of efficient pricing. Mises insisted it was not. Polanyi argued that a decentralized form of worker-led socialism could price necessities with good-enough accuracy.[4]

Mises had studied at the University of Vienna under Menger and Böhm-Bawerk. He spent six years at the university and was awarded his doctorate by the faculty of law. His first research project was a study of serfdom in eighteenth-century poverty-stricken Galicia. Mises developed Menger's theory in his first major work published in 1912, *The Theory of Money and Credit*, applying it not just to consumer goods and factors of production but also to money.

Mises argued that money should be regarded like any other good, and its value could be accounted for by the marginal-value theory. Mises integrated this theory of money and banking into the general theory of value and prices. Professor Böhm-Bawerk recognized the book's importance and devoted two entire semesters to Mises' ideas.

A short, but erect man, reserved and self-disciplined, Mises was no real aristocrat but the son of a Jewish nouveau riche. He belonged to a generation of Jewish intellectuals who had benefitted from the emancipation of the Jews enacted under Emperor Franz Joseph's rule. His parents had come from Lemberg, now Lviv, in western Ukraine. His father Arthur Edler von Mises had grown wealthy building and financing railroads. For this, he was ennobled with a title, hence the 'von', but they originated from backward Galicia.

By the age of twelve, Ludwig spoke fluent German, Polish and French, read Latin, and could understand Ukrainian. Due to the classical education provided by Austria's elite gymnasiums, Mises was able to pepper his works with quotations from Greek and Latin literature.

Throughout his life, Mises stuck to a motto taken from Virgil: *Tu ne cede malis, sed contra audentior ito*—'Do not give in to evil but proceed ever more boldly against it.' After 1918, he embarked on a life-long effort to reverse the tide of socialism and promote free market ideas.

As Mises battled ignorance, he also continued with his research, working evenings and weekends. Every second Friday, he hosted an influential seminar at his offices in the Chamber of Commerce. Afterwards, a dozen of them would go for dinner at an Italian restaurant, Anchora Verde, before finishing up at the Café Künstler, opposite the University of Vienna.

At the university, a new generation of economists had taken over after 1918. Mises was one of them, and so were his protégés, Joseph Schumpeter and Friedrich Hayek and others who after another great war would become much more famous in the English-speaking world. Mises appointed Hayek to lead a new think tank called the Austrian Business Cycle Institute. The Austrian school further developed the theory of business cycles and argued that it was foolish to allow banks to make borrowing too easy in an effort to avoid the peaks and troughs of the business cycle.

Curiously, these men had all once attended the same seminars, lectures and cafés together with Otto Bauer and Victor Adler, the so-called Austro-Marxists, who were now taking power. They all knew each other. It is even possible that Mises had rubbed shoulders with Bukharin when he was attending seminars and lectures at the University of Vienna.

In some ways, these contemporaries and ideological opponents, Mises and Bukharin, led parallel lives, ending up in exile or prison and then largely forgotten for a generation. Bukharin was eventually shot on the orders of Stalin, but his ideas about a mixed economy would later be taken up by Deng Xiaoping in China to great success.

As the Soviet empire crumbled, dissidents in the Soviet bloc turned to Mises and Hayek and found their explanations for what was wrong with Leninist economics illuminating. After the collapse of communism in Russia and Eastern and Central Europe, many of these people had the opportunity to put Mises' theories to the test.

Witnessing the magnitude of the disasters created in 1918 by the destruction of sound money and indeed any means of common exchange must have been immensely frustrating for Mises. Events proved he and the Austrian school were right, but it was hard to make anyone listen.

The former members of the Habsburg Empire at first tried to share the same currency, the krone. The Austrians and Hungarians held most of the war debt and used their control over the printing press to erode its value.

Then Yugoslavia decided to create a new currency, which it did simply by stamping the old krone notes with a two-headed eagle, its national symbol. Many thought this Yugoslavian currency was a safer bet, so they began pushing wheelbarrows of their cash across the open fields just to get their notes stamped in Yugoslavia.

Next, the Yugoslavs stopped anyone crossing over with their cash. Then the other three members of the currency union decided to copy Yugoslavia by rubber stamping their own currencies. Savers desperately began shifting cash from one country to another, searching for the best place to get their krone notes stamped.

Hungary, the last country to leave the krone, got stuck with railway wagons full of cash. At one stage, bizarre reverse bank runs occurred as savers stuffed money into banks. Then the authorities tried to confiscate cash and convert it into a new currency by fining anyone holding cash. Austria even tried creating two currencies, one for natives and another for foreigners.

Without a stable currency, all trade came to a standstill. Then each country began confiscating whatever railway wagons crossed their border. That meant there were no trains bringing Austria coal from the Czechs, nor food stuffs from agriculture-rich Hungary. And even when people sent food from Switzerland—shopkeepers in Zurich had thoughtfully put up placards saying 'Send food parcels to your friends in Austria'—nobody could afford the prices of the stuff that arrived on Swiss trains.

So it came about that many, perhaps most Germans, Austrians, Russians and Hungarians believed that the problem was not that their money was depreciating in value but that goods were becoming more expensive. For this, they blamed the old regime, not the new government. And that other currencies were unfairly rising, so pushing up the price of daily necessities.

Across the border in Hungary, things were even worse. There, a communist government led by Béla Kun for six months unleashed a flood of paper notes, dubbed white money, nationalized everything and caused widespread famine. Mises recounts his astonishment at hearing a Hungarian communist tell him that Kun's 'white money' ought to have a higher exchange rate than Russian roubles because after the socialization of all private property, the Hungarian state had the strongest credit base.

Mises partly succeeded in persuading the Austrian Christian Socialists, who were also anti-capitalist, to stop printing too much money and to balance the budget. 'It was to my merit alone that the Austrian Crown stabilized at 14,400 to one gold crown, otherwise it would have dropped to one million. The Austrian currency did not collapse like the German currency', he claimed. The middle classes, many of whom had bought war bonds that were now worthless, were plunged into poverty. They lost their jobs, pensions and all their savings. 'A man who had saved for forty years and had also patriotically put money into the war loan became a beggar, while a man who used to be in debt was free of it', Zweig recalled. 'There were no standards or values as money flowed away and evaporated.'[5]

Things never became as crazy as they would become in Germany. Even so, the currency collapse led to some extraordinary sights:

> Incredible as it may seem I can vouch for it that for a long time the famous, de luxe Hotel de l'Europe in Salzburg was entirely booked by unemployed members of the British proletariat, who live there more cheaply than in their slums at home thanks to the generous unemployment benefit they received.[6]

But later in Germany, the inflation rate was so extraordinary that 'you could buy whole rows of six-storey buildings on the Kurfürstendamm for a hundred dollars'.[7] This was the most prestigious boulevard in Berlin.

In Hungary, the short-lived communist regime made things even worse. Kun's worthless paper currency meant there was soon nothing at all to eat. There was widespread killing and looting, and the new regime began to fall part. The regime sent its militia, known as Lenin Boys, into the countryside to forcibly seize food from the peasants. This violent revolution was only ended when a Romanian army invaded and seized Budapest. Kun fled to Moscow.[8]

Mises could witness first hand what happened as people tried to live without a common means of exchange. As Zweig observed, no farmer would dream of selling his butter, eggs and milk at the legally fixed 'maximum prices' but instead asked four or six times as much:

> At first the farmers were happy with all the paper money coming in for their butter and eggs, but they in turn hoarded banknotes. But as soon as they took their fat wallets to town to buy things, they discovered ... the price of scythes, hammers and pots and pans they wanted to buy had risen by twenty or fifty times.
>
> After that they tried direct exchange for manufactured objects, bartering in kind. Humanity ... was now rejecting thousands of years of conventional financial transactions and going back to primitive exchange ...

> Every town began printing its own 'emergency currency',
> which would not be accepted in the next village ... everyone
> wanted real value rather than paper.[9]

Next Zweig said that a grotesque lifestyle of trading spread throughout the whole of Austria, with people wandering around bartering and trading anything they had because 'real goods were in demand, not money'.[10]

A housewife in Linz recorded the following in her diary: 'The wife of a doctor whom I know recently exchanged her beautiful piano for a sack of wheat flour. I, too, have exchanged my husband's gold watch for four sacks of potatoes, which will at all events carry us through the winter.'[11]

The government set up police cordons to stop this trading, but it was no use.

In Austria, hungry city dwellers also started going out to the farms and simply grabbing food by force. Bands of hungry people, often several hundred strong, took to riding out on bicycles to steal food. Those farmers that defended their land became very rich.

People were also angered that businessmen whose debts disappeared overnight could prosper if they retained their physical assets. Inflation encouraged them to borrow money and then quickly convert it into commodities, land, houses, machinery or even works of art. A fortunate minority could easily avoid taxes by simply waiting to pay until the value was eaten away by inflation. They could also deposit money abroad by under-invoicing their exports and over-invoicing their imports. Others became rich by speculating in stocks, currencies or commodities. So while the majority became poorer, rich people were to be seen ostentatiously flaunting their wealth in expensive restaurants, shops and nightclubs.

Mises could also see at first hand the folly of the imposition of rent controls. In 1917, the imperial government had introduced a Tenant Protection Act, which froze rents at the prices that existed in 1914. With high inflation, these rents were worthless, and housing was effectively free. No wonder many people would choose to flee to Vienna. At the same time, no property owner would repair any building, let alone invest in new ones to cope with the new demand if there was no rent.[12]

'No new building had been erected in Austria for four years, many houses were now in a dilapidated state, and now suddenly countless demobilized soldiers and prisoners of war were streaming back and had nowhere to go, so that a family had to be accommodated in every available room', Zweig recalled in *The World of Yesterday*:

> Most grotesque of all was the discrepancy between other expenses and rent. The government banned any rise in rents in order to protect tenants—who were the majority ... Soon the rent of a medium-sized apartment in Austria for a whole year cost its tenant less than a single midday meal. In effect, the whole country lived more or less rent free for five to ten years, since even later landlords were not allowed to give their tenants notice.[13]

The new municipal government organized emergency housing by expropriating vacant buildings or buying up what were now worthless buildings and real estate. By 1924, the Viennese government was the single largest property owner in the city. It soon set about a huge building programme, constructing over 60,000 new apartments between 1923 and 1934. More than that, it wanted to create a new communist utopia. The new apartment complexes were planned to offer communal laundries, health services, children's play areas, libraries, social clubs, swimming pools, sports centres—everything necessary to create a 'new man'. Community life and physical and cultural activities were facilitated and encouraged. New proletarian holidays and celebration days were created. Gas, water and electricity were also provided by the government, which gave family allowances to parents and municipal unemployment insurance to the trade unions.

One of these buildings is the Karl Marx-Hof, reputedly the longest building on earth, a complex with 1,300 one-bedroom flats, two central laundrettes, two public baths, two nursery schools, a dental clinic, a counselling service for mothers, a library, a youth centre, post office, its own health insurance services and so on. It looked like a fortress, and it became a real one during a brief civil war in 1934 when government forces attacked its defenders, the Socialist Defence Bund, with artillery.[14]

All this was financed by the Breitner tax, named after the councillor of finances, which taxed luxury goods, cars, horse racing and domestic servants, and another progressive housing tax that targeted villas and private homes. Still, Vienna's municipal welfare remained heavily reliant on funding from the national government.

Tenants of this social housing paid rent that barely covered operating costs—about 4 per cent of a worker's monthly wage. Apartment allocation was made by a points system that considered need, current housing situation, employment status and war injuries and place of birth.[15]

The achievements of Red Vienna were widely praised at the time, but Mises remained unconvinced by what he saw happening in Vienna. Mises attacked socialism of all flavours and insisted that no socialist commonwealth has ever had any chance of succeeding.

In 1920, he completed what his admirers believe is one of the greatest articles on economics ever written. It had the sombre title of 'Die Wirtschaftsrechnung im sozialistischen Gemeinwesen' or 'Economic Calculation in the Socialist Commonwealth'. Before it was published, he made a presentation to the seminar that included Schumpeter, Max Adler and Helene Bauer. Then he managed to have it published in the highbrow but influential German journal *Archiv für Sozialwissenschaft und Sozialpolitik*, edited by Max Weber, a towering figure in the social sciences.

'If compelled to single out the idea that best characterized Mises's overall contribution to human knowledge, one would have to name his general theory of economic calculation', his biographer Jörg Guido Hülsmann wrote in *Mises: The Last Knight of Liberalism*.[16]

Mises' paper on the socialist calculation problem was soon turned into a book. It was simply called *Socialism*, although the German title *Die Gemeinwirtschaft* means 'the common economy', and he wanted to include all kinds of utopian communal economies including anarchism and fascism.

Most economists start from the assumption that people act rationally, only after making an economic calculation of the benefits of a given action against another. Mises argues that this is not necessarily the case—you can only make a rational calculation in a market economy where private property is protected. This is even more true with a modern economy where there are capital-intensive production chains and a sophisticated division of labour.

A socialist economy has by definition no private property rights, so there are no prices. Prices can only emerge from the interaction of private property owners. These prices deliver the information that both a private businessman and a central planner need to direct resources efficiently and rationally. Money is essential because it serves as a standard of value, a measuring rod or *numéraire*. It measures the value of the commodities against which it is exchanged in the marketplace.

Mises stressed that money itself does not have any constant value, so it is not in itself a tool to calculate value. Prices are made by an individual who makes a valuation determined by the circumstances in which it is made. No socialist economy can deliver such prices because they can only happen in a market where two owners meet to make a trade.

In a socialist economy, there is by definition only one owner, which is the state—sometimes referred to as 'the people'—that controls all means of production. A socialist economy cannot allocate its factors of production on the basis of economic calculation because nothing is ever exchanged. Hence there could be no rational planning.

Economists in the twentieth century assumed that in general people act rationally, but they split into two schools. One held that those in a planned state-owned society would invest their wealth and industry rationally, while those that lived in a laissez-faire economy behaved more irrationally. In theory, an economy dominated by markets where investment is driven by irrational crowd behaviour would always perform poorly against an economy planned by rational officials. Only a few believed the contrary, and as the twentieth century progressed, that group became a dwindling minority.

In his paper, Mises turned the rational actor argument on its head. He predicted that socialist economies would suffer from irrational investment, or what economists term malinvestment. Planners would direct resources into projects, but in the absence of price signals, the returns would be poor, even if it might take a while before they realized it. Any state planning bureaucracy would operate in the dark because they made policy and investment decisions based on statistics rather than market prices. Without a reliable gauge to measure by, these statistics would be misleading. Socialism would be more arbitrary than a market economy.

'It was immediately clear to the audience that Mises was treading completely new ground. Socialism had been criticized from many angles, but hardly anyone had doubted that the central planners could achieve gains in efficiency', his biographer writes.[17]

Mises agreed that much depended on the subjective judgement of an entrepreneur, but even when the case involves the state directing its planning, any economic calculation requires the existence of prices for capital goods.

It was also true, Mises said, that in capitalism the relevant prices—future money prices—had to be guessed, but his point was that only in capitalism was there any basis for guesses. For this reason, he believed that in capitalism the division of labour is more productive than in socialism because only in capitalism can you make economic calculations. You need up-to-date prices to provide the information required to make a rational decision. Otherwise, you have no way of knowing whether you are making the most of your resources or squandering them. As he wrote:

> In any type of economy, an economic actor has to decide how to invest and plan for the future. If a society is static, without technological change, capital goods like factory machinery are always replaced by the same type of machines ...
>
> In this case, you have an identical physical yardstick, a unit. You can work out multiples of that unit; you can add one apple to another apple, or one grain of silver to another. Yet you cannot add a telephone to a piano concerto. You cannot add wittiness to silence. These items are unalike, so there is no way to assess their value.
>
> In a dynamic and changing economy—that is, a real life economy—old machinery is not replaced by the same model but by new ones that are usually better. So making calculations by adding up physical units is of no use. The only way is to use money to make value calculations.

In the real world a manager is constantly under pressure to replace capital goods because they get worn out or outdated. He can't keep things the way they are, so he has to decide which capital goods should be replaced and when. As with all economic decisions, this involves deciding priorities and making trade-offs. To do this rationally, the businessman has to weigh clear criteria in order to judge the extent of wear and tear on the current capital goods and assess the return on invested capital. Even in a planned economy, there has to be a way of doing the accounting.[18]

In the 1930s, these ideas were also explored by Hayek, who was to become famous for *The Road to Serfdom*, his attack on central planning. Yet Mises and Hayek differed on one essential question. Hayek considered that in theory, assuming one could gather the right knowledge without market prices, then one could calculate the correct prices for factors of production. Hayek admitted that obtaining such knowledge was very difficult and thought it unlikely that a socialist planning board could use mathematical equations to work things out. In 1938, Mises published an article demolishing this notion. It was hard to imagine how any socialist planning board could know future consumer preferences, but even if it did, it could not simply plug into a system of equations and solve the question of allocating resources properly. Prices were constantly changing.

Mises was also ahead of his time in disputing that the working class would be better off in a country run by socialists because they would enjoy more freedom and higher living standards. On the contrary, Mises said it was inevitable they would have less. The directors of any socialist commonwealth would have to decide the allocation of all factors of production, including people. They would not only decide how each stretch of land should be used but also how to allocate 'human resources'. The planners would have the power to order about all individuals and families, tell them where to move and live, and when to move on. This need not be malicious or a personal abuse of power but because in socialism the common ownership of all the means of production includes labour. The individual had to submit to the will of central planners; it was just like being in the army.

'It was obvious that socialism was anything but a reign of liberty', he said. 'The Socialist Community is a great authoritarian association in which orders are issued and obeyed.'[19]

Payment for work would also be arbitrary, and the individual could not challenge arbitrary decisions taken by the community or those at the centre who were in charge. Mises was certain this lack of freedom would spill into every area and end in absolute censorship and the absence of artistic creativity. Rather than socialist man striding forth, powerful and confident in a land of equals, Mises portrayed him as a tiny cog in a large, indifferent machine.

Mises also made a more basic point about the contradiction between the policy of class struggle and the end of labour specialization. Labour can only be divided among people who live in peace with one another. Violent conflicts, like waging class warfare, necessarily disrupt social cooperation. They split society into parties that work against one another rather than for one another. They destroy scarce resources rather than producing more resources.

Mises' thinking was informed by what he could observe from Vienna. He never witnessed first hand what was happening in Moscow as Lenin, with Bukharin at his side, seized untrammelled power and pushed through a six-month programme to introduce full-blown communism. The next chapter looks at how well Mises' diagnosis stands up.

3

WHY LENIN'S PROGRAMME FAILED AND THE EXCUSE OF WAR COMMUNISM

Many students are taught that after 1917, the communists' economic programme was never properly put into practice. As a backward country with an economy in shambles, it was not ripe for such an experiment, and then a civil war that raged for five years prevented anything other than 'war communism' from being implemented.

Leon Trotsky would later admit that in 1917 Lenin believed that he could reach full communism within six months.[1] And in 1921 Lenin conceded that the Bolshevik programme had not worked out and recognized this as a 'great defeat'. Then, before his death in 1924, he changed his line and instead wrote off the first five years as just 'war communism'.[2]

Until the archives were opened after 1991, many Western historians followed this war communism line, agreeing that the chaotic circumstances of the time prevented the communist programme from being properly tried.[3] Yet Bukharin himself admitted the programme had been tried and that it had failed: 'We conceived War Communism as the universal, so to say "normal" form of the economic policy of the victorious proletariat and not as being related to the war, that is, conforming to a definite state of the civil war.'[4]

The first excuse is easily dealt with. When the tsar abdicated in the spring of 1917, Russia was not considered especially poor. Russia had been a major food exporter, especially of grain, as well as the world's fourth largest industrial power. Up to 1914, the economy had been growing at 8 per cent a year, and foreign investment was pouring in. By 1916, Russia was churning out four times as many artillery shells as Austro-Hungary and 50 per cent more than imperial Germany. And it ended the war with the world's second largest gold reserves. Most of its 160 million people did still live in the countryside, but they were generally better off than in previous generations. They were poorer than their counterparts in Western Europe, but quite a few were prospering. Indeed, the underlying strength of the economy would serve to keep Russia's new rulers afloat in the first months of the revolution.[5]

The actions that Lenin took after the October Revolution (actually November 1917 in the Western calendar) matched their political programme. On 8 November 1917, the day after the coup that brought the Bolsheviks to power, Lenin began issuing the decrees designed to achieve full-blown communism within six months:

- He immediately abolished the right to own land, sell, lease or mortgage it.
- He nationalized all banks and set up a centralized state bank. On 19 December 1917, the Bolsheviks announced the abolition of all private banks and laid claim to all bank deposits in Russia.
- He decreed an end to all payments on investments and share dividends. All state loans were annulled. He appointed commissars to all the banks in Russia and demanded that anyone with a safe deposit turn up with a key, empty the deposit box and hand over the contents to the Party commissar.
- He declared a state monopoly over mining and trade in gold, silver and platinum and issued regulations controlling the allocation of coins, metal ingots and jewellery.

'In effect, the Bolsheviks had declared illegal the very fact of owing or being owed money, for any reason', notes Sean McMeekin in *History's Greatest Heist: The Looting of Russia by the Bolsheviks*.[6]

- By January 1918, Lenin had nationalized all the factories and all housing. Most private housing was divided and redistributed. People lived rent free, and the nationalized services like telegraph, post and telephone were also free.
- Trotsky launched the first campaign against 'speculators' in February 1918. Local soviets, railway committees and patrols had the right to enter and search any home. Speculators could be shot on the spot.
- The Bolsheviks had shut down all markets and established state monopolies for both internal and external commerce. By April 1918, commerce was directed by a Supreme Economic Council. All private trade in food was outlawed, and the state targeted all small traders and peddlers. All bakers, butchers, grocers, café and restaurant owners were forced to close.
- Everyone in the cities was ordered to register for labour under the direction of the state. In these industrial armies, all strikes were forbidden and discipline was strict.
- All inhabitants were ordered to join consumer communes; otherwise they could not obtain ration cards. In Petrograd, the state issued ration cards for thirty-three goods and services, including bread, milk, footwear and heating. These were only viable for one month and had then to be renewed.
- The population was divided into three categories. Each was entitled to different rations. The workers received a red ration card entitling them to three-quarters of a pound of bread per day. In the middle category were the bourgeoisie who had another card that merited them half a pound of bread a day. In the third category were the enemies of the people who had been stripped of all rights and who often received no rations at all. A proliferating number of state agencies took charge of procuring food for the cities, above all the flour baked into bread at state bakeries.
- All regions had to conduct trade by barter and could not use money. Urban factories had to obtain grain and other foodstuffs by bartering them for fabric, garments, processed leather, boots, matches, tea, sugar, salt and cooking oil. Each

factory also had to barter with other factories to get their supplies and parts.

Yet someone had to decide what the right trade off was between any industrial product and any agricultural product. It decided, for instance, that an *arshin* of fabric (an old Russian unit = 71.12cm) should be traded for 5 *pud* (another old unit = 16.38kg) of cereal. The state was free to decide whether each transaction favoured the farmer or the worker.

There was nothing half-hearted or tentative about these measures, and they brought the economy to a standstill. The industrial economy couldn't function in a barter economy. The farmers wouldn't trade their produce either. The example of the barter trade value of 1 *arshin* of fabric for 5 *pud* of cereal had to be calculated for thousands if not hundreds of thousands of different products and combinations, taking into account the quality and varieties of even basic commodities. And it needed to be updated all the time and adjusted to take in local circumstances. This was clearly impossible to do in the best of times.

The belief articulated by Engels, Lenin and Bukharin that anyone with rudimentary arithmetic skills could take over the management of factories, banks, insurance companies and so on proved to be a fantasy. Without a common currency and a banking system to allocate credit, enterprises that assembled hundreds of parts could not function. Nor could a network of statistical bureaux replace the pricing mechanism of the market. It is not surprising that neither Lenin nor Bukharin or anyone else in the leadership could understand this since none had ever worked in any commercial enterprise.

In May 1918, Lenin decided there was no alternative but to seize the grain by force if the urban population and the military were to be fed. A People's Commissariat for Food was set up with unlimited power to confiscate food. The first operations in the summer were rather disorganized. Armed detachments would drive into villages and grab whatever they could find. The Party recruited factory workers and committees of poor peasants to help. This sort of policy resembled the kind of thing going on in Austria at the same time, but it was quite unique in nature. What happened in Austria was largely spontaneous—markets did operate, and with the exception of real estate, private ownership was respected. What happened in Russia was the result of the deliberate application of the Party's ideology, and so it could not be allowed to be seen to fail.[7]

In January 1919, the Party attempted to establish a centralized planned requisitioning system. It set quota targets for every province, district, canton (*volost* in Russian) and village community determined by how big the coming grain harvest would be. Quotas were also set for potatoes, honey, eggs, butter, cooking oil, meat, cream and milk. If a village had met its quota, a Party official wrote a receipt that in theory allowed them to acquire manufactured goods.

In practice, these bits of paper had no value. The requisition quotas were arbitrary, based on inflated estimates of what the harvest would be. So instead of levying a tithe after the harvest was gathered, the Party simply took everything it could find. The following year, 1920, there were not enough planting seeds. In many places, the fields could not be sown, so by 1921, there was nothing to harvest.

The Bolshevik six-month programme met with enormous resistance from almost every sector of society. First, Russia's private banks shut their doors against the revolutionaries. The State Bank and Treasury refused to release cash to what they considered an illegitimate regime. Yet Lenin lost no time in robbing the banks, a strategy called 'looting the looters'. In one of those tragi-comic scenes of the revolution, the bankers in their wing collars managed to hold off the ruthless revolutionaries for quite a while. As Francis O. Lindley wrote in 'Report on Recent Events in Russia':

> Three times Lenin has sent down to the Bank to fetch ten million Rubles and three times he has failed to secure them. The last time ... a battalion of soldiers with a band at their head marched to the Bank with the necessary vehicles to carry off the spoil ... all began bawling and shaking their fists. ... For a time, things looked nasty, but the [Bank] Directors found their champion in a giant peasant, in soldier's uniform, who roared louder than any ten and had a larger fist.[8]

Finally, the Bolsheviks did wrest control of the banks, seize all the money and reward their supporters. Later, when they had run through the stock of banknotes, they ransacked the safe boxes and seized the stashed gold, silver and diamonds. When they had finished doing that, they fired up the printing presses until they stoked up a conflagration of hyperinflation. Everyone now had lots of paper money, but it was soon worthless. The Bolsheviks created a new State Bank and appointed twenty-nine-year-old Grigory Sokolnikov—who took pride in knowing nothing about banking— as its inaugural director.

The closure of the banks shut down the industrial economy, breaking the production chain at every point, shutting off the flow of funds to industrial enterprises so they could no longer pay suppliers or their workforce. Soon all the factory workers were on strike, and the peasants began taking up arms in a desperate fight for survival.

The Bolsheviks created a private army to enforce their decrees and crush all opposition. This was the Cheka, which became far more important to the Party's survival than either the Red Guards or the Red Army. The Cheka, or All-Russian Extraordinary Commission for Combatting Counterrevolution, Speculation and Sabotage, was founded in response to the bankers' strike on 20 December 1917, just six weeks after the revolution. Lenin ordered Felix Dzerzhinsky to create the Cheka because, he said, 'exceptional measures will have to be taken to combat these saboteurs and counter-revolutionaries'. It expanded rapidly to become an army and intelligence organization loyal to the Party and largely hidden from the rest of the country. It started with just forty officials, a team of soldiers and a group of Red Guards. By early 1921, it employed 280,000—around 105,000 civilians and nearly 180,000 troops of different types—including frontier guards, railway police and camp officials. By comparison, the tsar's secret police, the Okhranka, had never numbered more than 1,000.[9]

Keeping the Cheka well fed, clothed, mobile and armed became the top priority. In the spring of 1918, the Party secretly established a system of special privileges for both the Cheka and the Party elite. They became a special class, the fourth class, with unique access to food, clothing and housing, all distributed by secret shops and commissariats. They obtained chauffeur-driven cars, large apartments and dachas as well as special schools for their children. The Cheka forces invariably had superior weapons, clothing and communications to that of their enemies, who struggled just to get enough to eat, never mind essential weapons and transportation.

The Cheka could do whatever it wanted. It could arrest and execute almost anyone, seize their property or take hostages. Its members could keep any property they seized. In the first five years of Bolshevik rule, the Cheka probably executed 250,000 people, a number larger than those killed in civil war combat. The Cheka also created the world's first labour concentration camps, and the numbers imprisoned in work or labour camps increased steadily to more than 70,000 by September 1920.[10]

Just seven months after the October Revolution, the middle of 1918, industrial production had dropped by a third. By 1920, Russian industry's total production had crashed by over 85 per cent from a pre-war level of 6.059 billion gold imperial roubles to the equivalent of just 836 million, according to P. Popov of the Central Statistical Bureau of Soviet Russia.[11]

Desperate workers took to striking in most enterprises in Moscow, Petrograd, the Donbas mines, the metal-bashing Urals factories, the Baku oil fields and all the textile mills and railways. White-collar workers—telegraph and telephone workers, water transport workers, schoolteachers and municipal bureaucrats—joined them.

No one wanted to work in exchange for a worthless currency or equally worthless ration tickets. A worker in Petrograd in 1920 earned between 7,000 and 12,000 roubles, enough to buy a pound of butter (5,000 roubles) on the black market. Of course, workers had ration cards. A heavy industry worker in Petrograd was given a half-pound of bread a day, a pound of sugar a month, half a pound of fat and 4 pounds of sour herring.[12]

'They no longer have the physical strength necessary to continue working, and more and more often they are absent simply as a result of the combined effects of cold and hunger', said a secret police report in December 1919. Many other residents got no rations at all. In search of food, millions fled from the cities to the countryside. Petrograd and Moscow emptied.[13]

Colonel Edward Ryan, the American Red Cross commissioner for North Russia and the Baltic states, painted a devastating picture of Petrograd in the spring of 1920:

Both Moscow and St. Petersburg are indescribably filthy in outward appearance. ... [I] was told the streets had not been cleaned for more than three years. ... The dirt and rubbish is in all places at least ankle deep and in most places it is up to one's knees, and there are many places where it is as high as one's head. In Moscow a few women from time to time endeavor to clear up a little space by throwing and sweeping the dirt to the sides of the street so as to permit traffice [*sic*] to move in a narrow channel. There has obviously been no attempt to haul anything away ... Unable to bathe or dispose of trash properly, city dwellers were set upon by rats, cockroaches, mosquitoes and other vermin. In such conditions, epidemic disease was rampant. Those suffering from the outbreak of the flu, cholera, typhus or dysentery found little solace in the hospitals because the doctors and nurses were dying, too.[14]

At a hospital in a once wealthy part of central Moscow, he heard that three-quarters of the staff had died in the last three months. The hospital had sheets and mattresses, but surgeries were rarely performed because there were 'very few surgical instruments and few anaesthetics'. Ryan was not allowed to visit hospitals in poorer districts, which must have been even worse off. So many people were dying in Petrograd, he said, that 'morgues and cemeteries could not cope, and corpses lay around for months waiting to be buried'.

Workers in Petrograd staged a general strike on 2 July 1918, but it failed. They tried again in March 1919, angered by the arrest of the Socialist Revolutionary Party's leaders. Ten thousand workers at the Putilov factory adopted a resolution condemning the dictatorship of the Communist Party, calling for the release of political prisoners, free elections and an end to restrictions on the quantity of food that workers could bring into the city from the countryside. When Lenin went to Petrograd to address the striking workers, he was booed off the stage. Reprisals were not far behind. On 16 March 1919, Cheka detachments stormed the Putilov factory, arrested 900 and then executed 200 without trial in the Schlüsselburg fortress.[15]

Workers downed tools in Tula, Sormovo, Orel, Bryansk, Tver, Ivanovo-Voznesensk and Astrakhan. The demands made everywhere were always the same: more bread to avert starvation, the end of special privileges for communists, the release of political prisoners, free elections to the soviets and factory committees, the end of conscription into the Red Army, freedom of association, freedom of expression and freedom of the press. When soldiers refused to fire on protesting workers in Astrakhan, the Cheka was forced to retake the town by force. Afterwards, the Cheka loaded hundreds of prisoners, soldiers and strikers on to barges, tied stones around their necks and threw them into the Volga River. Between 2,000 and 4,000 strikers were shot or drowned in early March along with another 1,000 people identified as members of the 'bourgeoisie'.[16]

The Black Book of Communism describes what happened when, a month later, Cheka founder Felix Dzerzhinsky went to Tula to put down a strike at the munitions factories that produced most of the rifles in Russia. Dzerzhinsky arrested 800 'leaders', fired all the workers and cleared the factories. Next, he cancelled their ration cards so they could find nothing to eat. In order to get a new card, each worker had to sign a job application form stipulating, in particular, that any stoppage in the future would be considered an act of desertion and would thus be punishable by death. They could then return to work and get a half-pound of bread a day. Production resumed on 10 April. The night before that, twenty-six strike 'leaders' had been executed.[17]

A year later, another strike at Tula broke out. On Sunday, 6 June 1920, a number of metallurgy workers refused to work extra hours. The female workers refused to work on Sundays because it was the only day they could venture into the countryside and find food. The Party sent a large Cheka detachment to enforce martial law and arrest the strikers. A troika made up of Party and Cheka representatives denounced a 'counterrevolutionary conspiracy fomented by Polish spies and the Black Hundred to weaken the combat strength of the Red Army':

> While the strike spread and arrests of the 'leaders' multiplied, a new development changed the Cheka's calculus; in their hundreds, and then in their thousands, female workers and simple housewives presented themselves to the Cheka asking to be arrested too. The movement spread. Men demanded

to be arrested en masse as well in order to make the idea of a Polish conspiracy appear even more ridiculous. Within four days, more than 10,000 people were detained in a huge open-air space guarded by the Cheka. Temporarily overwhelmed by the numbers, and at a loss about how to explain the events to Moscow, the local Party hesitated ...

The Cheka finally persuaded the central authorities that an enormous conspiracy was afoot. A Committee for the Liquidation of the Tula Conspiracy interrogated thousands of prisoners in the hope of finding a few guilty conspirators. To be set free, hired again and given a new ration book, all the workers who had been arrested had to sign the following statement: 'I, the undersigned, a filthy criminal dog, repent before the revolutionary court and the Red Army, confess my sins, and promise to work conscientiously in the future.' In contrast to other protests, the Tula confrontation in the summer of 1920 was treated with comparative leniency: only 28 people were sentenced to camps, and 200 were sent into exile.[18]

Yet terror could not feed people in the cities. So in January 1921, the communists had no choice but to slash bread rations by a third in major cities like Moscow, Petrograd, Ivanovo-Voznesensk and Kronstadt. The starving workers rose up and were soon joined by the Red Army garrisons. Soon the rebellion spread across Russia, and Bolshevik authority collapsed in many provinces. In Petrograd, workers voted in a new 'Plenipotentiary Workers' Assembly' that demanded the end of the Bolshevik dictatorship and called for another general strike. On 24 February, Cheka detachments opened fire on a workers' demonstration, killing twelve men. That same day, the Cheka arrested more than 1,000 workers and militant socialists, yet more and more people joined the strikes, with troops deserting en masse to support them. The sailors on two warships at the naval base in Kronstadt mutinied.

This became the most critical moment since 1917. 'Of all the repressive episodes, the one most carefully hidden by the new regime was the violence used against workers, in whose name the Bolsheviks had first come to power', *The Black Book of Communism* notes. The whole city was on the brink of a general uprising against the Bolsheviks. The Cheka was forced to undertake a brutal assault in order to crush the same forces who had brought the Bolsheviks into power in 1917. Up to 10,000 people were subsequently arrested and were either shot or killed in concentration camps soon afterwards. The Kronstadt Uprising marked a turning point in the Bolsheviks' thinking.[19]

In the countryside, the barter system failed utterly. The Russian peasants, who lived in close-knit villages, had by then divided up the land and now farmed their own plots. They simply refused to barter surplus food for industrial goods, even when they were available. The Bolsheviks then tried to barter with the peasants collectively rather than individually by delivering a quantity of industrial goods to a district. They always tried to do this in a way that ensured that poorer peasants were given more for their grain than the richer ones, which made the peasants even angrier.[20]

Next, the government tried offering cash, but no farmer wanted bits of coloured paper that could not be exchanged for anything of value. The grain remained in the countryside, or it entered the black market, but even there, how much was a peasant going to get for his food? Fleeing émigrés, lucky looters and Bolshevik officials tried to swap jewels for food, but it was illegal to own gold or other valuables, so there were few takers. Baroness Meyendorff discovered that small pieces of jewellery, such as her favourite emerald and diamond rings, would fetch nothing. Finally, she bartered a brooch covered with 'six large diamonds the size of peas, the middle ones slightly smaller than the ones on either side, graduating from two to three carats each' for a single bag of white flour.[21]

Then the Party set out to tax the peasants in advance, so the peasants resisted and hid what they could. Otherwise, they too would soon be starving. Rather than change their ideas, the Party set out to seize the food with a campaign of extreme violence and terror— public executions, hangings and hostage taking. The Party justified this by claiming that a class of wealthy peasants were responsible for the food shortages, selfishly hiding food out of pure greed. This imagined group were called *kulaks*.

Cheka reports in archives, which only became available after 1991, revealed that this 'dirty war' against the peasants, who were known as the 'Greens', was bigger and far more important than the war with the 'Whites'. The peasants began to unite into armies. Instead of fighting a sporadic guerrilla war, the Bolsheviks were now engaged in pitched battles.

In Ukraine, many peasants had been armed and trained during the First World War to resist the invasion by German and Austro-Hungarian forces. By 1919, the Ukrainians formed a number of real armies, each with tens of thousands of peasants. They were commanded by military chiefs. These peasant armies drew up political programmes: land for the peasants, free trade and free elections to the soviets.

In the rich provinces of Samara and Simbirsk, where in 1919 the Bolsheviks wanted to requisition a fifth of the grain needed to feed Russia, a peasant army of 30,000 seized dozens of towns. The Bolsheviks lost all control of Samara for more than a month. In Tatarstan and Bashkortostan, another peasant army sprang up that in the spring of 1920 had 50,000 men. This pitchfork rebellion was called the 'Black Eagle Uprising'.[22]

The Cossacks of the Don and Kuban waged such fierce resistance that the Bolsheviks set out to eliminate them entirely. The Bolshevik leaders called this ethnic cleansing the 'Soviet Vendée', a reference to the French Revolution when a peasant counter-revolution was put down. In February 1920, the Bolshevik forces attacked for the second time with the intention of extracting 36 million *pood*, which was more than the area's normal harvest. According to a Cheka report, the local population was robbed not only of its meagre food and grain reserves but all its goods, including 'shoes, clothes, bedding, and samovars'.[23]

By 1922, the peasant resistance was defeated not so much by military force but by starvation. At least 5 million people died of hunger, and most of the country was starving. By comparison, during the last great famine in 1891, fewer than 500,000 had perished in the Russian Empire. With this man-made famine, the population had been starved into utter submission. In Samara, where tens of thousands had joined the armed resistance, the Party's provincial representative, I. N. Vavilin, reported:

There are no more revolts. We see new phenomena instead: crowds of thousands of starving people gather around the Executive Committee or the Party headquarters of the soviet to wait, for days and days, for the miraculous appearance of the food they need. It is impossible to chase this crowd away, and every day more of them die. They are dropping like flies. ... I think there must be at least 900,000 starving people in this province.[24]

Much of the grain seized never reached the cities because there were no granaries to store the grain and the railways were barely working thanks to a lack of coal.

The 'war communism' excuse, repeated in so many textbooks, does not hold up to scrutiny. The political programme that Lenin and Bukharin implemented failed for reasons that had little to do with the battles against the White Armies. These took place as far away as Siberia and the Caucasus.

Lenin was confident that his economic programme would work, and he believed too that the revolution needed to be supported by revolutions across the world. To achieve this, he ordered invasions of Poland, the Baltics, various Central Asian emirates and the nations of the Caucasus. The number of troops involved in these wars was immense. The Polish–Bolshevik War (February 1919–March 1921) involved 1.4 million troops on both sides. The Poles alone deployed 700,000 men, a far mightier force than the White Armies ever mustered. These immense armies pillaged food as they marched east, west and south. The White Armies never totalled more than 140,000 and were scattered around different corners of the former empire. And many of these White Army troops such as the Don Cossacks were not really 'Whites' but members of the 'Green' peasant rebellion.[25]

Since most of the fighting was taking place 1,000 or 2,000 miles away from key cities like Moscow and Petrograd, it should not have impacted the supply of potatoes, cabbages or eggs to the large industrial cities, which were usually supplied locally.

The Bolshevik experiment should have died in 1922. L. Kritsman, one of the architects of these policies, would later describe the first five years as a calamity 'unparalleled in the history of mankind'. Two million may have fled Russia, 5 million starved to death, there were over 600,000 war casualties and 250,000 civilian deaths from executions and imprisonment. The vast majority of the deaths and the fighting can be attributed to a terrible struggle over food almost entirely due to the shortages created by Bolshevik economic policies.[26]

In the summer of 1922, with some 30 million Russians rapidly starving to death, and factories and cities left abandoned and desolate, Lenin staged a strategic retreat. The barter system was abandoned, a new currency was issued and private trading was allowed. Food production began to recover.

The theory had failed to work, but despite the great losses, the Bolsheviks stayed in power. They had crushed their political opponents in a civil war in which their greatest weapon was food. Yet worse was to come. Some Bolsheviks were determined to try again.

4

HOW A GOLD-BACKED CURRENCY BROUGHT PROSPERITY TO MANY COUNTRIES IN THE 1920S

Leaders in Russia and in all the defeated countries of the First World War acted as if they could prosper by printing vast quantities of paper money or by abolishing money altogether. No one seemed to grasp the connection between a stable currency and inflation or price controls and food shortages. The Austrian economists had explained that when currencies became useless as a means of exchange and a store of value, the result was not social harmony but political chaos. Adam Fergusson puts it well in his book *When Money Dies: The Nightmare of the Weimar Hyperinflation*:

> If what happened to the defeated Central Powers in the early 1920s is anything to go by, then the process of collapse of the recognized, traditional, trusted medium of exchange, the currency by which all values are measured, by which social status is guaranteed, upon which security depends, and in which the fruits of labor are stored, unleashes such greed, violence, unhappiness and hatred, largely bred from fear, as no society can survive uncrippled and unchanged.[1]

The role of hyperinflation in destroying the Weimar Republic is taught in school history books, yet it is given little space in the story of Lenin's Russia, although it was equally important. Rampant inflation undermined the popularity of first the imperial government and then the provisional. To pay for the war, the Russian government began printing money and soon quadrupled the money supply. By the start of 1917, the rouble had lost nearly half its pre-war value, measured against the gold-backed currencies traded in Stockholm and London. Then in April 1917 the new provisional Kerensky government started printing money in earnest. By the time of the Bolshevik coup, the money in circulation had gone from 2 billion in 1914 to 19.6 billion. The imperial roubles were known as *nikolaevki* or *romanovki*, but the script issued by the Kerensky government, the *kerenki*, were much plainer and easier to counterfeit. They were printed on one side without a serial number, signature or name of issuer.[2]

To persuade the peasants to sell food, the Bolsheviks chose in mid-1918 to start printing even more *kerenki*. By January 1919, the supply had tripled to 61.3 billion roubles. The following month, the Bolsheviks started printing their own money, which they termed 'accounting tokens'—abbreviated as *sovnarki* from Sovnarkom, the name of Lenin's Council of Commissars. The new currency circulated along with imperial roubles and *kerenki* but at a steep discount. Then in May 1919, the floodgates really opened. The State Bank was authorized to print as much money as it judged the national economy required. By the end of 1919, it issued 225 billion *sovnarki*. In 1920, the money in circulation rose to 1.2 trillion. In 1921, it rose to 16 trillion, and in 1922 the number of banknotes in circulation hit an astonishing 2 quadrillion—that is to say, 2,000 million millions.[3]

The Bolsheviks regarded hyperinflation as a positive development. On one occasion, the Soviet commissar of finance, Isidor Gukovsky, declared that his job served no purpose: 'Finance should not exist in a socialist community and I must, therefore, apologize for speaking on the subject.' But he also admitted as early as April 1918 that '[a]ll our efforts to induce the peasant to give us his foodstuffs have been rather fruitless, because in exchange for his produce we offer him paper money which cannot buy anything'.[4]

Economist Evgenii Preobrazhensky (the co-author of *The ABC of Communism*) memorably described the banknote-printing press as that 'machine gun of the Commissariat of Finance which poured fire into the rear of the bourgeois system and used the currency laws of that system to destroy it'. He argued that inflation was a highly effective policy for diverting resources from the private to the socialized sector and for expropriating the money capital of the bourgeoisie.

As the historian Richard Pipes writes in *The Russian Revolution 1899–1919*, at the Tenth Party Congress, held in March 1921, before inflation reached its apogee, Preobrazhensky boasted that whereas the paper 'assignats' issued by the French revolutionaries had depreciated 500 times, the Soviet rouble had already fallen to 1/20,000 of its value. 'This means', he said, 'that we have beaten the French Revolution 40 to 1.'[5]

Russia was even more reckless than Germany. During the war years, the money in circulation had doubled in Britain, tripled in France, but it had quadrupled in Germany. Next the post-war Weimar Republic began printing money with even greater speed. The head of the Reichsbank, Dr Rudolf von Havenstein, employed twenty paper mills, 150 printing firms and 200 printing presses that operated round the clock to supply an avalanche of banknotes. But there was never enough. People panicked when the printers staged a strike, and crowds, some with wheelbarrows, descended on the Reichsbank head office calling for more banknotes. In less than a year, the exchange rate of marks to American dollars jumped from 9,000 to 4.2 trillion. Banknotes worth 1 million marks were followed by the issuance of the 100 trillion-mark banknote. After the war ended, German families had spent half their money on food, but they were soon spending three-quarters of their budget on food.[6]

In those circumstances, it didn't take much to bring people on to the streets. The revolution in Munich in November 1918 started when 100,000 people protested that the price of a litre of beer had risen by just 6 *pfennigs*. By 1922, the Bavarians needed ration cards just to get things like bread and sugar, and in every major town in Germany, large numbers were reported to be malnourished and suffering from rickets, pneumonia and tuberculosis.[7]

As politicians did not understand the role that money played, they took absurd counter-measures to deal with the crisis. The

German government threatened anyone who hoarded food or money, prevented the payment of taxes, or impeded the distribution of food or fodder with unlimited fines and a month in jail. The prime minister of Bavaria wanted to make gluttony a criminal offence and to punish any caterer who abetted or connived at this crime. Germany tried to confiscate people's foreign currency and even sent the police into Berlin cafés, where they forced customers to open their wallets and then trousered any foreign banknotes.

Although the hyperinflation allowed governments to erase their war debts, it also made it impossible to raise taxes. Since they had no meaningful tax revenues, governments had to print more money to pay for salaries and services. In Russia, the state could not raise taxes, since there was nothing to tax, so it took the absurd decision to try—naturally without success—to tap into the illegal black-market trade by ordering a 40 per cent tax on all items sold for more than 5,000 roubles.[8]

Yet finally, the monetarist view of the world re-asserted itself. A new currency was successfully issued in Germany. Countries such as Britain and France returned to the gold standard, and international trade revived. In fact, it was gold that kept the Bolsheviks in power, another story omitted from most history books. It's remarkable that the Bolsheviks were able to survive so long as 1922 and were not forced out as they were in Hungary.

It was only when the archives were opened after 1991 that it became clear how the Bolsheviks had been able to retain their hold on power. It was gold, the ultimate currency, that saved them. The Bolsheviks had inherited the imperial gold reserves, the second largest in the world. At first, the gold could not be sold because Russia was shut out of world markets after Lenin had repudiated the country's foreign debts and confiscated foreign-owned assets.

The Bolsheviks initially tried selling the gold in Sweden and importing the goods through Tallinn by negotiating a treaty recognizing the independence of Estonia. The real breakthrough came when, at the end of 1919, British Prime Minister Lloyd George unexpectedly decided to abandon the British Baltic blockade and open trade relations with Russia. This was a great stroke of luck, because it meant that the gold could be imported and sold in London, the biggest market for gold. Other countries followed Britain's example.[9]

At the same time, Lenin tried to find more gold. He declared a policy of 'looting the looters'. Teams of safe-crackers forced open deposit boxes in every bank, and all the gold, silver, diamonds and foreign banknotes were sent to a central depository. A campaign against the Russian Orthodox Church snatched up the accumulated treasures of Russia's churches and monasteries. In all, the Bolsheviks collected 500 tons of silver and half a ton of gold, most of which was melted down and sold. And when the Bolsheviks had completed the conquest of the Central Asian khanates, they were stripped of their gold and other treasures as well. The Bolsheviks were suddenly able to barter the vast hoard of gold, diamonds and other assets they had accumulated and buy whatever they needed.[10]

Lenin was so desperate to rush in new supplies and secure the loyalty of his troops that the Bolsheviks sold the gold at a third below the prevailing market price. Within weeks of Lloyd George's decision, they spent at least $200 million, the equivalent of some $20 billion today, on importing war materiel.

In less than two years, the Bolsheviks traded 500 metric tons for over 2,000 locomotive engines and rolling stock, needed because much of the grain collected simply rotted by the railway in warehouses even as the surrounding population starved. As the American historian McMeekin says, they also bought tens of millions of boots, greatcoats and woollen uniforms; rifles, artillery shells and hundreds of millions of machine-gun rounds; ferrous metals and ball bearings to reinvigorate Russia's own ailing arms factories; spark plugs and spare parts for military vehicles and for the luxury cars driven by high Party officials like Lenin; an entire fleet of armoured airplanes; Scandinavian fish, European delicacies, Persian fruit, tobacco and opium, to satisfy the tastes of Bolshevik elites; and not least, enormous volumes of paper, chemicals to treat it, along with ink and film stock to print both money and propaganda.[11]

Lenin and the Cheka also benefitted from another unexpected stroke of good fortune. Germany became the only state willing to extend trade credits to the Bolshevik state when in 1922 the two outcast countries signed the Rapallo Treaty in Italy. Although

Germany had just suppressed a violent communist uprising, Lenin allowed Germany to hide its illegal rearmament by allowing it to train its troops and build weapons factories in Russia. This was of course a complete breach of the terms of the Versailles Treaty. In return, Germany gave Moscow trade credits worth 500 million gold marks, with which the Cheka could buy modern munitions, tanks and aircraft made in these German factories.[12]

Lenin had once declared that after the revolution, gold would lose its value to such an extent that it would be used to make urinals, but now he learned why gold has played such a central role in the economic history of the world. Only by secretly selling off the country's gold could the Bolsheviks save themselves by importing the war materiel that enabled the Cheka to defeat its enemies. The Bolsheviks were fighting peasant armies in Ukraine and elsewhere who could not even pay their troops let alone import aeroplanes, railway stock, lorries, radios and modern armaments.

When the fighting was over, the Russian communists made frantic efforts to find more gold to sell. Millions of semi-slaves were despatched 10,000 miles to the Russian Arctic, where they were worked to death in the newly discovered Kolyma gold mines. These mines alone produced 200 metric tons of gold a year, equal to 15 per cent of world gold production. The resulting exports were worth around $10 billion a year to Moscow. At its height, Gulag labour provided the Soviet Union with most of its nickel, tin and gold, a quarter of its lumber, much of its coal, as well as all its platinum and diamonds. These raw materials enabled the state to keep importing more materials and luxuries for its elite.[13]

It is not surprising that the Bolshevik leaders, who sacrificed millions of lives for a revolution dedicated to the abolition of all forms of money, kept very quiet about the essential role gold played in keeping them in power.

When the gold finally ran out, they decided to blame the weather for the disaster that their policies had caused. At first, Lenin thought that he could keep the state going with foreign loans and by selling concessions to foreign businessmen. When this did not work, he decided to appeal for international famine relief. This started after June 1921, when eminent economists Nikolai Kondratyev and Sergei

Prokopovich, once a minister of food in the provisional government, and various writers, doctors and agronomists, established a Fight against Famine Committee. Lenin's government begrudgingly recognized the committee, naming it the All-Russian Committee for Aid to the Starving. In the 'Appeal to All the Citizens of Soviet Russia', published in *Pravda* on 12 July 1921, Mikhail Kalinin, president of the Central Executive Committee of Soviets, blamed the famine on bad weather, stating that 'in numerous districts, the drought this year has destroyed the harvest'.

The committee contacted Patriarch Tikhon, head of the Russian Orthodox Church, who immediately set up an All-Russian Ecclesiastical Committee for Aid to the Hungry, which wrote to the Red Cross, the Quakers and the American Relief Association (ARA), presided over by Herbert Hoover. However, six days after this committee had signed an agreement with the ARA, the Bolsheviks dissolved it and exiled or imprisoned all those involved. As the food arrived from abroad, the government set up its own 'Central Commission for Help for the Hungry' and took control over the delivery and distribution of the food. The food aid supplied about 11 million people per day, but at least 5 million of the 29 million Russians affected died of hunger and disease in just two years, 1921 and 1922.[14]

It goes without saying that the Bolsheviks could easily have sold their gold to import food and clothing for the general population and save millions from starving to death instead of waging war against their own people and those of neighbouring states. And finally, as the next chapter explains, it was a return to a gold-backed currency that allowed food production to increase.

5

HOW BUKHARIN LOST HIS LIFE BUT SAVED
MILLIONS OF LIVES IN CHINA

After the bloody uprising at Kronstadt in 1921, Lenin began to signal a very hesitant retreat. A little over a year later, in May 1922, he suffered his first stroke, after which he was increasingly incapacitated. Lenin was still able to argue that the reforms should be relatively modest, and the state must always retain its control over what he called the 'commanding heights' of the economy. He had announced that forcible grain requisitioning would be replaced by a fairer tax in kind, leaving all surplus produce to the individual. Yet the initiative now fell into the hands of other leaders. The last of the gold reserves were being sold, and the reality was sinking in that the 1917 programme would have to be jettisoned. Bukharin became bolder in admitting what had gone wrong.

Hitherto, Bukharin had been a leading figure in the group closest to Lenin and had enthusiastically backed almost everything that Lenin had decreed and applauded the most violent Bolshevik policies, calling them the 'midwife' of revolutionary change. When the country was descending into economic catastrophe, he said this was a good thing because it would thoroughly demolish the legacy of capitalism and clear the way for communism. Lenin had once described him as a son, and he had often been called the 'darling of the Party'. During the previous decade, his books had made him the official theorist of the Bolsheviks, he had edited *Pravda* and controlled the rest of the Party's propaganda machinery. He also directed Comintern, which controlled the international communist movement, and so he was well known all over the world.[1]

As Lenin's influence weakened, Bukharin changed. He openly admitted that the 1917 programme had been tried and that it had failed. Bukharin told the Fourth Comintern Congress in December 1922: 'We will say frankly, we tried to take on ourselves the organization of everything—even the organization of the peasants and the millions of small producers ... from the viewpoint of economic rationality this was madness.' He also admitted that 'war communism' had been an attempt to implement communism and that the New Economic Policy (NEP) 'represented the collapse of our illusions'. 'We conceived War Communism as the universal, so to say "normal" form of the economic policy of the victorious proletariat and not as being related to the war, that is, conforming to a definite state of the civil war', Bukharin wrote.[2]

He knew that the Party had only clung on to power thanks to the gold that they had managed to sell abroad and that only when the gold ran out in February 1922 was Lenin forced to retreat.[3]

When Lenin died in 1924, a weeping Bukharin helped carry his coffin into the House of Trade Unions and many expected him to succeed Lenin. In his final testament, Lenin had warned against giving Joseph Stalin, the Party's general secretary, too much power. In 1925, Bukharin was still only thirty-seven and seemed poised to emerge on top since his popularity was bolstered by the success of the NEP. Bukharin became famous for telling the peasants to 'enrich themselves' and promising that the new policies would last twenty years. He declared: 'We must say to the peasants, and its strata, enrich yourselves, accumulate, develop your own economy.' This made him popular both within the Party and the country. He was one of the few who could freely walk around Moscow without a bodyguard.[4]

The partial reintroduction of the market economy had an almost magical effect. It ended the worst hunger by lifting grain production by 40 per cent, industrial production recovered and the violent class struggle abated. Given his authority on ideology, second only to

Lenin, Bukharin's statements carried great weight. He had admitted that the push towards full communism had failed and that for a long time to come Russia needed to stick to a mixed economy, officially termed 'the development of capitalism under the control of the proletarian state'.[5]

Bukharin now envisaged a gradual evolution into socialism. Under the NEP, peasants and urban residents were free to buy and sell their goods and services at market prices. The attempt to create a barter economy was abandoned. To make the market work, the Bolsheviks needed to establish a new and trustworthy currency. In 1923, Russia minted gold coins that were called the *chervonets*. The state later issued gold-backed notes, which initially traded at 50,000 old roubles for one gold-backed rouble. This worked: even though the state had secretly sold off most of its gold reserves, it was enough that the Russians believed the currency was backed by gold.

After Stalin forced him into exile in 1928, Trotsky wrote a book, *The Revolution Betrayed*, in which he described his conversion to the mixed economy policies espoused by Bukharin. 'It is clear that in the transitional economy, as under capitalism, the sole authentic money is that based on gold. All other money is only a substitute.' Trotsky argued that a stable monetary unit is essential for both domestic and foreign trade, and there must be a long transition between capitalism and communism:

> Money cannot be arbitrarily 'abolished', nor the state and the old family 'liquidated'. They have to exhaust their historic mission, evaporate, and fall away ... We shall be able to speak of the actual triumph of socialism only at that historical moment when the state turns into a semi-state and money begins to lose its magic power.[6]

He advanced the deadline for the end of money to a time when Homo sapiens had evolved into a superior creature:

> The death blow to money fetishism will be struck only upon that state when the steady growth of social wealth has us bipeds forget our miserly attitude towards every excess minute of labour ... having lost its ability to bring happiness or trample

men into dust, money will turn into mere bookkeeping receipts for the convenience of statisticians, and for planning purposes. In the more distant future, probably these receipts will not be needed. But we can leave this question entirely to posterity, who will be more intelligent than we are.

Trotsky probably spoke for many veteran Bolsheviks when he argued in favour of continuing to use money for the foreseeable future:

> In the meantime, the more elementary functions of money, as a measure of value, a means of exchange and medium of payment, are not only preserved, but acquire a broader field of action than they had under capitalism … The role of money in the Soviet economy is not only unfinished but, as we have said, still has a long growth ahead. The transitional epoch between capitalism and socialism taken as a whole does not mean a cutting down of trade, but on the contrary, its extraordinary extension.

But Stalin believed that the NEP was a betrayal of the revolution and that Lenin had only authorized a short-term retreat to cope with an emergency. One of Stalin's supporters was the theorist Preobrazhensky, Bukharin's fellow author of the *ABC of Communism*, and he developed an alternative economic policy that Stalin seized upon. Preobrazhensky argued that Russia's economy didn't need markets but a large investment programme to accelerate industrialization, and the only way to find the capital for this was by squeezing it out of the agricultural sector. He dressed this up as the 'law of primitive socialist accumulation'. He claimed it was different from the 'law of primitive capitalist accumulation' that Marx believed had taken place in England when capitalists had pushed peasants off the land to create a landless proletariat. This capitalist accumulation had also supposedly taken place when England and other nations established overseas colonies, violently seized territory and imported slaves to work on plantations or to mine gold and silver. Preobrazhensky thought the Bolsheviks needed to do the same, but rather than venturing abroad to find slaves, the Russian peasants could be forced off their land and become a landless proletariat. A slave army would be sent to colonize virgin lands to the east. The capital for industrial investment would come from paying the remaining peasants the lowest possible prices and charging higher prices for industrial products. This programme of naked exploitation became the foundation of Stalin's policies.[7]

Bukharin dismissed these ideas as a 'lunatic utopia' and vigorously opposed industrialization at the expense of agriculture. He favoured balanced economic growth and what he called 'socialist humanism'. Stalin began a sly campaign to destroy all those who like Bukharin and Trotsky had come to terms with reality. Stalin had Trotsky expelled from the Party in 1927 and drove him into foreign exile in 1929. The same year, Stalin ousted Bukharin from the Politburo as a 'right-wing deviationist' and established himself as the supreme leader. Stalin went on to murder or imprison a million and half of the old Bolsheviks, including Preobrazhensky, because he believed (or feared) that they did not support what he was doing. Between 1936 and 1938, he staged the famous Moscow Show Trials, putting the leading figures of the 1917 revolution on trial, where they confessed to the most astonishing crimes and were executed.

Stalin carried out what he termed a 'revolution from above', overturning the NEP and resuming the war against the peasants by forcibly seizing their grain. He reintroduced rationing, shut down markets and created massive collective farms. Stalin claimed that these 'extraordinary measures' were necessary to overcome a grain collection crisis because farmers refused to sell grain to the state at low prices. He blamed the rich farmers, the *kulaks*, for hoarding their harvest and ordered their arrest and deportation. Some 2 million were sent into the wilderness to starve.[8]

Bukharin, not yet imprisoned, attacked these policies as demanding 'a military-feudalistic tribute' from the peasants. He warned that their exploitation was not only wrong but would threaten the Party's grip on power. Forcible grain collection would alienate the poor and middle-income peasants and create a wave of unrest. 'Stalin's policy is leading to civil war. He will have to drown the revolts in blood', Bukharin warned. He travelled across Ukraine and witnessed the horror of mass starvation. At each train station, he saw children with swollen stomachs begging and returned to Moscow in a deep state of depression. He asked his father-in-law, the veteran Bolshevik Yury Larin: 'What was the point of the revolution?'[9]

Many millions starved to death in Ukraine, plus a million Kazakhs and many more elsewhere. Again the farmers tried to resist, but the Cheka was well prepared with German Mausers, machine guns and motor cars. This time, Stalin did not appeal for international aid but instead began exporting the seized grain to pay for imports of machinery. In one respect, though, Stalin did not repeat the mistakes of the first period. He carried on printing and using money. He also tolerated the black market, where managers of state enterprises could purchase whatever was in demand.

Meanwhile, Bukharin was arrested and tortured until he confessed at his trial that he was working towards the restoration of capitalism and had tried to murder Lenin.[10] Bukharin begged Stalin to save him, believing he would do so because they had been close friends ever since they had met in Vienna. When Stalin came there to work on his theory of nationalism, Bukharin (along with Trotsky) had shown Stalin around. They called each other by affectionate nicknames— Koba and Bukashka—and later went on holidays together. One of Bukharin's wives was the closest friend of Stalin's wife, Nadya. After 1917, Bukharin often stayed at Stalin's dacha in Zubalovo. Their children played with each other, and Bukharin taught his and Stalin's children to ride bikes and shoot an air gun.[11]

While in prison, Bukharin wrote thirty-four letters to Stalin, who never replied, although he kept them in a drawer. In these letters, Bukharin retracted his confessions, and there is no sign that he thought he was making a last service to the Party. On the contrary, he was hoping that if he cooperated, Stalin would spare his new wife, Anna Larina, and his own life. In his last message to Stalin, Bukharin wrote: 'Koba, why do you need me to die?' The note was found in Stalin's desk just after his death in 1953. Three days after the court sentence was passed, on 15 March 1938, he was taken at dawn from his cell in the basement of the Lubyanka prison in Moscow. He had asked to die by drinking morphine but was instead forced to watch others die before being shot himself. Anna Larina and their children were arrested and sent to penal labour camps. She was released after many years and survived long enough to see her husband officially rehabilitated by the Soviet state under Mikhail Gorbachev in 1988.

After 1938, every effort was made to bury Bukharin's memory, but his words, 'peasants enrich yourselves', were not forgotten. More than forty years later, Deng Xiaoping would tell Chinese peasants that to 'get rich is glorious' when he re-opened markets after the failures of Chairman Mao's collective farms. Mao had cursed Bukharin after his collectivization ended in famine, but Deng still knew all about his ideas for a mixed economy and set out to put them into practice after Mao's death.

6

WHY WESTERN INTELLECTUALS WERE FOOLED
BY SOVIET STATISTICS

Stalin had planned the new famine, and he was able to hide it so well that for decades many people continued to dispute that it had even happened. The first famine had been impossible to hide because the Party had, as a last resort, been forced to appeal for international food aid. In 1921, there was no choice but to let the foreign press into Russia along with the relief workers. Journalists like Walter Duranty saw the empty, ruined cities, encountered some of the millions of ragged, abandoned orphans, and interviewed the starving families wandering the countryside in search of food.

This time round, the State Political Directorate (GPU, the intelligence service formed out of the Cheka in 1922) was fully in control. Stalin was able to destroy or silence opposition within the Party. After ousting Bukharin, he seized control of the propaganda machinery and used it to manipulate the reports filed by resident correspondents and visiting experts. Visitors were taken on Potemkin tours and returned praising the success of Stalin's industrialization programme. It renewed faith in the Marxist dream around the world, and some may have believed this was more important than reporting truthfully what they had seen. In addition, Stalin claimed that he was implementing a five-year plan, and its success was demonstrated by a flood of statistics calculated according to a unit measure of a rouble. How it was used to hoodwink visitors will be described later.

Duranty went on those organized tours around Russia, now called the Soviet Union, even visiting farms in desperate Ukraine. He returned declaring that he saw no evidence of any famine. He also remarked in 1933: 'It may be said without fear of contradiction that the Stalinist machine is better organized for the formation and control of public opinion in a great country than anything history has hitherto known.'[1]

The greatest triumph of this 'Stalinist machine' was to parade an estimated 20,000 foreigners, including many of the world's leading intellectuals, around Russia to see for themselves. Almost every one of them returned to write a book, do an interview or give a lecture about their findings. Intellectuals who at home would never have dreamed of visiting factories or schools returned rolling off the statistics for the output of cars, tractors, locomotives, shoes, shops, coal, oil, pig iron and rolled steel, electric power kilowatts per year, acres under cultivation, trees planted and canals. They were almost without exception wildly enthusiastic, and they became known as the fellow travellers.

In her book *Western Intellectuals and the Soviet Union, 1920–40: From Red Square to the Left Bank*, Ludmila Stern notes that the fellow travellers arrived already primed by having watched films or listened to lectures on Soviet achievements presented by organizations like the Society for Cultural Relations between the Peoples of the British Commonwealth and the USSR. This had on its board the philosopher Bertrand Russell, Fabian economist G. D. H. Cole, economist Professor Harold Lasky, playwright G. B. Shaw, Beatrice Webb and the Bloomsbury group of writers E. M. Forster, Leonard and Virginia Woolf, and Aldous and Julian Huxley.[2]

These people would be offered a guided visit, often free of charge and with inducement of generous royalties from their book sales in the Soviet Union. Once in the country, they were feted and flattered and taken in chauffeur-driven cars to numerous banquets and concerts where they had the chance to meet famous writers and artists. Many felt privileged to be granted rare interviews with

Soviet leaders. Then they were taken on a fixed itinerary of model collective farms, the Bolshevo Commune for underage criminals, the Central Park of Culture and Rest (the future Gorky Park), the Moscow Metro with its chandeliers, the Lenin Museum, the ballet, the Institute of Child and Adolescent Health, model factories, schools, hospitals and prisons. Everywhere they were accompanied by helpful interpreters who ensured that no one they spoke to ever had a negative word to say.[3]

'There is no doubt that providing special conditions for resident and visiting foreign writers did significantly affect their perception of the USSR', wrote Stern. She cites the example of French writer Jean-Richard Bloch and his wife, Marguerite, who attended a writers' congress in 1934 and published a volume of their daily letters documenting their tour.

'There are still prisons here,' wrote Marguerite Bloch, 'and, despite everything, they are still not charming places. But I believe they are nothing like those in capitalist countries.'[4]

They met Soviet writer Ilya Ehrenburg, who told them life in the Soviet Union had improved dramatically: 'When I see people laugh and sing, I am not used to it yet; I say to myself, "It was worth it, no one is hungry, no one is in rags and everyone feels like dancing and singing." Two or three years ago, this wasn't the case.'[5]

Another classic example was the German (and Jewish) playwright Lion Feuchtwanger, a fierce critic of Hitler who moved to France and later the United States. He wrote a glowing report of his visit to the USSR in *Moscow 1937* and felt it would be disloyal to air any doubts he had:

> I was at first surprised and dubious when I found that all the people with whom I came into contact in the Soviet Union, and this includes casual and obviously spontaneous conversations, were at one with the general scheme of things, even if they were sometimes critical of minor points. Indeed, everywhere in that great city of Moscow there was an atmosphere of harmony and contentment, even of happiness.[6]

Yet he suspected they were too frightened to say anything about the shortages he saw. He noticed the terrible lack of living space, the queues outside lavatories and the primitive lifestyles even of eminent writers. But Feuchtwanger nevertheless came back and trumpeted that life in Moscow was far better than anywhere in the West.

Some of the foreign communists who came in their thousands to be trained as revolutionaries were more honest in noting what they witnessed. Yueh Sheng, one of the famous thirty-seven Bolsheviks who returned to China and a member of the Chinese Communist Party Central Committee, wrote a memoir of his years in Moscow from 1926 to 1932:

> We were wonderfully well fed and clothed. At the same time, I could not help but see the long, pathetic queues of Russians, standing all night long in front of shops from which they hoped, often unrealistically, in the morning to be able to get a tiny bit of meat. Nor could I ignore the Russian student from Moscow University who worked part time at Sun Yat-sen University carting wood for the stoves that kept us comfortably warm. In temperatures far below zero he wore only a threadbare cotton jacket. I could see him shivering in the cold, and I knew that he probably had an unheated home to return to. Every day, moreover, while we ate our excellent meals, I knew that our professors could not dream of eating so well.[7]

Stalin's programme inspired fierce loyalty in most people. Arthur Koestler, who resigned from the Party in 1938 after Bukharin's execution, believed, as he wrote in a personal letter to the Party: 'Whoever goes against the Soviet Union goes against the future.' The black American singer Paul Robeson declared: 'From what I have already seen of the workings of the Soviet Government, I can only say that anybody who lifts his hand against it ought to be shot.'

In October 1931, at the height of the famine, playwright George Bernard Shaw declared in a BBC broadcast:

> Russia flaunts her budget surplus of 750 millions, her people employed to the last man and woman, her scientific agriculture doubling her harvest, her roaring and multiplying factories, her efficient rulers, her atmosphere of such hope and security for the poorest as has never been seen in a civilized country on earth.[8]

Among the most influential enthusiasts were Beatrice and Sidney Webb. The Webbs were among the founders of the British Labour Party, the London School of Economics and the influential *New Statesman* magazine. As a measure of their immense influence on British society, especially the creation of Britain's welfare state, their ashes lie in the nave of Westminster Abbey. The Webbs planted an enduring faith in a planned and nationalized economy that led directly to the 1945 Labour Party manifesto and the nationalization of the commanding heights of the British economy enshrined in Clause IV of the party's constitution. Clement Attlee, the post-1945 Labour prime minister, was chairman of the New Fabian Research Bureau that the Webbs set up in the 1930s. William Beveridge, who designed the British welfare state, was also an avid reader of the Webbs' book on the Soviet Union.

Future generations of Labour leaders became enthralled by Stalinism at an early age. Some, like future chancellor Denis Healey, joined the British Communist Party while a student at Oxford. The Webbs' enthusiasm for the USSR helped convince the famous 'Cambridge Five' spies to become active servants of Stalin. Anthony Wedgwood Benn, Richard Crosland and future Labour Party leaders James Callaghan and Michael Foot all believed that central planning must inevitably take the place of capitalism. Clause IV would not be altered until 1995. It was not so different in the United States, where, in the 1930s, Stalin enlisted many future spies, including prominent economists such as Harry Dexter White, the top treasury official who became the key American figure behind the post-war economic order established at the 1944 Bretton Woods meeting.[9]

Beatrice Webb was in her mid-seventies when they set off for the Soviet Union in 1932. After they returned to England, they spent three years writing a thousand-page book, *Soviet Communism: A New Civilisation?*, stuffed with facts and figures. Sidney Webb returned for a second visit in 1934. The book came out in 1935, and a second edition in 1937 dropped the question mark. By 1939, their book had sold 40,000 copies, mostly to the trade union members who made up the backbone of the Labour Party.[10]

The Webbs toured the Soviet Union at the height of the famine, even visiting Ukraine, yet they saw no evidence of any famine. When he was taken to a giant collective farm in the lower Volga, Sidney Webb had even seen boxcars full of families being transported, but he was satisfied with the information that either these were seasonal workers or peasants whose labour was no longer needed thanks to mechanization. They were, he noted with approval, sent fares and food paid for by future factory employers.[11]

In a postscript to the 1937 edition, the Webbs said: 'Now the tables groaned under the weight of cheese, butter, eggs, meat and other foodstuffs ... The shops which four years ago boasted only cosmetics and cobwebs, which had not an ounce of sugar or cereals or herring, were now crammed with sugar cigarettes and tinned fish and meat.' In Ukraine in 1936, it was the same story everywhere of 'abundant crops and fewer and fewer families without their own cow, pigs and chickens'. Elsewhere, they say: 'We must, however, repeat that queues do not necessarily imply short supply. There are, in the USSR, constant queues at the post offices where the supply is unlimited.'[12]

The Webbs refused to believe the eyewitness accounts written by their nephew, Malcolm Muggeridge, who toured Ukraine and reported for *The Guardian*. He called the famine 'the most terrible thing I have ever seen'. Beatrice called his reports 'hysterical' and suggested they were motivated by 'poor Malcolm's complexes' and 'a well of hatred in [his] nature'. In her diary, Beatrice wrote: 'Malcolm has come back with stories about a terrible famine in the USSR. I have been to see Mr. Maisky [the Soviet ambassador in Britain] about it, and I realize that he's got it absolutely wrong.' However, Muggeridge wrote the following in his memoir:

> My wife's aunt was Beatrice Webb. And so one saw close at hand the degree to which they all knew about the regime, knew all about the Cheka and everything, but they liked it. I remember Mrs. Webb, who after all was a very cultivated upper-class liberal-minded person, an early member of the Fabian Society and so on, saying to me, 'Yes, it's true, people disappear in Russia.' She said it with such great satisfaction that I couldn't help thinking that there were a lot of people in England whose disappearance she would have liked to organize.[13]

The Webbs also denied that Stalin could in any way be described as a dictator and claimed the Soviet Union was a fully fledged political democracy. They denied that Gulag slave camps existed and later rejected all evidence of the purges and show trials. They asserted that 'there does not seem to be any implication of slavery in a planned economy. The government of the USSR has indeed no need to employ compulsion to fill its factories or state farms, or even its lumber camps.' They would staunchly support Stalin through the Great Purge, the show trials and even the Hitler–Stalin Pact.[14]

The Webbs' views were confirmed by many great academics. In 1937, the great Cambridge historian E. H. Carr paid a second visit to the Soviet Union and returned so impressed by what he saw that he was convinced there was no alternative, informing an audience at Chatham House that

> the German and Russian regimes, today, represent a reaction against the individualistic ideology prevailing at any time in Western Europe, for the last hundred and fifty years. ... The whole system of individualist laissez-faire economy has, as we know, broken down. It has broken down because production and trade can only be carried out on a nationwide scale and with the aid of State machinery and State control.

Carr produced a fourteen-volume history of the Soviet Union that concluded that Stalin's industrialization policies were the only way to modernize a backward country. He thought that Lancelot Lawton, another British historian who in his work *An Economic History of Soviet Russia* had correctly concluded that the Soviet economy was a failure, was utterly mistaken. Carr also rejected the view that Bukharin and the NEP could ever have represented a viable alternative to Stalin's policies.

Carr, whose essay *What Is History?* was for a long time on the reading list of every history student, was backed by many other influential historians and writers. Among them were the popular historian A. J. P. Taylor and Isaac Deutscher, author of a three-volume biography of Trotsky that presented him rather than Bukharin as the key ideological rival to Stalin.[15]

Yet Stalin's five-year plans produced exactly the dystopia that Mises had predicted in 1920. They resulted in irrational and arbitrary management of the economy. The population was treated as an industrial army and commanded to relocate at the whim of Party officials. Millions of the farmers labelled as *kulaks* were transported en masse and dumped in a wilderness. Millions of others were relocated into cities and towns to work on large-scale industrial projects. Yet there was no housing for them or any transport or other services. Huge numbers were imprisoned on spurious charges and sent to work as forced labourers.

The new collective farms into which the rural population was compelled to work did not produce more food but less. So in 1929 rationing was reintroduced and continued until 1935 and then resumed from 1941 to 1947. Even in non-rationing periods, local authorities were likely to impose rationing locally, without central approval, whenever supply problems got out of hand. In the centrally planned economy, goods shortages were endemic. Letters to Stalin and reports by the NKVD reveal that most of the population queued for hours every day to purchase the basic necessities of life. Even in good years, breadlines in various cities and regions were sufficiently alarming to be included on the Politburo's agenda. The most serious and widespread recurrence of breadlines occurred in the winter and spring of 1936–7, after the harvest failure of 1936. Per capita urban consumption of meat and lard in 1932 was less than a third of what it had been.[16]

Sheila Fitzpatrick's study *Everyday Stalinism: Ordinary Life in Extraordinary Times; Soviet Russia in the 1930s* describes how both the factories and farms malfunctioned:

> The 1930s was a decade of enormous privation and hardship for the Soviet people, much worse than the 1920s. Famine hit all the major grain-growing regions in 1932–33, and in addition bad harvests caused major disruptions in the food supply in 1936 and 1939. Towns were swamped with new arrivals from the villages, housing was drastically overcrowded, and the rationing system was close to collapse. For the greater part of the urban population, life revolved around the endless struggle to get the basics necessary for survival—food, clothing, shelter.

She quotes from the account of an American engineer who returned to Moscow in June 1930 after some months' absence:

> On the streets all the shops seemed to have disappeared. Gone was the open market. Gone were the nepmen [private businessmen of the NEP period]. The government stores had showy, empty boxes and other window-dressing. But the interior was devoid of goods. Living standards dropped sharply at the beginning of the Stalin period in both town and countryside.[17]

According to Fitzpatrick:

> Clothing, shoes, and all kinds of consumer goods were in even shorter supply than basic foodstuffs, often being completely unobtainable. In the 1920s, artisans and craftsmen had been either the sole or the dominant producers of many necessary everyday items: pottery, baskets, samovars, sheepskin coats and hats, to name only a few. All these goods became essentially unobtainable at the beginning of the 1930s, while in public cafeterias, spoons, forks, plates and bowls were in such short supply that workers had to queue up for them as well as for their food; knives were usually unobtainable. Throughout the decade, it was all but impossible to get such ordinary necessities as basins, oil-lamps and kettles because it was now forbidden to use nonferrous metals to manufacture consumer goods.[18]

The poor quality of the few goods available was a subject of constant complaint, she reports. Clothes were sloppily cut and sewn, and reports abounded of gross defects like missing sleeves in state stores. As Fitzpatrick writes: 'Handles fell off pots, matches refused to strike and foreign objects were baked into bread made from adulterated flour. It was impossible to get clothes, shoes and household items repaired, to find a locksmith or a painter.'[19]

The shortage of shoes was dire. Farmers had slaughtered their animals rather than see them confiscated by the state for collective farms. So there was no leather. Besides, after 1931 the state had banned private shoemakers from working. There were state shoe factories, but the output was poor and quality so bad they often fell apart days after purchase. The shortage of shoes was particularly lamentable, and Fitzpatrick cites the case of Yaroslavl, the famous town on the Volga, where parents struggled to find even a single pair of shoes for the new school year in 1935.

Things didn't get better. People couldn't find clothes, shoes or any kinds of textiles. Not even needles and thread. The NKVD reported that even in Leningrad up to 6,000 people queued up to buy things. There was such a long queue outside one shoe shop that no one could move along the street, and the shop windows were broken by the press of bodies. Russian sources quoted by Fitzpatrick relate how thousands of people queued all night outside clothing stores in Kiev, and when they opened in the morning the police escorted shoppers into the store in batches of five to ten people who had to link arms so that nobody could jump the queue. They looked just like convicts.[20]

The state wasn't any better at building housing than it was at supplying consumer goods. As Fitzpatrick explains, people lived in communal apartments, dormitories and barracks, usually with one family to a room. This meant that home life was 'miserably overcrowded and uncomfortable and often poisoned by quarrels with neighbours'. Matters were inflamed by the 'continuous work week', which abolished the Sunday holiday and often meant that family members had different days off. In Moscow, average living space was 5.5 square meters per capita in 1930, dropping down to just over 4 square meters in 1940. In new and rapidly industrializing towns, the situation was even worse: Magnitogorsk and Irkutsk both had under 4 square meters, and in Krasnoyarsk the per capita norm in 1933 was a mere 3.4 square meters.[21]

Using public transport was also a horrible ordeal. People spent long periods trying to get to and from work or trying to carry their shopping on shabby, densely packed buses or trams. Or they walked along unpaved streets that in winter were piled high with snow or were turned into a morass of mud by spring or autumn weather.

Hidden from the world, the mass of the Soviet population survived on near starvation rations. The economy performed even more badly than it had done in the miserable 1920s, but you wouldn't know from reading the official statistics. Statistics had become the sacred litany of socialism and were endlessly cited with breathless enthusiasm by the Westerners who came back from touring Stalin's Russia. As David Caute explains in *The Fellow-Travelers: Intellectual Friends of Communism*, these statistics were a fetish for those like the Webbs who believed in Soviet planning. Their bible was the 300 pages of statistics published in English by Gosplan as the 'Summary of the Fulfilment of the First Five Year Plan'. It claimed that the five-year plans produced annual industrial annual growth of 30 per cent.[22]

If the statistics were to be believed, as the Webbs wrote,

> the deliberate planning of all the nation's production, distribution and exchange. ... for increasing the consumption of the whole community was a triumph. In fact, it was the great hope for mankind: a rational planned economy based on collective welfare and altruism instead of the scramble for private gain, individualism and irrational markets.

The Webbs took it for granted that socialism was by its nature morally superior in every way to capitalism. Such a system of governance appealed to man's better instincts and would bring into being a new socialist man. So the Webbs dismissed the possibility that the statistics were just propaganda:

> It is, we suggest, sheer prejudice to pretend that the statistics of the USSR are to be disbelieved because, like all other public statistics in the world, they are compiled and published by the government concerned. In fact, they command greater credence than the published statistics of any other government because, in the USSR, they form the basis of all economic and financial action, which, if it were taken upon 'cooked figures' must inevitably result in patent failure.

As Beatrice and Sidney Webb were well aware, Mises in *Die Gemeinwirtschaft* had argued that in a socialist economy, any planner would be taking decisions in the dark. They devote an entire chapter in *Soviet Communism: A New Civilization* to refuting the socialist calculation problem and arguing that his premise was wrong. The Soviet Union had successfully replaced economic calculus, dependent on price in a competitive market, with a utilitarian calculus based on the greatest happiness: 'While the western economists count as success solely the maximizing of exchange values in relation to production costs, the Soviet planner takes account of every purpose of an enlightened community', the Webbs claimed. 'The socialist planner has higher objectives, namely the welfare of the human race, now and for all time.'[23]

The trouble was that the Webbs did not recognize that Soviet statistics did not allow for any useful planning. As Mises had predicted, they often listed physical quantities of steel or coal or wool or kilowatts—all of which seemed impressive until they were studied more closely. Coal output supposedly went from 36 million tonnes to 130 million, iron from 3 to 15 million tonnes and electricity from 5,000 million to 36,000 million kilowatts. Grain production tripled to 10 million tonnes.

One trick was to manipulate the grain harvest reports by declaring a 'biological yield', an estimate of the harvest of the field that was always far larger than the actual harvest gathered, and inflated further by the amount that was delivered and held in a granary. And the quantities gave no idea of their value, such as whether the steel was the right kind needed at that time and place.

Other statistics and targets used roubles. In contrast to the first phase of communism after 1917 when the government tried to do without money and create a pure barter economy, Stalin accepted that money was a necessary evil. At the Seventeenth Party Congress in 1934, he explicitly declared that money was there to stay 'until the completion of the first stage of communism—the socialist stage of development'. As he explained:

> The money economy is one of those few bourgeois apparatuses of the economy which we, socialists, must use *ad fundum* ... and we will set about it in our own way, to make it serve our cause, rather than capitalism's. Under our circumstances, it is unthinkable to organize the exchange between city and countryside without commodity circulation, without buying and selling.[24]

When, in 1936, Vyacheslav Molotov reminded him that, according to Marx and Lenin, the first stage of communism was supposed to be a system without money and commodity production, Stalin answered that although this was desirable in theory, life dictated otherwise. This also meant that since money continued to be used, the Party had to allow market exchanges. Most of the urban markets were closed down during the first five-year plan, but in May 1932 a decree recognized the existence of so-called *kolkhoz* (meaning collective farm) markets. Only peasants and rural craftsmen were allowed to trade.

In fact, an entire black market economy sprang up and was tolerated. This informal distribution system, known as the 'second economy', distributed goods produced and owned by state enterprises. Industrial enterprises employed an army of second-economy procurement agents or 'pushers' to get hold of the necessary raw materials and equipment. Ordinary citizens also used pull or *blat* to buy food or clothing, obtain an apartment, railway ticket or a pass to a vacation resort. In other words, they continued to trade with each other in a way Adam Smith would have recognized.

What was also apparent was that any five-year plan required a unit of account, a notional currency, still called the rouble. Enterprises had to do business with each other, and various factories in nationalized enterprises had to settle accounts with one another. Without the rouble, how could different nationalized units work out what to pay each other for their supplies? As Bukharin had originally imagined, this meant that the banking system transferred notional roubles from one bank account to another. Yet an enterprise with surplus roubles in its account could not spend them. It did not repay any loans because there was no credit or debt. As these notional roubles were no longer tied to gold or anything else, they could not be used for trade. In any case, these had largely stopped after Stalin defaulted on his debts to Germany. The state enterprises paid their employees roubles, but these official salaries gave no indication of what could be bought with them. Many necessities were either free or tightly rationed.

Until 1928, the Soviet Union had enjoyed a real currency backed by gold, the chervonets, but when the five-year plans started Stalin abandoned this. In order to cheat the peasants and underpay them for their grain, he started circulating roubles that were not backed by anything. They were just bits of paper. In 1928, the total issue of currency in circulation was 1.7 billion real roubles, but by early 1933

83

there were 8.4 billion roubles. The peasants who sold goods in the *kolkhoz* markets received roubles whose purchasing power dropped rapidly. Urban wage earners needed more and more roubles to buy the same goods. As the peasants realized there was no point growing things to sell, either as employees on the collective farm or on the private allotments, the shortages began to worsen. The shortages drove prices ever upwards in an inflationary spiral. As Trotsky colourfully put it: 'Inflation is the syphilis of a planned economy.'[25]

The planners couldn't rely on any price signals because there were so many prices for the same item—one in the peasant market, another on the urban black market, a third in a state shop, still yet another in the special shops reserved for top Party officials or often another in a hard currency shop for those who had somehow obtained foreign currency or gold. In 1923, the going rate for meat in the Moscow markets was 10 to 11 roubles a kilo, but in state stores it was 2 roubles. The market price for potatoes was 1 rouble a kilo but 18 kopecks in the state shop. Naturally, these different prices were an invitation to corruption, which soon infected the whole system and created a new class of criminals, later known as the Russian Mafia. As Mises had predicted, every part of life was now arbitrary, unfair and irrational.[26]

It was equally inevitable that the government struggled to motivate anyone to work hard even by raising their salary. This in turn meant that the state had to rely on other means to incentivize people—encouragement via propaganda campaigns or fear induced by a reign of arbitrary terror. For instance, workers arriving ten minutes late for work risked being sent off to labour camps for five or ten years. The easiest part of the planned economy to manage was the Gulag economy because prices didn't matter. The prisoners were mostly cutting timber, mining or digging reservoirs and canals, so quality did not matter either. In the 1930s, around 7 million were sent to the camps.[27]

In the meantime, visitors to the Soviet Union marvelled at its impressive statistics, which they barely understood. The rouble prices quoted in the plans and statistics, far from illuminating anything, sowed utter confusion. The value of the rouble relative to domestic goods and foreign currencies changed every year, making comparisons impossible. Despite these vagaries, a few scholars began to ponder what they actually meant. Their conclusions would lead to disastrous miscalculations in America and Britain. The statistics that were supposed to reflect scientific facts actually shrouded the truth.

7

WHY EVEN THE CIA BELIEVED SOVIET STATISTICS

Three months after Bukharin was taken from his cell and shot, a young American economist from Harvard arrived in Moscow curious to discover the truth about the Soviet Union's 20 per cent annual growth statistics. Over the next fifty years, Abram Bergson would reign as the dominant authority on the art of interpreting Soviet statistics and hence the top expert on the Soviet economy, a career in which he completely misled the US government.

By nature, Bergson was a scholarly, reserved, pragmatic, cautious man whom no one would ever accuse of any emotional commitment to the ideals of socialism, let alone the reckless enthusiasm of the fellow-travellers. This made his endorsement of Soviet economic planning all the more credible, but it would lead to calamitous misjudgements by American economists and CIA analysts.

Bergson was the son of Russian immigrant Jews. His older brother, Gus, studied physics at Harvard. In 1933, Abram went to Harvard Graduate School to study economics after undergraduate training at Johns Hopkins. He was a prodigy who started graduate work at nineteen and made his mark at twenty-three when in 1938 he wrote an extraordinarily influential, highly technical paper on social welfare. This looked at the issue of how to judge whether it is better or worse to choose a policy like free trade or rent controls that invariably help some people but hurt some others. He established the chain of reasoning that underpins all applied welfare economics.[1]

A year earlier, he had taken a crash course in Russian and then spent the summer in Russia on a research trip. 'In the mixed-up world of the 1930s, how socialist planning functioned in the one country where it was being applied on any scale seemed a rather momentous matter', he said later. It was indeed the great question. Enlightened opinion agreed that capitalism was outdated and doomed. Some praised Mussolini's corporatist state, others Hitler's economic policies, and many were bedazzled by the image of the Soviet Union.[2]

In such a milieu, it was understandable that Bergson would want to use his talents to shed light on Soviet statistics. During his stay in Moscow, he found that the experts he went to see were plainly terrified of speaking to a foreigner and he could discover very little. Once back in the United States, he located some musty publications in the Library of Congress that would become the basis of his dissertation. These were reports on Soviet wages that led Bergson to compare the worst-paid workers with those making top wages. In his Harvard PhD on the structure of Soviet wages, he concluded that the wage structure in 1928 was fundamentally similar to that of capitalist countries, and therefore Soviet wages were paid according to 'capitalist principles'. Hence, they must reflect productivity. The notion that wages adhered to capitalist principles enabled the application of the economist's full set of economic tools: micro-economic measures of supply and demand, along with macro-economic efforts to measure the size and scope of the economy. Wages are, after all, income for the workers, but they are also prices, which are central to both micro- and macro-economic analysis.[3]

Bergson's second item of faith was that the Soviet wage statistics for 1928 and 1934 must surely be reliable because they were consistent with each other. The work that Bergson did on Soviet wages would qualify him as one of the few American authorities on the Soviet economy. So when America joined the Second World War, and the Soviet Union became a key ally, Bergson was recruited into the fledgling US intelligence organization, the Office of Strategic Services (OSS), the forerunner of the CIA. At the age of twenty-seven, Bergson was made the leading figure in the group of academics recruited by the OSS for its Research & Analysis branch. Their job was to measure the size and growth of the Soviet economy to answer two vital questions: could the Soviets hold off the German invasion, and could its factories supply enough war materiel? Only then could the American government plan how much Lend-Lease aid to provide (i.e., how many tanks and trucks to make and ship to arm Stalin's armies).[4]

As head of the Soviet analysis section during the war years, Bergson's views carried huge weight in Washington; after all, the Red Army was committed to battles that would destroy the bulk of Hitler's war machine. Without it, Hitler could not be defeated. Yet Bergson's influence grew even greater as the Cold War deepened. American intelligence quickly ballooned from two dozen tweedy professors in a few rooms helped by secretaries with typewriters to the equivalent of an aircraft carrier manned by 30,000 analysts and supported by satellite surveillance costing many billions every year. The CIA would be surrounded by a flotilla of think tanks, like the RAND Corporation, and university research centres, to which it outsourced much of its work.

When the CIA was founded in 1947, a year after Churchill's Iron Curtain Speech, its primary mission was to assess the size of the Soviet economy and detail Soviet military spending. By then, Bergson had left intelligence to teach at Harvard, where he directed its Russian Research Center, and so much of the work inside and outside the CIA was done by his protégés and disciples.

This meant they used the methodology Bergson had developed in the late 1930s based on wage statistics. The CIA employed hundreds of people to work out the Soviet labour costs of building, say, a tank with that of American labour costs, adding an estimate of the raw material inputs to arrive at a dollar equivalent. Bergson was thus the pioneer of a new field that came to be known as comparative economics.

Bergson knew that the Soviet statistical system was based on the Marxist concepts of labour value rather than market value. So analysing labour costs and labour productivity made more sense than analysing, say, the official rouble costs of anything. Bergson also knew that Soviet statistics, even when applied to labour, had to be treated

89

with caution because of exaggeration and error. He thought he could make reasonable assumptions, though, and conjured up something he called 'adjusted factor cost'.[5]

Bergson explained his reasoning in a short but incisive article, 'Reliability and Usability of Soviet Statistics: A Summary Appraisal', published in 1953: 'Contrary to a common supposition, the Russians seem generally not to resort to falsification in the sense of free invention and double book-keeping. I have explained that there is falsification of a local sort. ... I am now concerned primarily with falsification of a comprehensive character at the centre.'[6]

Bergson was certain that what he was doing with Soviet labour statistics was a form of 'empirical analysis' based on scientific principles, whereas the research other people did was mere anecdotal observation. 'He had little patience with anecdotes or stray evidence. He believed that one must first define a problem analytically and then look for the necessary evidence to derive one's conclusions', wrote one of his disciples, Padma Desai of Columbia University.

One of Bergson's first pieces of research was judging the performance of Soviet agriculture in the 1930s. He concluded that the level of Soviet consumption in 1937 had surpassed that in 1928. In other words, people were as well off, if not better, after Stalin's forced collectivization than during the NEP period even though there had been a massive famine and terrible purges. Further, in 1948, he wrote that 'there can hardly be any room for debate; of course, socialism can work ... the Soviet planned economy has been working for 30 years. Whatever else may be said of it, it has not broken down.'[7]

The Soviet Union continued to exist, but it never functioned in the way that Bergson and many others thought it did. Yet its survival was enough to convince leading economists that Mises was utterly wrong. As Bergson was celebrating Stalin's achievements, Mises' life was unexpectedly thrown into turmoil. His influence had risen steadily after much of the world reverted to the gold standard in the mid-1920s and enjoyed an economic recovery. Austrian economics was held in high regard until an obscure Polish economist, Oskar Lange, devised a theory that seemed to demolish the arguments of Mises and bolster the claims of Stalinist planning.

In the late 1920s and early 1930s, Mises was recognized as Austria's greatest monetary theorist and the most influential voice defending nineteenth-century laissez-faire capitalism, often dubbed the Manchester school. He helped establish the famous Institute for Business Cycle Research in Vienna and joined the board of the prestigious German academic body, Verein für Socialpolitik.

As chief economist at the Austrian Chamber of Commerce, Mises lobbied the Austrian government with some success. Compared to its neighbours, the Austrian government was prudent, cutting foreign debt, balancing the budget and reducing unemployment. Mises urged the government to end price and rent controls, lower taxes and free up labour markets. Yet he felt it was not doing enough and warned that the Austrian banking system was unsafe and could collapse. The system was only being kept afloat by a steady stream of loans from America and France. He refused to keep his own money in an Austrian bank because he was sure they were all bankrupt.[8]

He was proved correct. In early May 1931, Austria's largest bank, the Rothschild-dominated Credit-Anstalt, defaulted. It was bailed out by the central bank, but even so, the repercussions spread through all Austrian banks. On 13 July 1931, customers in next-door Germany panicked. One of the German banks considered to be among the safest, the Darmstädter und Nationalbank, closed its counters, triggering a chain reaction that quickly froze all payments within Germany. The subsequent banking crisis and a sharp rise in unemployment as many companies went under helped bring the Nazis to power.

Until the Great Depression, the ideas of the Austrian school had begun to attract converts in the Anglo-Saxon world. One of the leading professors at the London School of Economics, Lionel Robbins, had the ambition of building a department to rival the influence of Cambridge, where John Maynard Keynes reigned supreme. It could have been the British home of Austrian thinking. First, Robbins invited Mises to London to lecture. Then in 1931 he appointed his protégé, Friedrich Hayek, to a post in his department. He would go on to write an influential counterblast to Keynesianism. Sir William Beveridge, the post-war founder of Britain's welfare state, was another adherent, and even Hugh Gaitskell, the future

Labour chancellor and Labour Party leader, came to Vienna and started to translate Böhm-Bawerk's book, *Capital and Interest*.[9]

As the Great Depression unfolded, though, enthusiasm for the economic policies of both Stalin and Hitler grew. A fateful blow to the popularity of Mises' ideas was delivered by another economist whom Robbins invited to London. This was Oskar Lange, an enthusiastic Stalinist who had been born in Poland in 1904 when it was part of the Russian Empire, then studied law and economics at the University of Kraków and worked briefly at the Ministry of Labour in Warsaw. In 1934, he wrote an interesting paper about a planned socialist economy explaining how it could work with government-determined prices. It was an explicit attack on Mises and his economic calculation theory. By the late 1930s, most economists accepted that Lange had proved the case against Mises.

After 1945, Lange returned to communist Poland, a country that would be so badly managed in the post-war years that it would become the epicentre of the earthquake that brought down the Soviet Union. When Lange returned to Kraków University, that was still far in the future. With another economist, Marek Breit, he outlined a version of socialism in which the government owned all plants, and each industry was organized as a monopoly but called a public trust, in which the workforce was given a large say. That year, he arrived at the London School of Economics courtesy of a Rockefeller fellowship. During the next few years, he wrote several academic papers that demonstrated how socialism could be made to work. His ideas, later reprinted as *On the Economic Theory of Socialism*, drew on the work of other economists such as H. D. Dickinson at Oxford, Abba P. Lerner at London and Professor Fred M. Taylor at Michigan University. Lange started by sneering at Mises:

> Socialists have certainly good reason to be grateful to Professor Mises, the great advocatus diaboli of their cause. For it was his powerful challenge that forced the socialists to recognize the importance of an adequate system of economic accounting ... the merit of having caused the socialists to approach this problem systematically belongs entirely to Professor Mises. Both as an expression of recognition for the great service rendered by him

and as a memento of the prime importance of sound economic accounting, a statue of Professor Mises ought to occupy an honourable place in the great hall of the Ministry of Socialization or of the Central Planning Board of the socialist state … I am afraid that Professor Mises would scarcely enjoy what seemed the only adequate way to repay the debt of recognition incurred by the socialists.[10]

Economists found Lange's work so interesting because he opened the door to marrying Marxist planning to the Austrian school's theories on prices. The concept was eagerly embraced by politicians. Lange suggested that eventually the central planning board could employ mathematicians and computers to run complex equations that would magically coordinate inventories, prices and manufacturing. Robbins took this so seriously that he endorsed it in his study of the 1929 crash, *The Great Depression*:

> On paper we can conceive this problem to be solved by a series of mathematical calculations. We can imagine tables to be drawn up expressing the consumers' demands … And we can conceive technical information giving us the productivity … which could be produced by each of the various possible combinations of the factors of production. On such a basis a system of simultaneous equations could be constructed whose solution would show the equilibrium distribution of factors and the equilibrium production of commodities.[11]

Hayek took it seriously too, agreeing that if one could gather the right knowledge without market prices, then indeed one could calculate the correct prices for factors of production. Yet he also said that it would not work in practice:

> It would necessitate the drawing up of millions of equations on the basis of millions of statistical tables based on many more millions of individual computations. By the time the equations were solved, the information on which they were based would have become obsolete and they would need to be calculated anew.[12]

In *Collectivist Economic Planning*, Hayek reemphasized the point:

> This means that, at each successive moment, every one of the
> decisions would have to be based on the solution of an equal
> number of simultaneous differential equations, a task which,
> with any of the means known at present, could not be carried
> out in a lifetime. And yet these decisions would ... have to be
> made continuously.

In a 1936 article, Lange dismissed these objections as nonsense:

> Neither would the Central Planning Board have to solve
> hundreds of thousands ... or millions ... of equations. The only
> 'equations' which would have to be 'solved' would be those of
> the consumers and the managers of production plants. These
> are exactly the same 'equations' which are solved in the present
> economic system and the persons who do the 'solving' are the
> same also. Consumers ... and managers ... 'solve' them by a
> method of trial and error ... And only a few of them have been
> graduated in higher mathematics. Professor Hayek and Professor
> Robbins themselves 'solve' at least hundreds of equations daily,
> for instance, in buying a newspaper or in deciding to take a meal
> in a restaurant, and presumably they do not use determinants or
> Jacobians for that purpose.[13]

Lange came back to this issue before his death in 1965, claiming that
computers would do the hard work:

> Were I to rewrite my essay ['On the Economic Theory of
> Socialism'] today my task would be much simpler. My answer
> to Hayek and Robbins would be: 'So what's the trouble? Let us
> put the simultaneous equations on an electronic computer and
> we shall obtain the solution in less than a second. The market
> process with its cumbersome *tâtonnements* appears old-fashioned.
> Indeed, it may be considered as a computing device of the pre-
> electronic age.[14]

Lange presented a world where a central planning board would
allocate investment and capital goods but retain a market for wages
and consumer goods that would produce useful price signals. There

would be no market for capital goods; instead, a central planning board would create a 'pretend market' in capital goods and by trial-and-error adjust capital outlays or set prices in response to shortages and surpluses.

Lange, Dickinson and others argued that whatever the system, a political and economic elite was always going to decide how to allocate capital, and surely central planners would be just as good or bad at doing the job as stock market investors. It was true that at first the planning official would have to rely on his own judgement to set a price for any product made in a government factory. Yet by watching inventories, they could spot a shortage or a glut, and intervene by hiking or cutting prices. If they raised prices, the factory manager would step up production so the shortages would disappear. And if the planning official noticed a glut, he would slash prices, and the factory manager would cut back output to avoid losses until the surplus disappeared. Having successfully solved the problem of matching up supply and demand, the central planning board's next task would be to wisely reinvest these factory profits and distribute 'social dividends' to everyone as the entire population would be treated as equal owners of the capital.

In 1937, Lange went to live in America, and at the University of Chicago he drew up a plan for a future Polish government. It should nationalize key industries but keep small enterprises like farms, shops and the like in private hands. A large private sector, he wrote, was necessary to preserve 'the kind of flexibility, pliability and adaptiveness that private initiative alone can achieve'. These notions amounted to a 'third way' between socialism and capitalism rather like the socialism proposed by Bukharin and the NEP.

In his 1920 paper, Mises had considered the possibility of socialist officials simulating market prices but argued that the core problem is how investment decisions are made and then evaluated. No matter who the owner is, any enterprise has to decide how to deploy their land and capital resources. In a socialist economy, the state is both the buyer and seller in each transaction involving land and capital goods, and this is precisely why decisions are not guided by meaningful price signals. The most important transactions occur between state monopolies. A market economy succeeds because the decision-making is made by entrepreneurs, investors and private owners, but in a planned economy, the managers of state enterprises behave very differently. He explained it like this:

> One may anticipate the nature of the future socialist society. There will be hundreds and thousands of factories in operation. Very few of these will be producing wares ready for use; in the majority of cases what will be manufactured will be unfinished goods and production goods. All these concerns will be interrelated. Every good will go through a whole series of stages before it is ready for use. In the ceaseless toil and moil of this process, however, the administration will be without any means of testing their bearings. It will never be able to determine whether a given good has not been kept for a superfluous length of time in the necessary processes of production, or whether work and material have not been wasted in its completion. How will it be able to decide whether this or that method of production is the more profitable? At best it will only be able to compare the quality and quantity of the consumable end-product produced but will in the rarest cases be in a position to compare the expenses entailed in production.[15]

In short, a government knows what it wants, what goods are most urgently needed, but it cannot know the other crucial element required for rational economic calculation: valuation of the various means of production, which a capitalist market does by giving monetary prices for all products and their factors.

Mises concluded that in a socialist economy there is no way for rationality to intrude on the vast number of decisions made when making capital goods. In a market economy, entrepreneurs are strongly motivated to make greater profits and avoid losses, but this does not happen when all capital goods, land and other resources are controlled by the government. The manager of a socialist enterprise is an administrator obeying orders, fulfilling quotas and avoiding risks. As Mises explains:

> The cardinal fallacy implied in [market socialist] proposals is that they look at the economic problem from the perspective of the subaltern clerk whose intellectual horizon does not

extend beyond subordinate tasks. They consider the structure of industrial production and the allocation of capital to the various branches and production aggregates as rigid, and do not take into account the necessity of altering this structure in order to adjust it to changes in conditions … They fail to realize that the operations of the corporate officers consist merely in the loyal execution of the tasks entrusted to them by their bosses, the shareholders … The operations of the managers, their buying and selling, are only a small segment of the totality of market operations. The market of the capitalist society also performs those operations which allocate the capital goods to the various branches of industry. The entrepreneurs and capitalists establish corporations and other firms, enlarge or reduce their size, dissolve them or merge them with other enterprises; they buy and sell the shares and bonds of already existing and of new corporations; they grant, withdraw, and recover credits; in short, they perform all those acts the totality of which is called the capital and money market. It is these financial transactions of promoters and speculators that direct production into those channels in which it satisfies the most urgent wants of the consumers in the best possible way.[16]

Mises argued that it was absurd for any socialist planning board to tell their managers to 'play market', to act as if they are owners of their firms in trying to maximize profits and avoid losses. Speculators and investors expose their own wealth and their own destiny to risk. Nor could any socialist market system envisage a role for stock and commodity exchanges, trading in futures or the bankers and money-lenders.

Further, the issue does not revolve around knowing or understanding past prices but calculating future prices and wants. Even if accurate information about past prices were fed into the computer, this could not help much to appraise future prices, future technologies and the many, many other factors, known or unknown, that determine the future. A stock and commodity market delivers prices that are constantly reflecting changing beliefs in the success or failure of enterprises in delivering future goods and services. Simply put, you need a basically unchanging static world for socialist planning to work, or as economists put it, one in a state of equilibrium. But Mises grasped that the world is constantly changing. As Heraclitus, the Greek philosopher said, no man steps into the same river twice, for it is not the same river and he is not the same man.

The only thing that mattered was what happened in the real world. And since the real world economy is always in a state of flux, it is continually in disequilibrium. Even a dictator in a communist state had to work in the real world, where general equilibrium equations, hypothetical future consumer preferences or any kind of theoretical construction was of little use. Just like an entrepreneur, he had to make investment decisions to bring supply and demand closer to an equilibrium. He had to speculate about the future just as an entrepreneur did, always knowing that most assumptions about the future are overturned, often daily, by unforeseen changes.

These issues were not just of concern to obscure economic theorists writing in journals with tiny circulations. Real dictators were in charge in Germany, Russia and elsewhere. And their achievements were receiving near universal approbation.

Faith in Stalin's central planning reached a feverish pitch. Many, like George Orwell, who flocked to Spain to fight in the civil war were ready to sacrifice their lives in the cause of the anarcho-syndicalists' moneyless economy. Enthusiasm among Western intellectuals and politicians for the economic policies of Italy's Mussolini reached a peak. In America, President Edgar Hoover signed the Revenue Act of 1932, which ushered in the largest peacetime increase of tax rates in US history. Then, in 1933, a new president, Franklin Delano Roosevelt, launched the New Deal policies that had begun with the Smoot–Hawley Tariff Act imposing high tariffs on imports of agricultural products and manufactured items. These soon had a devastating impact on international trade. In Britain, Keynes declared that laissez-faire economics was dead, and in 1936 he published *The General Theory of Employment, Interest, and Money*, which quickly became the cornerstone of new policies. Keynes argued that the level of employment was determined not by the price of labour or supply and demand but by the spending of money, that is, government money. He argued that it was the responsibility of governments, even in a mixed economy, to maintain full employment by investing or spending during a slump, thus smoothing out the ups and downs of the business cycle. Keynes was not especially enthusiastic about the Soviet Union, but his books helped convince many that state intervention worked.

It certainly seemed to be working in Germany. As Harvard economic guru Professor J. K. Galbraith wrote in the 1970s:

> The elimination of unemployment in Germany during the Great Depression without inflation—and with initial reliance on essential civilian activities—was a signal accomplishment. The economic policy involved large scale borrowing for public expenditures, and at first this was principally for civilian work— railroads, canals and the Autobahnen [highway network]. The result was a far more effective attack on unemployment than in any other industrial country.[17]

By late 1935, unemployment was at an end in Germany. By 1936, high income rates were pulling up prices or making it possible to raise them: 'Germany, by the late thirties, had full employment at stable prices. It was, in the industrial world, an absolutely unique achievement.' Galbraith praised Hitler for 'recognizing that a rapid approach to full employment was only possible if it was combined with wage and price controls'. In fact, Hitler took Germany off the gold standard and quadrupled the supply of banknotes in just twelve years, introduced price and wage controls, and launched a four-year economic plan devoted to military spending, which was later bolstered by a slave economy.

In March 1938, Hitler was riding a wave of popularity and confidence, and his forces were poised to annex Austria in the Anschluss. Mises knew he was high on the Nazi enemies' list, and he left Vienna the very day SS Chief Heinrich Himmler arrived with an advance contingent to make the first arrests. Two days later, when the German army reached Vienna, a group of men broke into Mises' apartment and searched it. The Gestapo came and took twenty-one boxes full of Mises' possessions and sealed the apartment. His belongings would be rediscovered by the Red Army in 1945 and would only be recovered in 1991 in an archive in Moscow.[18]

Mises had previously moved to Geneva to take up a teaching job, but he went back to Vienna to marry Margit von Sereny, a beautiful former actress from Hamburg. They had met in 1925, and he had proposed a year later, but they never married because Mises' mother objected to him marrying a gentile. His mother died on Christmas Day, 1937, and although he was by then fifty-seven, they decided to get married. As soon as they could, they went back to Geneva, where the ceremony was held.[19]

Soon even Switzerland was considered too dangerous, and they crossed occupied France for Portugal, where they could board a ship for America. Mises arrived in 1940, hoping to take up a temporary position at the University of California at Berkeley, but by that time the offer had been withdrawn. Although many other émigré economists assumed key posts in leading universities or government, no one wanted to give him a job. His English was not the best, and everyone knew his old-fashioned ideas had been disproved by Lange. Moderates favoured Keynes, radicals favoured Stalin.

At last he received a small grant from the Rockefeller Foundation, gave occasional lectures and hosted seminars. Yet his followers were few and far between. The couple spent the rest of their lives in America, but Mises never regained the influence he had once enjoyed. He refused to moderate his ideas to suit the times. He became an isolated and embattled figure. Even fellow Austrians thought him extreme. Hayek, Schumpeter and Milton Friedman espoused some forms of state intervention. In his 1942 book *Capitalism, Socialism and Democracy*, Schumpeter predicted that capitalism would not survive.[20]

Meanwhile, Lange continued to flourish. He had a professorship at the University of Chicago and then accepted a personal invitation from Stalin to join the post-war communist government in Poland. Despite Stalin's record of invasion, and the murder and imprisonment of millions of Poles, Lange accepted. He became a professor at the University of Warsaw and chairman of the Polish State Economic Council. Stalin never allowed him to put any of his theories into practice, and instead Lange wrote articles enthusiastically praising Stalin's economic policies. After becoming so prominent in the 1930s, both Lange and Mises were to become largely forgotten figures by the end of the 1950s. Lange's ideas would be forgotten even in his native Poland and were never tried and put to the test.[21]

8

HOW THE CIA CREATED PHANTOM SOVIET
GNP STATISTICS

The creation of GNP as an economic measuring tool in 1937 is hailed as one of the great American inventions of the twentieth century. GNP is a large-scale measure of a nation's total economic activity. It tallies up the value of all finished goods and services produced in a country. While it was devised for free-market economies, it was also put to work as a way of gauging the success of Stalinist economics. Bergson produced the first report estimating Soviet GNP. In 1943, Bergson's team sent off a report that concluded that since 1929, Stalin had quadrupled Soviet GNP.

Only a very clever person could ever have entertained this absurd notion for more than a moment. Stalin's policies had overturned a successful recovery policy, killed over 8 million in a massive famine and then exiled, purged or imprisoned tens of millions of the best cadres, intellectuals, officers and farmers in the Great Terror. Bergson may not have known all the details, but the broad outlines of what happened during the 1930s were widely reported. Even if he preferred to believe the accounts of fellow travellers, what country in history has ever quadrupled its economy in just over a decade? Not even America in its best periods like the roaring 1920s had come anywhere near that. Such spurts of growth were accompanied by a flood of high-quality goods for the world's consumption, but for a quarter of a century Russia had not exported much of anything except bullion.

The timing of the announcement was also peculiar. Bergson's team reported that despite the immense devastation of the Nazi invasion, the Soviet economy remained a 'highly stable' society with little risk of imminent collapse. A background paper produced before the Yalta Conference of February 1945 asserted that even relying on its own resources, the Soviet Union would recover strongly. This was soon shown to be wrong, since the Soviet Union suffered another horrific famine in 1947 in which perhaps 2 million starved to death.[1]

GNP as a measuring tool was an invention that came into use during wartime partly because it was perfectly suited to measuring a wartime economy. Up until 1937, American leaders had depended on sketchy data like stock prices, freight car loadings and incomplete indices of industrial production to make policy. Then the Department of Commerce commissioned Simon Kuznets of the National Bureau of Economic Research to develop a set of national economic accounts. The first set of accounts arrived in a report to Congress in 1937. Next, Wassily Leontief developed the first US input–output accounts. Both he and Kuznets would be awarded Nobel Prizes for this work.

Over in Britain, Keynes complained in 1940 that '[e]very government since the last war [the First World War] has been unscientific and obscurantist, and has regarded the collection of essential facts as a waste of money'. Without hard statistics, he wrote in *How to Pay for the War*, it was impossible to calculate what the British wartime economy could produce with its available resources. So a new official statistical agency, the Central Statistical Office, was set up. The first modern set of British national accounts appeared in 1941. Following suit, Washington decided it needed annual GNP estimates to facilitate wartime planning. In 1942, Kuznets set out to capture all economic production by individuals, companies and the government in a single figure. Gross Domestic Product (GDP), which adds income from sales and overseas investments, came a little later.

At the 1944 Bretton Woods Conference that established the post-war global financial system, including the World Bank and the

International Monetary Fund, GDP was adopted as the standard tool for measuring a country's economy. It became a mainstay in the Cold War, giving everyone a way of comparing the performances of the two rival systems, the free world and the communist bloc. It was supposedly a neutral scorecard uncoloured by moral or political issues.[2]

Since it had no market economy, the Soviet Union could not adopt the system for compiling its national accounts. Its statistics could at best measure government spending as output. Not to be deterred, the Bergson team devised another way of producing a GNP-like figure. It pioneered the techniques of Soviet national income analysis and comparisons that became standard tools both in American academia and in the CIA. After 1945, the RAND think tank in Santa Monica took over the work of the OSS team, but it remained under Bergson's influence. In 1952, the CIA took over research on the Soviet Union. Bergson became a tenured professor at Harvard, where he supervised the Russian Research Institute and taught the theorists and Kremlinologists recruited by the CIA.

A minority of critics immediately pointed out that the GNP concept had inherent flaws. For example, events that are extremely destructive or wasteful such as hurricanes, typhoons, earthquakes and above all wars actually make a country's GNP go up, not down. Put another way, if a government opted to stimulate demand for goods, it could have officials go around and break every window in sight. That would produce the same statistical effect. Similarly, if a government, like the Soviet Union's, chose to divert its wealth into wasteful or useless projects, GNP would also go up. So even if it spent huge sums either preparing for war or actually waging war, the statistics would not record the destruction of wealth but an economic stimulus. Applied to the United States, its GNP statistics showed that it had grown out of the Depression by waging destructive wars with its former economic partners in Europe and Asia.

The GNP calculations also count private property twice: once when it really is private property and again when it becomes government property after the citizen or company has paid taxes. It is biased towards output and government expenditure. The GNP figure supports the belief that if government spending boosts growth through a so-called multiplier effect, then the more government spending the better. Conversely, it hides the fact that much government spending detracts from growth by diminishing the size of the private sector through taxation.

Although the Soviet economy had outlawed all private investment and property, this did not matter. Any GNP statistic would inevitably flatter the performance of the Soviet economy, since the only investment and spending came from the government. Of course, it is true that waging war may sometimes be necessary or even desirable, so defence spending is not per se a waste of money. It is also possible that wars of conquest can be profitable in the short term, and that may have been true for the Soviet Union with its conquests in Eastern Europe.

The GNP statistic is not very good at revealing what happened in the past, but its real damage was that it gave credence to those who claimed that governments could plan the future. It led economists to believe they could make useful forecasts by sifting government spending plans through an economic model of any state. Once GNP had been invented, economists could advise governments on how to manage the business cycle because they could show economic growth rising and falling. So one could hope to plan, or at least intervene and direct, an economy.

As these ideas became accepted by economists and politicians, no one felt any need to pay attention to Mises and the arguments of the Austrian school. Mises was no longer treated as a leading thinker. He was written out of American textbooks and appears, if at all, as a curious footnote. For example, Robert Heilbroner's *The Worldly Philosophers: The Lives, Times and Ideas of the Great Economic Thinkers*, which sold over 2 million copies, fails to even mention him.

This was a pity, because Bergson, and hence the CIA, made assumptions about the Soviet Union that turned out to be wildly erroneous. First, they believed that the Soviet statistics were meaningful. Second, that they could use the statistics for a socialist economy equivalent to those used to calculate GNP, so they could compare the Soviet and American economies. Last, they assumed that Soviet statistics enabled its central planning board to direct meaningful investment. Once they had calculated the equivalent

GNP figure for the Soviet Union, Bergson concluded that since they were investing more than the United States, its GNP would be growing faster. Inevitably, the Soviet economy would overtake the US economy.[3]

Bergson published three major Soviet national income studies—in 1953, 1954 and 1961. Even prior to these, in 1948, Bergson was so confident about his ability to interpret Soviet data that he said it conclusively showed that Stalinist economics worked. He bluntly declared that Mises was just plain wrong: 'By now it is generally agreed that [Mises'] argument is without much force', he wrote.

On the contrary, he asserted, the Soviet Union was growing very fast under its five-year plans, faster than the United States. He did not go as far as to believe official Soviet data that claimed that aggregate national income had risen by an average of 16 per cent every year during the first two five-year plans. Bergson calculated that annual growth was really 5.5 per cent a year, if measured in 1937 rouble prices, or 11.9 per cent if measured in 1928 rouble prices. Bergson created tables of the adjusted Soviet GNP for 1937 broken down by sector of production and use. By his calculation, defence spending accounted for a mere 8 per cent of the economy, agriculture was 30 per cent and 21 per cent was spent on investment. In one of his early studies of Soviet national income, Bergson argued that the Russians were better off after forced collectivization, famine and rationing.[4]

Bergson did not try to convert his Soviet data into dollar equivalents. He came up with his figures by calculating estimates measured in roubles, and where possible he factored in physical measures of output like steel tonnage. Spotty Soviet figures about output and prices were used and then refined by multiplying production by the prices for hundreds of items. Then he used what he called an 'adjusted factor cost system' to take into account government subsidies and taxes. All this was supposed to reveal the true producer's price for any given item—that is, how many roubles' worth of labour, capital and materials went into creating a product. Armed with these 'adjusted prices', he went on to compute national income.[5]

It was a distorted system from the start. Bergson was trying to input a wide range of real market prices, not in a simple rural economy, but an industrial economy with thousands of products whose prices changed all the time. As the Cold War developed, policy-makers demanded reports expressed in dollars. That way, they could compare Soviet with American military spending. While Bergson insisted on working with rouble-denominated estimates, the men who had invented GNP took up the challenge, namely Kuznets and Leontief. Both these men, incidentally, had strong family connections with Russia. Kuznets had left Russia in 1921 to become a professor at Harvard University. Leontief had left Russia in 1925 and also worked at Harvard, where one of his doctoral students was the famous economist Paul Samuelson.[6]

Leontief had worked on estimates of the Soviet economy at the OSS, and in 1940 he concluded that Soviet production was 53 per cent of America's. Although his report cautioned that this was probably an overstatement, from then on it became repeated as an established fact that the Soviet economy was half the size of the American economy. After 1945, others tried to devise input–output tables for the Soviet economy. Another Russian émigré, Alexander Gerschenkron, who worked at the Federal Reserve's research department and later at Harvard, produced a thick document called 'A Dollar Index of Soviet Machinery Output 1927/1928 to 1937'. He tried to work out how many dollars it cost to make 128 different types of machines and over forty types of farm machinery. Then he tried to do the same for Soviet machine tools. The next leap was to use machine production as a proxy for overall economic growth. At the end, Gerschenkron concluded that overall the Soviet growth rate was not nearly as high as Soviet propaganda claimed, but it was still very high.[7]

All these Harvard experts reached the same conclusion. If any outsider doubted their figures, then they could read in the papers how the Soviet Union had destroyed the German war machine, detonated its own nuclear bomb, launched the Sputnik into orbit in 1957 and sent the first man to space in 1961. When the CIA started reporting on the Soviet Union, its staff were confident in saying that its economy was growing faster than America's and Soviet per capita growth was much faster, too. It held fast to that view for the next forty years.

9

NO ONE WAS ALLOWED TO CHALLENGE
ABRAM BERGSON

Apart from Mises, only a handful of other voices dared question the findings of the Bergson school. One of these was another Russian émigré, Naum Jasny, who thought the five-year plans were largely a façade designed to create useful propaganda. Jasny was sure that the first five-year plan was an economic disaster—not only in terms of consumption and food production but also industrial growth. In 1949, Jasny published *The Socialized Agriculture of the USSR*, which directly challenged Bergson's work. He found it astonishing that Bergson could claim that '1937 was for the Soviet consumer a year of relative prosperity.'[1]

The conflict between Jasny and the Bergson/RAND school became so bitter and personal that after 1954, largely because of opposition from RAND, Jasny was unable to publish anything in American professional journals and found it difficult to get research grants. The only place where Jasny managed to get published was in *Soviet Studies*, a humble journal produced by the University of Glasgow. For twenty years until his death in 1967, he lived in a tiny apartment in Washington and worked at the Library of Congress without any salary or funding. Yet before he died, he found himself fully vindicated by Khrushchev's admission, after Stalin's death, that

Soviet agriculture was not producing enough food for the shops. Khrushchev cited numbers very close to those that Jasny had come up with.[2]

Jasny was an agricultural specialist born in Kharkiv, Ukraine, in 1883, whose early career gave him first-hand experience of how the Soviet Union really worked. He obtained a doctorate in law in St Petersburg and, after practising law for a short time, became director of a flour mill in Kharkiv. After 1917, he designed food policies for the Soviet government. He then went to Germany, where he joined a famous Berlin think tank, the Institute for Business Cycle Research. After 1933, he fled the Nazis for the United States and joined the Department of Agriculture. From 1939, he worked at the Food Research Institute of Stanford University, where he prepared forecasts of food availability in allied and enemy countries.[3]

Jasny demonstrated that at best consumption had reached 60 per cent of the level in 1928. He tried to recalculate the Soviet statistics by basing them on 1928 rouble prices. Yet he discovered so many prices for any given item that it led to tortured statements like this one, taken at random from his book *Soviet Industrialization 1928–1952*:

> The official price established for unrationed bread effective January 1 1935 was about half the price in state commercial and *kolhoz* trade at the beginning of 1934, but 4 times the rationed price at the same time and double the rationed price immediately before derationing. Thus, the meeting of the 'low' rationed prices and high unrationed prices at derationing—the official assertion—occurred nearer to the high prices in state commercial trade and *kolkhoz* trade than to the price on rations.[4]

Jasny also challenged Bergson's judgement on other issues by asserting that an astonishing proportion of Soviet national product went to investment and defence rather than consumption. He estimated that personal income had only gone up by a third between 1928 and 1952, but funds for investment and the military went up eight times.[5]

'Large-scale falsification of statistics was resorted to in order to make the rates of growth seem much bigger than they really were and especially to conceal the fact that instead of rising greatly, as promised and claimed, the level of personal consumption had declined', he concluded.[6]

Jasny tried to demonstrate that the Soviet statisticians simply made up figures whenever it suited them. He didn't believe either that there ever was a planned economy. Stalin just ordered campaigns and projects. Judging by how much was published each time, the plans certainly became less and less important. The first plan took up four volumes, the second two volumes, the third one volume. The fourth merited just six pages in *Pravda* and the fifth plan (1951–5) a scant three pages. Jasny argued that it was more realistic to calculate in terms not of five-year plans but economic trends. So he designated periods with names like the Warming Up (1928–31), All-Out Drive (1932–4) and Three 'Good' Years of 1935–7, which he put in quotes to emphasize how bad the preceding years were.[7]

Bergson was horrified by this doubt and quickly dismissed it. In his 1953 article 'Reliability and Usability of Soviet Statistics: A Summary Appraisal', he wrote: 'Contrary to a common supposition, the Russians seem generally not to resort to falsification.'

Bergson argued that Soviet data held up to tests of internal consistency. Soviet data corresponded to other Soviet evidence, such as when a certain industry experienced low growth rates, what followed was a personnel shake-up in that industry. He said that Soviet data was broadly consistent with reports from foreign observers, and that Soviet plans in classified and unclassified versions of the 1941 economic plan matched each other closely. His strongest point was that Soviet statistical data did not have to be accurate but only inaccurate in systematic ways so that scholars could make appropriate adjustments.

In fact, Soviet statisticians did completely fabricate figures. The 1937 Soviet population census, for instance, was not released because it showed the large numbers of famine deaths. Instead, a new census in 1939 reported false data.

Bergson and his school dismissed as unscientific the evidence from other American researchers that showed how Soviet statistics were really made. American academic Joseph S. Berliner conducted interviews with Soviets displaced in Germany and examined the handful of Communist Party archives that fell into Western hands during the Second World War. Based on this information, he published *Factory and Manager in the USSR* in 1957. The forty-one former Soviet managers told the interviewer about the perennial shortages of almost everything and the routine falsification of statistics at every level. The planning process involved 'an enormous amount of falsification in all branches of production and in their accounting systems', reported one manager. 'Everywhere there is evasion, false figures, untrue reports.' Managers hoarded materials, chronically underreported supplies and exaggerated output and otherwise fulfilled the plan according to quantity targets. Since steel was measured in tons, managers produced it in bulk instead of the various steel products, such as the thin rolled steel, that were actually needed.

Managers deliberately misrepresented their firms' costs and capacities in their reports to the ministries that supervised them. They exaggerated their needs of labour, materials and equipment; failed to report improvements in techniques; concealed the productivity of new machines; understated the number of engineers on hand; and overstated the time needed for a task. Similar misrepresentation occurred at all levels of the hierarchy. Inside the firm, production-floor supervisors padded their reports to middle managers, as did middle managers to top managers. The misreporting did not end there. The bureaucrats in direct charge of a firm understated its capacity to the central planning commission. The result was a cumulative divergence between actual and reported capacities. The entire Soviet economy therefore ran according to a plan built on biased information.

One manager described the ways in which the planned targets were influenced:

> When the shop engineer receives an order he begins to discuss it with the foreman, the dispatcher, and all the responsible people in the lower level. The foreman knows that the job will be done in the first machine row. He can compute the number of machine hours there, looking for reserves. If 2,000 machine hours are needed for the assembly, he will say 2,200 are needed.

The planner thinks that perhaps the foreman did not allow enough, so he raises it to 2,400. Then the planning sector gets it and there it is discussed, and allowance is made for breakdown, etc. They allow for such things as an order from the chief electrical engineer of the district to economize on electricity. In this case all the electrical power may be cut off for two hours a day in all the factories in the district. ... In consequence of all these possibilities, the chief of the planning sector increases the number of required machine hours to 3,000 in order to secure himself. And even the resident ministry representative may add something besides, because he is responsible for the production program also, and he may add a few hours. This they called insurance (*strakhovka*). Misappropriation of funds was routinely covered up in reports to the centre, as was spoiled production and unfulfilled targets.[8]

Bergson operated on the premise that the Soviet Union worked much as Lange thought it would: a central planning board stimulated a market in capital goods through a trial-and-error process. He also imagined that Stalin would put in place a framework of general directives to guide subordinates on how to implement the plans. And that even under a dictator's rule, the government would follow a plan and try to maximize the potential of the economy as best it could.

When the Soviet archives opened after 1991, the notes taken of Politburo meetings during Stalin's twenty-five-year rule were uncovered. As the following examples show, he ran the Soviet economy much as Mises had predicted, not Bergson and Lange. In 1947, Mises had restated his argument in a new book called *Socialism*: 'A socialist management of production would simply not know whether or not what it plans and executes is the most appropriate means to obtain the ends sought.' Without market prices, there would be economic chaos.

Stalin administered the economy by issuing decrees, thousands of them every year. As Paul Gregory explains in *The Political Economy of Stalinism*, even Politburo members were too terrified to decide anything for themselves, so they pushed all decisions, even trivial ones, up to Stalin. In a typical year, 1934, Stalin spent some 1,700 hours just in private meetings, the equivalent of more than 200 eight-hour days.[9]

Gregory shows how he worked: in one memo, Stalin would order officials shot, the minister of transport fired, issue instructions on foreign exchange, order vast organizational changes, cut back investment or order major foreign policy initiatives. In another, Stalin discussed the production of vegetables near Moscow, the amount of lanes a particular bridge should have, whether a Soviet author should write books about Soviet industry, which products should be sent to send to Baku, which articles published in various journals and newspapers included ideological errors, the price of bread in various regions, and the renaming of a square in Moscow. When the politburo members met in one of their endless meetings, they had discussed everything—tons of steel, peat, truck designs, freight loadings and so on, and Stalin always had the final say.[10]

When taking economic decisions, Stalin sometimes talked about physical quantities like grain collection targets, and sometimes made investment decisions which were calculated in nominal roubles. One example is the proposal that Stalin received on 2 September 1936:

> We [the Politburo] discussed with the ministers the fourth quarter plan. The volume of production of union and local industry was set at 19.7 billion roubles, which gives a 17.3 percent increase relative to the third quarter. The ministries proposed to establish tasks for each main administration, trust and enterprise for the production of completed production and a detailed assortment of production with high quality parts and corresponding to established standards. The Council of Labor and Defense is charged with approving this more detailed plan. We set the average daily loading of the rail system at 91,000 cars, the transport of commercial freight at 131 million tons, and the volume of passenger transport at 12 billion passenger kilometers. The volume of water transport is set at 12 billion tons and of sea transport at 7.8 billion tons. We set the volume of capital work at 7,909 million roubles and financing at 7,048 million roubles, taking into account the lowering of construction costs. Retail trade of state and cooperative stores is set at 28 million roubles. The market fund for grain is set at 3,100 thousand tons,

for grits at 230 thousand tons and for sugar at 360 thousand tons, for vodka at 20,300 thousand deciliters. We ask you to send your opinion.[11]

No one ever attempted to fix the value of these roubles on a base year, so that made all comparisons meaningless. When various state agencies such as a ministry or a republic would be given 'investment roubles', no one could tell what 'real' investment these roubles produced. The definition of a ton of grain or sugar or whatever was also vague and open to manipulation.

Once any agency obtained its investment budgets, it could do as it pleased. Their investment projects were usually approved without cost estimates, despite clear-cut rules requiring them. When the central planning agency, Gosplan, or the finance ministry or the state bank tried to supervise the costs, they were accused of sabotaging key state projects. Even the defence ministry could not examine the costs of its suppliers.

The Soviets employed none of the general rules for administering a planned investment that Bergson envisaged. Any rule or procedure was liable to be overridden by a superior. Each year's or each quarter's planning process was initiated by new guidelines rather than an established set of planning rules. No 'plan' was final; all were tentative and subject to intervention. The few accounting and loan administration rules that existed were easily ignored.

Yet by the time Stalin died in 1953, the belief in the marvels of Soviet planning had taken firm root in every university economics department in the West. When the future leaders of the Third World or nonaligned movement studied at the London School of Economics or at Harvard, they naturally took Stalinism as their inspiration. Once in power, they too announced five-year plans, introduced price controls, tried to squeeze their country's peasants by herding them into state farms in order to generate the capital to build steel plants and dams. 'Planning and development have become a sort of mathematical problem which may be worked out scientifically', as India's first prime minister, Jawaharlal Nehru, enthused in 1960.

of each good, then asked each factory to deliver its own sub-quota.

All the 5,000 cotton and textile factories were then merged and consolidated into 1,000 state companies and placed under central control. Many small factories were closed and the employees lost their jobs.

The workers were organized into new labor unions, and each branch was invited to elect a well-paid official, who set the piece-work rates under for their employees. The employers were required to submit their accounts to the accountant and then had to pay their [...........]. Foreign businessmen were not allowed to leave until all small businesses lost all their property, sometimes after [...........] struggles on their own.

China's foreign trade collapsed and was cut off to the [...........] to do with other socialist countries. The closure of markets and export markets caused particular [...........] [...........] self-reliance came to be highly prized, a goal that [...........] of factories, small businesses, [...........] lost [...........] the model of small [...........] became [...........] factories and railways. [...........] of the country. The [...........] of workers was [...........] [...........] prices reduced to [...........] compared to [...........] advanced societies in Shanghai, [...........] factories found it difficult to remain interior markets, further inland to the west of factories was subordinated to the [...........] to the [...........] further interior where food was [...........] distribution services all served to [...........] other [...........] when transportation and travel, [...........] to [...........] reduced to develop.

When Mao introduced [...........] and property owners in China peasants could no longer hire extra hands, nor could without to dispose of their work outside the village or their seasons. The employers no point production in the collectives and the [...........] restrictions discouraged handicrafts, silk cultivation, and wool production that had previously helped peasants supplement their incomes. All the small-scale private enterprises of village life withered, leaving the peasants dependent on what the state could supply from its factories.

The most damaging policy was the closure of grain markets after 1953, when the Party mandated compulsory grain procurement prices. These prices were deliberately set too low in order to subsidize

10

WHY AMERICAN ECONOMIC TEXTBOOKS
WERE WRONG

By the time Stalin died in 1953, most American experts had convinced themselves that he had created a socialist economic system that was outperforming American capitalism. Better yet, it was destined to overtake it within ten to twenty years. The consensus was promulgated by top American universities and repeated in virtually all popular economics textbooks. It was reinforced by the further research carried out by think tanks working on behalf of the CIA and by the resulting intelligence estimates read by politicians and diplomats.

This mutually reinforcing belief system was bolstered by the advance of Soviet technological feats—its first nuclear bombs, first satellite in space, Sputnik, followed by Yuri Gagarin becoming the first man in space. The Russians were clearly overtaking the Americans in technology and know-how. In October 1963, the leader of the British Labour Party made a famous speech at a party conference in Scarborough in which he warned of 'the formidable challenge' posed by Soviet scientists and technologists and the ruthless application of scientific techniques in Soviet industry. Behind the propaganda curtain, though, Khrushchev was struggling to find ways of turning the Soviet Union and his allies away from

Stalin's slave labour economy towards one based on international trade, consumer spending and high agricultural investment. There was less to Soviet technological achievements than met the eye. The Russians had stolen nuclear know-how from Britain and America, Britain had given it jet engine technology for nothing, and former Nazi scientists were behind the success of Soviet rockets.

The transmutation of Bergson's work on Soviet statistics into established fact was largely the creation of the scholars who went to work for the OSS during the Second World War. Afterwards, they and their disciples went on to become professors at top universities, or they directed the work done by leading think tanks and advised the CIA on how to conduct its research. Bergson's beliefs were accepted without question by Professor Paul Samuelson, who would win a Nobel Prize for Economics and who wrote the all-time bestselling textbook: *Economics: An Introductory Analysis*. It was first published in 1948 and would go on to sell over 4 million copies in fifteen editions with translations into forty-one languages. Samuelson was a Keynesian who influenced students all over the world, many of whom went on to work in business or as economic analysts and lecturers. Samuelson famously remarked, 'I don't care who writes a nation's laws—or crafts its advanced treaties—if I can write its economics textbooks.'[1]

Over the years, as the textbook grew into an 800-page opus, it found no space for the ideas of Mises or even Hayek. Their warnings about socialist central planning and the impossibility of calculating quantities are only briefly mentioned in editions nine to twelve but not before or afterwards, as Professor David Levy and Dr Sandra Peart explore in an article, 'Soviet Growth & American Textbooks', published in 2009.

Samuelson and Bergson became friends in the late 1930s while attending graduate school at Harvard when they were still in their early twenties. Bergson was two years ahead of Samuelson, and together they penned a highly influential article on welfare economics. After graduating, he became an assistant professor of economics at the Massachusetts Institute of Technology (MIT) when he was twenty-five and a full professor at age thirty-two. Samuelson spent his career at MIT, and when he died in 2009 aged ninety-four, he was lauded as the 'father of modern economics'. He served as an advisor to Presidents John F. Kennedy and Lyndon B. Johnson and was a consultant to the US Treasury, the Bureau of the Budget and the president's Council of Economic Advisors.

Bergson returned to Harvard, where he directed the Russian Research Center, now the Davis Center for Russian and Eurasian Studies. Harvard was also home to other influential opinion-makers such as Arthur M. Schlesinger Jr, professor of history, and the prolific writer and economics commentator Professor J. K. Galbraith. Another key member of the Harvard faculty, Galbraith wrote numerous best-sellers, including *The Affluent Society* and *The New Industrial State*. After touring China in 1972, he wrote a short book, *China Passage*, in which he praised all of the alleged accomplishments of Mao's economic system. Professor Galbraith returned from a visit to the Soviet Union in 1984 and penned an article in *The New Yorker* saying:

> That the Soviet system has made great material progress in recent years is evident both from the statistics and from the general urban scene. ... One sees it in the appearance of well-being of the people on the streets. ... Partly, the Russian system succeeds because, in contrast with the Western industrial economies, it makes full use of its manpower.[2]

Separately, he said that standing on the Berlin Wall: 'Looking in either direction it really makes no great difference.'

Another enthusiast who visited both the Soviet Union and China was John K. Fairbank, professor of Chinese history at Harvard University and the leading Sinologist of his generation. He, too, had worked for OSS during the Second World War and wrote sympathetically of the communist revolution, claiming that it was the best thing that had happened to the Chinese peasants, dramatically improving their standard of living.

All these authorities took for granted that any enlightened scientific planner or development planner could alter the allocation of resources in a rational manner and produce a 'better' economic outcome than relying on markets. They stressed that a large government should provide 'built-in stabilizers' to the economy, such as taxes, unemployment compensation, farm aid and welfare payments in order to even out the ups and downs of the business cycle, and most of all, prevent unemployment. Harvard became the top university in the world for studying economics.

By contrast, American academics treated Mises as a relic of a pre-scientific age and either ignored or ridiculed him. His laissez-faire ideas were considered unscientific, lacking both methodology and unsubstantiated by the sort of empirical data that could be used for the macro-economic modelling that became fashionable. Mises received no higher position than as a visiting professor at the New York University's Graduate School of Business Administration, where his salary was paid by donations from wealthy businessmen. For most of the twenty-four years after he arrived in New York, he gave a monthly seminar, but in all this time he only supervised four postgraduate students.

However, the public was far more receptive to the ideas of the Austrian school than anyone in academia. Hayek's book, *The Road to Serfdom*, became a runaway success after it was published in 1944. *Reader's Digest* condensed the book, and the Book-of-the-Month Club distributed more than 1 million copies. Hayek became an international celebrity for arguing against increasing government powers. In 1947, Hayek founded the Mont Pèlerin Society, named after a Swiss village where the first meeting was held. The society brought together libertarian thinkers, including of course, Mises.[3]

The older man had his own success with an English version of his work *Nationalökonomie*, which was published by Yale University Press as *Human Action*. It came out in 1949 and, despite being 900 pages long, went on to sell 4,000 copies in the first three months. It made Mises a central figure on the American right. 'Mises now appeared to the public not merely as a scholar of the old school, but as one of the great minds of western civilization, a creative genius who had not only mastered all aspects of his science, but had completely transformed this science to offer a new way of looking at social processes and relationships', says his biographer. The success of *Human Action* paved the way for a new edition of his book *The Theory of Money and Credit* in 1953 and another book, *The Anti-Capitalistic Mentality*, which investigated why so many intellectuals, especially in America, were so drawn to socialism. However, unlike Schumpeter or Hayek, Mises never received any high honours or any important prizes.

The popularity of the Austro-libertarian movement in America reached a peak in the mid-to-late 1950s when Ayn Rand published her novel *Atlas Shrugged*, which became a runaway success. This was accompanied by the rise of a fervent anti-communism movement in the United States amid a red scare and a hunt for communist spies and infiltrators. The House Committee on Un-American Activities targeted communist sympathizers in Hollywood, while Senator Joseph McCarthy ran a Senate sub-committee that targeted fellow travellers in the State Department and other institutions.

Partly as a backlash, university campuses swung ever more to the left in the 1960s. Students expressed strong sympathies for communist revolutionary movements and voiced great hostility towards capitalism. The pendulum swung so far that academics like Fairbank who had praised the achievements of the Soviet Union and Mao's China came under attack either for collaborating with the CIA or for not being sufficiently radical and left wing. Younger academics formed a pressure group called the Committee of Concerned Asian Scholars. The war in Vietnam made a generation sympathetic to Mao, the Vietnamese communists and left-wing liberation movements.

The textbooks written by Samuelson and other economists played a significant role during this decade. They consistently favoured a big role for the state and endorsed the success of the Soviet model. To help support his position, Samuelson pioneered the use of what he called the 'productivity possibility frontier' or the 'production possibility curve', a curious statistical trick that enabled him to compare market and socialist economies and project their future growth.

This invention derived from certain assumptions for which he offered little justification. One was that the Soviet economy invested much more of its GNP into industrial production because in a market economy like that of the United States, politicians divert resources into consumption. In this supposed trade-off between 'guns and butter', a Stalinist economy would inevitably grow much faster than one that wasted its resources on idle consumption. In the first 1948 edition of his textbook, *Economics: An Introductory Analysis*,

Samuelson wrote: 'The Russians, having no unemployment before the war, were already on their Production-possibilities curve. They had no choice but to substitute war goods for civilian production—with consequent privation.'[4]

The idea was given a spurious scientific validity in 1961 by a chart showing the Soviet economy overtaking the US economy. This made a second unmerited assumption that the Soviet economy was half the size of the US economy in 1960, although, of course, there was no way this assertion could be measured. This belief also assumed that all economic systems were equally efficient, so that what principally mattered was where any country chose to invest its energies. He also assumed that there was no major difference between the share of GNP that each country devoted to defence, a fallacy that will be discussed in more detail further on.

Building on this shaky foundation, Samuelson confidently forecast that Soviet GNP would surpass that of the United States by 1984. In the 1967 edition, his graph forecast that within ten years the USSR could overtake the United States. By 1970, Samuelson said that the United States had been growing towards the top of its projected range of growth rates, but the USSR had slowed down because bad weather had caused poor harvests and Soviet workers were working shorter hours.[5]

In the 1973 edition, he predicted that as the Soviet Union's per capita income continued to grow, it would probably match that of the United States by 1990 and overtake it by 2010. In later editions, bad weather was still blamed, but he claims that technical improvements would soon boost agricultural efficiency. By 1980, the cross-over date was expected to come before 2012.

In the 1985 edition, Samuelson posed the rhetorical question of whether or not Soviet repression was 'worth the economic gains', which he thought of as 'one of the most profound dilemmas of human society'. He argued:

> It is a vulgar error to think that most people in Eastern Europe are miserable. Although it is undoubtedly true that few citizens of the West would trade their degree of economic comfort and political freedom for life in the Soviet Union, it is also true that a

Soviet citizen thinks that he is living in a paradise in comparison with life in China or in earlier times. Remember that life under the czars was no bed of roses for most classes, and to the eye of the traveler from impoverished Asia and Africa, the rising degree of Russian affluence must seem impressive.[6]

As Professor Mark Skousen points out, the twelfth edition replaced the graph with a table, declaring that between 1928 and 1983, the Soviet Union had grown at a remarkable 4.9 per cent annual growth rate, faster than the United States, the United Kingdom or even Germany and Japan. In the thirteenth edition, published just before the fall of the Berlin Wall in 1989, he, along with his fellow author, William Nordhaus, wrote: 'But it would be misleading to dwell on the shortcomings. Every economy has its contradictions. ... What counts is results, and there can be no doubt that the Soviet planning system has been a powerful engine for economic growth.' That's because, the book declared, 'The Soviet economy is proof that, contrary to what many skeptics had earlier believed, a socialist command economy can function and even thrive.'[7]

Samuelson's economics textbook was not the only one during this era to make unsupported claims about the Soviet economy. Another publishing success was Campbell McConnell's *Economics: Principles, Problems and Policies*, which came out in 1960. For the next thirty years, the author claimed that 'the annual rate of growth in the Soviet Union is two or three times as great as that now achieved in the United States because investment as a proportion of GNP has in many years been put at over 30 per cent, twice that of the United States'. In the 1990 edition, he was still asserting that Soviet GNP had been expanding at about 7 per cent per year compared to 3–4 per cent per year for the United States. Although he recognized the tendency of Soviet planning to become less efficient in an increasingly complex economy, one must take into account 'the likelihood of significant breakthroughs in the techniques and mechanics of central planning'. Curiously, although over ten editions it was claimed that the Soviet economy was growing much faster than America's, the 1990 edition still showed Soviet GNP at half that of the United States'.[8]

121

Another popular textbook, Professor George L. Bach's *Economics: An Introduction to Analysis and Policy*, first published in 1954, said: 'No other nation in history has industrialized at anything like the rate of the Soviet economy since the early 1920s. From a backward, rural economy, in less than three decades Russia has become the world's second greatest industrial power.' All through the next ten editions, the USSR remained the second greatest industrial power in the world.[9]

For more than thirty years, all these textbooks insisted on the success of Soviet economic management, which was described in some detail, while the truly successful post-war economies of Germany and Japan merited only brief mentions. Samuelson devotes just a paragraph to West Germany, and of Japan he simply says that its 'recent sprint has been astounding'. Also neglected were East Asia's tiger economies until the thirteenth edition in 1989, when they are given just two paragraphs of coverage.

All across academia, it was hard to find an economics expert or a student in the United States or elsewhere who did not believe either that the Soviet Union was an economic giant that posed a great threat to national security or that it was such a successful alternative to Western capitalism that the United States should adopt socialist planning. The enlightened view was often that the two systems were busily converging on each other. There would be more planning in the United States and more consumerism in the socialist world.[10]

As enthusiasm for left-wing dictatorships swept through American campuses in the 1970s, some American Sovietologists increasingly presented the Soviet Union as a 'developmental dictatorship', devoted to creating an equal society that was making the Soviet people not only more prosperous but also freer. Stalinism was presented as a necessary cultural revolution, and all the stories about purges and the Gulag were alleged to be greatly exaggerated. In this view, the Soviet Union was just a variant of democracy, and the West had a great deal to learn from it.

Inevitably, the positive view of the Soviet Union and its economic achievements swayed key foreign policy debates in the 1970s. If the Soviet Union was poised to overtake the United States, then it could not be defeated. The only possible way forward was a succession of summits and negotiations known as détente, and those who thought otherwise were only endangering world peace. The United States therefore recognized the Soviet Union as an equal superpower.

As much influence as institutions like Harvard had, though, the real debate about the Soviet Union's true economic achievements took place not in the universities but inside the CIA. A fierce struggle erupted as some people produced evidence to show that Bergson's data was hopelessly flawed. The reputations of too many important figures were now chained to his authority and the illusions he had helped foster for any challenger to win.

11

WHY THE GULAG ECONOMY WAS ABANDONED

For fifteen years, Lavrenty Beria, a short, pudgy Georgian with soft hands and *pince-nez*, ran Stalin's vast Gulag slave economy, and no one knew better why it was an economic failure. Gigantic projects on which millions had toiled on starvation rations were either never finished or turned out to be completely unproductive. Just as Mises had predicted, the Soviet system led to irrational investment.

Only after the collapse of the Soviet Union did conclusive evidence emerge that not even Beria, often hailed as a brilliant administrator, could find a way to make the Gulag pay. Even more shocking, he declared after Stalin's death that the whole Soviet economy did not work and should be abandoned. In 1953, Beria called for an end to the 'forced construction of socialism, the compulsory collectivization of agriculture and the elimination of private capital in the economy'. Within days of Stalin's death, he released 1.5 million prisoners and set about overturning many of his domestic and foreign policies.[1]

In 1938, Stalin had replaced Nikolai Ezhov as the NKVD chief with Beria, who had presented Stalin with a plan to make the camps the most productive part of the Soviet economy. In the 1930s, about 7 million prisoners worked building dams, railways and large industrial plants. Their low cost, expendability and reliability made the Soviet Union's dramatic strides in industrialization possible. The slave laborers spearheaded Stalin's grandest projects, building everything from the Moscow Metro to giant metallurgical complexes, hydropower schemes, huge canals, railways, roads and aircraft factories. Huge numbers were thrown into the nuclear weapons programme, working in uranium mines or digging out vast underground reprocessing plants and the reactors housed in networks of tunnels and caverns excavated inside mountains. At its height, the slave labour provided the Soviet Union with most of its exports of nickel, tin, gold, timber, coal, platinum and diamonds.

When Stalin collapsed at Blizhnaya, a north Moscow dacha, after an all-night dinner with his four Politburo comrades in March 1953, Beria, then fifty-four, may have poisoned him, possibly with warfarin. Beria may also have prevented any doctors reaching him in time and instead watched his dying moments with pleasure. Two months later, Beria reportedly boasted: 'I did him in! I saved all of you', according to Vyacheslav M. Molotov and as recorded in Khrushchev's 1970 memoirs, *Khrushchev Remembers*.

Stalin died when he was seventy-four and had just ordered the construction of four new giant labour camps, possibly in preparation for a purge of the ethnic Jewish population. He was also preparing for a war against the United States. Beria swiftly began reducing tensions with the United States over Germany, aware that the USSR's economy was in a shambles. In May 1953, Beria overturned Stalin's plans for East Germany and replaced the Russian military commander in East Germany with a civilian commissioner and said he wanted to work towards a democratic unified Germany. Despite such promises, in June large-scale protests in East Germany erupted, which the Soviet leadership crushed with tanks. Nine days later, Beria was arrested at a Politburo meeting in the Kremlin by rivals who felt that events in Germany proved his reforms had moved too far and too fast, threatening to bring down the entire system.[2]

Marshal Georgii Zhukov unexpectedly entered the room, drew a pistol and shoved it against Beria's head. Beria was marched out of the room and then smuggled out of the Kremlin to the Lefortovo Prison. He was then kept in an underground bunker at the headquarters of the Soviet high command for five months until a closed trial was held on 18 December. A few days later, he was shot in the head by a General Batitiskii and his remains buried in secrecy. The man who organized the coup against him was Nikita Khrushchev, the man who had overseen the destructive collectivization of Ukraine. Naturally, little could be found out about Beria after his downfall. It was only after 1990 when the Soviet archives were opened that we learned why Beria had moved so quickly to dismantle the Gulag system.

There were two main reasons why the Gulag failed. First, Beria realized that the schemes were poorly thought out and produced no good return on investment. And secondly, the Soviets realized that slave labour was inherently costlier than free labour. Huge projects were started on the spur of the moment without any proper engineering feasibility studies or financial costing. And even when these were done, it was impossible to calculate the returns on investment in an economy that did not use money. It was simply assumed that because the labour was free, they must be viable.

American academic Paul Gregory and Oleg Khlevnyuk, a senior researcher at the State Archive, wrote in *The Economics of Forced Labor: The Soviet Gulag* that Stalin's major engineering projects were ill-conceived, wasteful investments. Many were either left unfinished or brought few returns. In his work *The Economy of the OGPU, NKVD and MVD of the USSR, 1930–1953: The Scale, Structure and Trends of Development*, Khlevnyuk observed that by creating so much cheap and mobile manpower, the state could undertake expensive but economically dubious projects without much thought or preparation. In Gregory's words:

> The countries of the former Soviet Union are cemeteries of failed construction projects, which would never have been started if project analysis had not been distorted by the absence of market pricing in the national economy and by the country's isolation from international markets. Many such projects came into being merely because of fleeting political considerations.[3]

The first of these mega-projects, the White Sea–Baltic Canal and the Moskva–Volga Canal, never fulfilled their potential because they were never properly linked—the Mariinsk and Moskva River systems were never modernized to allow traffic. In 1940, the canal was being used at only 44 per cent of its capacity, and in 1950 this had fallen to just 20 per cent. 'The canal's value to the region's economic development, as soon became clear, was minor. And strategically, the waterway's value was negligible', according to Gregory. It remained as an expensive monument to the mismanagement of the Soviet system.

Another great OGPU/NKVD project was to build a new railway line north of the trans-Siberian starting from Tayshet, which was never finished. Individual sections were put into operation but proved to be of little use. Many other railway lines were started and then abandoned. The disorganized construction of many railroads without the necessary feasibility studies was enormously wasteful. By 1938, work on 5,000 kilometres of track (excluding railroads that had been built but not used or only partially used because they weren't needed) was suspended. The total increase in the rail system from 1933 through 1939 was only 4,500 km.[4]

After Stalin's death, the government halted the construction of various plants and hydraulic-engineering installations, where work costing roughly the annual capital investment budget of the MVD (Ministry of Internal Affairs) had already been done. One of these was the never finished Chum–Salekhard–Igarka railroad across the Arctic, which cost the lives of tens of thousands of prisoners. It started in April 1947 and used a maximum of 130,000 people working along its 1,200-kilometer length. Normal construction methods in the Arctic tundra were impossible, so the prisoners used wooden rails instead of steel. These promptly sank into the permafrost surface mud. By 1953, 500 kilometres had been built at one end, 200 kilometres from the other end. As soon as Stalin died, the project was abandoned at a total cost of 40 billion roubles and unimaginable human misery.

A similar fate befell the Kuibyshev hydroelectric system, started in September 1940. By the time construction at the Kuibyshev project was suspended, a huge sum—126.7 million roubles—had already been spent—and 30,000 to 40,000 prisoners had been concentrated at the Samara camp.

The camps were first built in Lenin's time as instruments of political and moral reform. Only after Stalin launched the first five-year plan in 1929 did the Gulag come to assume its truly sinister proportions. It expanded rapidly in size and importance during the 1930s. Stalin's priorities fluctuated. Sometimes he wanted to use the system to punish and indeed liquidate his enemies, but at other times he wanted a slave labour army to construct his ambitious industrialization projects.

The scale of the Gulag labour system was staggering, even when set against the Atlantic slave trade. Over the space of several centuries, between 10 and 12 million Africans were transported the 4,000 miles from Africa to the New World. By comparison, between 1918 and 1956, twice as many passed through Soviet prisons and labour camps, at least 25 million, and many of them perished before they could do any useful work. Some, like the Poles and citizens of the former Baltic republics, were brought 7,000 miles to Magadan in the Russian Arctic only to die within a year or two after journeys that lasted four or five months.[5]

The Far North Construction Trust, better known as Dalstroy, was established in 1931 to mine gold during the first five-year plan. The deposits along the Kolyma River in the Russian Far East were richer and cheaper to mine than those of Alaska. Lenin's former bodyguard, Eduard Berzin, founded Dalstroy. He had a Rolls Royce presented to him by Nadezhda Krupskaya, Lenin's widow, and, clad in a bearskin coat, he drove it around the eighty camps scattered throughout the vast region. In 1937, he was recalled to Moscow, arrested and then executed at the Lubyanka.

Dalstroy was considered an economic success because output doubled every year, and the gold was vital for paying for imports of machinery essential for the industrialization drive. In 1992, when I visited Magadan, the capital and port of the Kolyma region, just after the dissolution of the Soviet Union, it still felt very remote. It required a flight from Moscow that crosses five time zones. In the 1930s, prisoners were taken on a journey even longer than that of the black slaves shipped along the Middle Passage from Africa to the New World. They were brought along the trans-Siberian to Vladivostok, after which they spent months on a ship. In the 1990s, Magadan resembled a provincial city in Mitteleuropa. After Japan's surrender, huge numbers of Japanese POWs arrived there and replaced the old wooden buildings with neo-classical apartment blocks. The road out of Magadan is still called the road of bones. In the 1930s, the prisoners trudged hundreds of miles on foot to reach the mines, dressed in rags and sleeping in canvas tents. This far north, it is dark and bitterly cold most of the year. The temperature rarely rises above minus 20 C, but in the brief summer, it is surprisingly hot and humid, and prisoners suffered agonies from the clouds of midges and mosquitoes that breed in the swampy taiga.

I was taken to the last surviving building from the Stalin era, a small prison block in the town centre. Each cell was stacked from floor to ceiling with shelves of brown foolscap personal files of the prisoners. Underground were special cells for executions with a drain in the middle of the concrete floor for the blood. The largest spate of executions took place during Stalin's Great Terror campaign after 1937, when prisoners were shot after a brief trial by a so-called troika of NKVD officers. Files picked at random yielded some factory workers sentenced to ten years for arriving late for work and then shot for being Trotskyists or Japanese spies. Later prisoners were foreigners sentenced for anti-Stalin protests. In one was a faded piece of sack cloth from a bag of wartime grain delivered as part of US aid during the Second World War marked by crudely daubed anti-Stalin slogans. It was written in clumsy Russian because the author was one of the million Poles arrested after the Red Army invaded under the Soviet–Nazi pact to divide Poland.

The Kolyma camps boasted so many famous actors and musicians that some were recruited to perform in a theatre built to entertain the guards and commandants. Other famous inmates included Mikhail Kravchuk (Krawtschuk), a Ukrainian mathematician well known in the West, and Léon Theremin, an inventor, who voluntarily returned to the Soviet Union from America and was soon sent to Kolyma. Later, Theremin was sent to a *sharashka* or secret research laboratory, together with other scientists and engineers, including aircraft designer Andrei Tupolev and rocket scientist Sergei Korolyov, another Kolyma inmate. Apart from these few exceptions, the men and women were grimly worked to death. Even the top ration of 800 grams of bread was not nearly enough to sustain anyone doing twelve-hour days of hard manual labour in Arctic conditions.

It was hard to grasp the economic rationale for anything that happened there. Unlike the African slaves who were bought and sold, the Soviets placed no value on the prisoners' lives. Of the 16,000 sent in the first year to Kolyma, only 10,000 survived. Only half survived the following year. Between 1932 and 1953, when the camps operated at full strength, over a third of the prisoners died in their first year either in transit or from the shock of working twelve-hour days in the deadly cold. The death toll in those two decades has been estimated at around 900,000, but the toll was quite possibly two or three times as much. If sent to Kolyma, you were reckoned to have just a 10 per cent chance of survival.[6]

Throughout history, slave-owning societies like the Romans treated slaves quite differently. Records recovered from Pompeii showed they were valued and well treated. Many of them were able to buy their freedom and became Roman citizens and often prosperous ones at that. The Bolsheviks transported millions halfway round the world and either shot them or starved them to death within months of their arrival. Why?

Adam Smith argued that the plantation slavery common in the Americas was a mistake, not just for moral reasons. In 1776, he wrote in *The Wealth of Nations*:

> From the experience of all ages and nations, I believe that the work done by free men comes cheaper in the end than the work performed by slaves. Whatever work he does, beyond what is sufficient to purchase his own maintenance, can be squeezed out of him by violence only, and not by any interest of his own.

He argued that slavery created an inefficient market. Slave owners were forced to purchase and maintain slaves year after year, since slaves had a high mortality rate. The cost of purchasing slaves was then passed on to the common consumer. This cost could be avoided by switching to a wage-labour economy and providing decent working conditions for former slaves.

The Bolsheviks ignored this because they believed in class warfare, with those arrested being categorized automatically as class enemies whose lives were therefore worthless. And because of Marx's convoluted thinking about the value of a product being the accumulated labour that went into making it. His reasoning went like this: the industrial wage-earning proletariat were slaves. There was no essential difference, though many secondary ones, between the wage contract and the purchase of a slave:

> [W]hat the employer of 'free' labour buys is not indeed, as in the case of slavery, the labourers themselves but a definite quota of the sum total of their potential labour. But what number of labour hours enters into the 'production' of the stock of potential labour that is stored up within a workman's skin? Well, the number of labour hours it took and takes to rear, feed, clothe and house the labourer. This constitutes the value of that stock, and if he sells parts of it—expressed in days or weeks or years— he will receive wages that correspond to the labour value of these parts, just as a slave trader.[7]

Engels went further by declaring that workers are in fact slaves. In one passage, he writes:

> [T]he worker is, in law and in fact, the slave of the property-holding class, so effectually a slave that he is sold like a piece of goods, rises and falls in value like a commodity. If the demand for workers increases, the price of workers rises; if it falls, their price falls. If it falls so greatly that a number of them become unsaleable, if they are left in stock, they are simply left idle; and as they cannot live upon that, they die of starvation. The only difference as compared with the old, outspoken slavery is this, that the worker of today seems to be free because he is not sold once for all, but piecemeal by the day, the week, the year, and because no one owner sells him to another, but he is forced to sell himself in this way instead, being the slave of no particular person, but of the whole property-holding class. ... The bourgeoisie, on the other hand, is far better off under the present arrangement than under the old slave system; it can dismiss its employees at discretion without sacrificing invested capital.[8]

This kind of mad theorizing held that all labour was a form of slavery and thus from the Bolshevik point of view the less that was spent on feeding and housing the labourer, the more value that could be squeezed out of him. Hence the 'primitive socialist accumulation' proposed by Preobrazhensky would do much better than the 'primitive capitalist accumulation' of the imperialist world.

Marx also believed that the division of labour enabled the capitalist to enslave the worker, and he envisaged that in the communist future 'the enslaving subordination of the individual to the division of labour' would end. With no division of labour, the Bolsheviks reduced the meaning of 'labour' to physical manual labour whose output could only be measured by quotas of physical quantities—how much earth was moved, or timber cut, that sort of thing, all assuming they had no tools or machinery more sophisticated than a shovel or an axe. No other kind of labour counted. So, once arrested, musicians, composers, inventors, philosophers were only valued in terms of their physical brawn.

Beria discovered the truth of Smith's observation that slaves are not productive, hard to motivate and costly to manage. To guard them, the Gulag required at least 200,000 able-bodied soldiers who could have been better employed doing something else.[9] Further, during the 1941–4 war years when productive labour was at a premium, the death rate among the inmates accelerated. Camps had become so overcrowded by the influx from the purges that the living space of each prisoner fell from 1.5 square meters to 0.7—prisoners had to take turns sleeping on boards. Beds became a luxury reserved for workers with special status. The average daily calorific intake fell by 65 per cent from pre-war levels. In 1942, there were major outbreaks of typhus and cholera that killed nearly 19,000 prisoners a year, according to official figures. In 1941, there were nearly 101,000 deaths in the labour camps alone, not including the forced-labour colonies. In 1942, the Gulag administration registered 249,000 deaths and in 1943, 167,000 deaths. If the executions of prisoners and deaths in the prisons and in the forced-labour colonies are included, then there were 600,000 deaths in 1941 alone and perhaps a total of a million for the whole war period.[10]

The survivors were in a pitiful state. Only 19 per cent of all prisoners by the end of 1942 were capable of performing heavy physical labour, 17 per cent were capable of medium physical labour and 64 per cent were only able to perform 'light work'. In other words, they were sick. The deteriorating conditions led the state to give 420,000 inmates early release and to send another 157,000 to the army. Between 1 July 1941 and 11 February 1945, for example, the population in the camps and colonies dropped from 2.3 million to 1.4 million. Hundreds of thousands of prisoners were drafted into the armaments factories to replace the men conscripted into the army. Prisoner manpower was responsible for nearly a quarter of all production in certain key sectors of the armaments industry, notably in metallurgy and mining.[11]

After the war, new prisoners filled the Gulag camps who were much more difficult to manage than those arrested in the 1930s. The latter were former Party cadres who felt they had been mistakenly arrested and still hoped to be released. The new prisoners were Ukrainian and Baltic 'nationalists', some from defeated guerrilla organizations, 'foreign elements' from newly incorporated regions, real or supposed 'collaborators', and other 'traitors to the fatherland', including repatriated Russian prisoners of war. From 1939 onwards, the Gulag filled up with Finns, Poles, Germans, Italians, Romanians and Japanese, plus some 3.4 million German POWS. These new inmates, who were given twenty- or twenty-five-year sentences with no hope of early release, had nothing to lose. They were put in special camps and separated from the common criminals who had controlled the political prisoners in the past. Now these special camps quickly became hotbeds of resistance and revolt. Strikes, hunger strikes, mass escapes and riots, especially by Ukrainian and Baltic prisoners, became increasingly common. There were at least sixteen large-scale riots and revolts in 1950–2, each involving hundreds of prisoners. Aside from the increasing number of violent confrontations between prisoners and guards, gangs of prisoners fought among each other. Deaths from stabbing were more common than deaths from hunger or disease.[12]

In 1951, General Sergei Kruglov, the minister of internal affairs, worried by the constant decline in productivity among penal workers, began a vast inspection campaign. The resulting reports have since been uncovered in the archives. In 1951, a million work days were lost to protests and strikes by prisoners. At a conference of Gulag commanders held in Moscow in January 1952, it was acknowledged that 'the authorities, who until now have been able to gain a certain advantage from the hostilities between various groups of prisoners, [are] beginning to lose their grip on the situation ... In some places, certain factions are even beginning to run the camp along their own lines.'[13]

To break up groups and factions, it was decided that prisoners should be moved between camps more frequently. The biggest penitentiaries, which often held between 40,000 and 60,000 people, were permanently reorganized into separate sections. 'In addition to noting the considerable problems generated by the different factions, many inspection reports from 1951 and 1952 acknowledged a need both for a complete reorganization of the prisons and their systems of production, and for a considerable scaling down of the entire operation.'[14]

His investigation called into question the economic value of what he recognized as an outdated system. The infrastructure in many labour camps was more than twenty years old and needed new investment. All the giant Stalinist projects that depended on prison labour, including the hydroelectric power stations in Kuibyshev and Stalingrad, the Turkmenistan Canal and the Volga–Don Canal, fell behind schedule. Many camps had been designed to house a big labour force conscripted to work on such giant projects, so they were extremely difficult to break up into smaller production units. Furthermore, machinery was now becoming available to replace muscle. Power saws cut logs instead of axes and were hauled by trucks rather than chain gangs. Excavators and bulldozers replaced picks and shovels.

After the war, the state tried to use the prisoners in a more rational way. To motivate them, bonuses and salaries were introduced, and food rations were increased for prisoners who met their quotas. Some were released early to motivate the others. On 13 March 1950, the government introduced wages for all prisoners except those in the special camps for 'especially dangerous' common and political criminals. Yet even in these camps, the authorities eventually came round to paying wages.[15]

'These and similar measures pointed to a post-war trend to transform prisoners into partly free employees—a kind of conversion of slaves to the category of serfs', notes Oleg Khlevnyuk, senior researcher at the State Archives in Moscow and author of *The History of the GULAG: From Collectivization to the Great Terror*.

By the time Stalin died in 1953, the Gulag administrators knew it was unprofitable. The truth could not be hidden by the padded statistics. The tiny salaries given to prisoners, generally a few hundred roubles per year, proved too small an incentive. Its revenues were not enough to cover the cost of both its active labour force and the non-working part of the population. Gulag managers were aware that the labour productivity of their workers was 50 to 60 per cent lower than that of free workers. Near its end, the Gulag employed one guard for every ten workers. The NKVD (as the KGB was then called) and the Ministry of the Interior, which between the 1930s and 1950s had become one of the largest economic ministries, had to plead for subsidies from the state budget, and the subsidies grew until they reached 16 per cent of the state budget.

Beria's successors retreated more gradually, but even so, within three years of Stalin's death the Gulag had largely been dismantled. Khrushchev, who won the resulting power struggle, now tried to find other ways to make socialism work. One of these initiatives was foreign trade, as the next chapter describes. As Khrushchev struggled to plot a way to make Soviet planning more viable, belief in the efficacy of Soviet economics was riding high in America.

Had Beria stayed in power, one can only wonder whether he might have dissuaded the leaders of other communist regimes like Mao Zedong from replicating Stalin's labour camp systems, thus preventing millions of unnecessary deaths. Mao biographer Jung Chang claims that during Mao's rule, around 27 million died in Chinese prisons and labour camps. In his book *Laogai: The Chinese Gulag*, Harry Wu, who spent nineteen years as a prisoner, believes 50 million passed through the camps, most of whom were political prisoners. It is reckoned that in any year Chinese prisons held 10 million people and every year one in ten died. As for North Korea, the Gulag death toll since 1947 is put at over a million. No one has computed the total from all thirty-two countries run by communist parties, but possibly 100 million people were sent to them in the twentieth century.

12

MOSCOW'S FAILED GLOBAL BARTER SYSTEM

Since the CIA believed the Soviet economy had been powering ahead under Stalin's five-year plans, the intelligence agency assumed it would do even better after 1945. In the late 1940s, Stalin created a second empire, bringing East Germany, Poland, Bulgaria, Romania, Czechoslovakia, Yugoslavia and Albania under Moscow's sway. The 100 million people of Eastern Europe were soon joined by North Korea, Vietnam and China, totalling over a quarter of the world's population. Many other countries in the so-called Third World or nonaligned movement ranging from Cuba to India also embraced central planning and joined the network of bilateral barter trading. Most post-colonial leaders, inspired by the reported success of Stalin's efforts to modernize a backward rural economy, chose to launch their own five-year plans and started building massive steelworks and hydroelectric dams. They also created national monopolies over the domestic trade in key commodities, and this inevitably led to state-to-state barter trading of commodities.

After the Second World War, Moscow switched from being a largely autarkic state to pioneering an alternative global trading system that did not use money. It can be described as the first recorded civilization to be based on barter trade. Although some economic historians believe that primitive human societies passed through a barter phase system before adopting a common currency to facilitate trade, no one has yet discovered any trace of such a civilization. The Soviets' barter trade lasted for forty years, and during all those years it strove to avoid using the dollar, which at the 1944 Bretton Woods Conference had been adopted as the base currency for the rest of the world. It was stable because it had a fixed value to gold.

The American dollar became a hated symbol of capitalism and American hegemony. Naturally, it is hard to put a dollar value on the size of socialist international commerce, but the United Nations created a special unit called UNCTAD largely devoted to supporting barter trade. It reckoned that by the 1970s barter trade accounted for 30 per cent of world trade. Many around the world hoped that it could rival and even replace the capitalist global trading system.[1]

Far from being an asset that helped the Soviet Union grow and prosper, however, the international trade it advocated became a massive drain on resources that played a role in its economic collapse. The first admission came during the 1980s when Gorbachev's government revealed that the Soviet Union was losing $12 billion each year in trade with allies. Of course, the Soviet Union could no more work out a reliable figure on its trade than it could for the cost of its military. Without real currencies and market-driven exchange rates, it used prices for its trade that were inherently irrational. It was impossible for those involved to work out what exactly to adjust or how that might be done.

During the 1930s, the USSR had been almost completely uninvolved in world trade. It did export some grain during the collectivization famine, along with gold, platinum, diamonds, cotton, timber and other foodstuffs. It occasionally sold gold or works of art, but the severe shortages of almost all goods and the lack of any hard currency or gold prohibited the development of any ongoing trade relationships. In response, the state created the Torgsin stores in 1931, where citizens could buy food if they had any gold, jewellery, medals or coins. The Torgsin stores steadily widened their remit to accept silver, platinum, diamonds, antiques and eventually any hard currency acquired abroad or sent as remittance from families abroad.

During the Second World War, the United States and Britain delivered a substantial amount of aid, including entire factories to enable the Red Army to keep fighting. After 1945, Stalin would forcibly seize more factories. He expected the countries of Eastern Europe to contribute to the country that had liberated them from Nazi tyranny and set about pillaging the conquered territories. Moscow stripped them of raw materials and factories. It did the same in Manchuria. Then Stalin's operatives uprooted factories and moved them to Soviet soil. They also forced countries to sell resources to the Soviet Union at very low prices, and they took a 50 per cent stake in many large firms throughout Eastern Europe. At least two ministers of foreign trade, one in Bulgaria and another in Czechoslovakia, were executed for bargaining too hard with the Soviet Union.

In 1949, the Soviets created the Council for Mutual Economic Assistance (CMEA) to coordinate production and help integrate the economies of the Eastern bloc into Soviet planning. Western strategists like former US National Security Advisor Zbigniew Brzezinski believed that Moscow was skilfully exploiting its vassal states through unfair trade deals. In his book *The Soviet Bloc, Unity and Conflict*, he says that full economic integration meant the small countries would become absorbed into the USSR. Given national feelings, it is not hard to understand why they would be reluctant to go that far.[2]

The CMEA was based in Moscow and followed policies determined by Soviet leaders, but as the trade developed, the smaller states turned the tables. They were able to manipulate the Soviet Union into delivering low-cost energy and raw materials in exchange for shoddy manufactured goods. As political scientist Randall Stone observes in *Satellites and Commissars: Strategy and Conflict in the Politics of Soviet-Bloc Trade*: 'The politics of trade in the Soviet bloc swirled and eddied around opportunities created by the distorted prices mandated by the Council for Mutual Economic Assistance.'[3]

After Stalin's death, Khrushchev tried to raise living standards and encourage a consumer society. One way this would work, he thought, was by expanding trade and importing consumer goods and manufactures from the relatively more developed economies of Eastern Europe. As a result, Soviet trade turnover quadrupled between 1950 and 1965.

Khrushchev's other policy initiatives stressed the development of agriculture rather than heavy industry, domestic consumption rather than military hardware. As the Soviet government curbed military spending for the first time, it stressed peaceful coexistence with the West. Khrushchev promised to outdo the West economically, famously stating, 'We will bury you.'[4]

Russia's new role as a trading power made it seek closer ties not only with CMEA allies but also China and much of the developing world. After 1956, India became heavily involved in barter trade and a major trade partner when it suffered a hard-currency crisis. The same was true for other newly independent post-colonial countries. If they ran up foreign debts too quickly or their currencies fell in value because of a political crisis or because a drop in commodity prices led to a crisis of confidence, then an easy way out was a barter deal with the friendly Russian giant. In marble palaces the world over, president would meet president to barter over how many tons of tea would buy a power station or how much palm oil would net them a submarine. Top leaders began to spend an inordinate amount of their time negotiating the pernickety details of these trade dealings or tackling the trade disputes that inevitably followed. The tricky nature of socialist trade negotiations meant that fundamental issues were often lost in the haze of socialist friendship prices.

In the following passage, Khrushchev recounts his negotiations with Fidel Castro, who wanted to swop sugar cane for an iron and steel works. Khrushchev spoke about the request to his colleagues in the Presidium a few weeks after Castro's return to Cuba:

I said: 'So you want to build an iron works, well we could build one for you, but how much is a ton of cast iron going to cost you? Do you know how much it will cost you? How competitive would that be? You don't have coking coal. Where are you going to get the coal from? From us? You are going to ship that coal 11 thousand kilometers. So how much is a ton of cast iron going to cost you?

'When things are built, you must know what profit you get. So what profit do you get, what goal do you set for yourself? To rely on your own and build a defense industry?'

'No,' he says.

'So then what?'

'We need cans to can food,' admitted Castro.[5]

This meeting resulted in commissioning studies on the merits of expanding Cuba's existing nickel plant or investing in a new steel and iron works. The Soviets built both under long-term payback contracts. It was one of the foreign trade deals that helped doom the Soviet Union. Its trade experts didn't know how much it cost to produce anything, and then it didn't know how to value the end products, so most of the time it ended up losing money on such deals. They never knew if they were making a profit or not. In this case, the only commodity Cuba could offer in exchange was sugar, which the Soviet bloc did not need because it already had plenty of sugar beets. Yet the Soviets kept importing the Cuban sugar they didn't need, and they then started forcing the Finns to buy their surplus sugar, 120,000 tons of it. The 4 million Finns couldn't possibly eat so much sugar—33 tons per person—but they wanted to keep their giant neighbour happy. So the Finns then had to offload this sugar mountain on to the world market, which they finally managed to do.

The quality of the manufactured goods the Soviets exported was so poor that even developing countries were reluctant to accept them in barter deals. Not for nothing did some describe the communist bloc's trade as a vast exchange of rubbish.

Take Ghana, which became independent in 1957. It decided to barter its cocoa crop for Soviet manufactures like airplanes. Soviet purchases of cocoa quickly climbed from 2 per cent of world imports in 1958 to about 8 per cent by 1968. Ghana's leader, Kwame Nkrumah, created a state export monopoly that he imagined would finance the building of a heavy industrial sector under Soviet-style planning. Seven years later, however, the country was deeply in debt and had run through its reserves of hard currency. It had no recourse but to barter away more and more of its crop to the Soviet Union. In the early 1960s, Ghana swopped its cocoa for eight Soviet IL-18s, a 100-seater turbo-prop passenger plane, but found out they were next to useless. A Soviet delegation went to Ghana to check out the complaints and discovered that only four of the eight planes

141

worked regularly, and even these were clocking on average a mere fifteen hours of flying time each month. By comparison, the single Bristol Britannia airplane in the country's fleet was flying 113 hours monthly, as well as costing the government less in repairs. The difference between the perceived value of the Soviet plane and its real value was also revealed. By this measure, one British plane was worth almost twice that of the eight Soviet planes.[6]

Further, the barter transaction left both sides unhappy. Under the bilateral deal, the value of the eight planes was fixed in terms of the tons of cocoa that Ghana agreed to deliver over several years. Ghana realized it had overpaid for the planes because although the quantity was delivered, the quality was poor. On the other hand, if Moscow had waited, it could have bought the cocoa it wanted on the world market anyway but at a lower price. For much of the 1960s, the global market cocoa price was going down, but Moscow was stuck with the fixed price it had arranged.

By the late 1950s, the Soviet Union had exhausted its hard currency reserves because of its need to import Western technology. In the 1960s, the discovery of huge reserves of oil and gas, especially in Western Siberia, handed the Soviet Union a way of paying for more imports of Western machinery and consumer goods. It was a blessing because in this sector quality was relatively unimportant. Soviet oil production skyrocketed from 155 million barrels in 1945 to 1.78 billion barrels by 1965. Even so, importers still complained about the quality of many commodities being offered. In 1959, Western importers of timber, coal and chromium rejected Soviet deliveries of these products, as they found the timber unseasoned and the coal and chromium riddled with impurities. One document found in the Soviet archives names other factories that had failed to provide competitive products. The authors especially single out car parts from the automotive industry, particularly engines and tires produced at the automotive combine in Yaroslavl, as well as tractors from the Kharkiv tractor factory.[7]

The Soviet Union tried to improve the reliability of its products by setting all kinds of quality targets, but this was no substitute for the judgement of the market, governed by competitive pricing. The only way trade officials could evaluate the stuff they imported from the Soviet Union was to resell it to buyers in the international market. As for deals conducted between socialist countries, no one had a way to work out equivalent values even with reference to world market prices.

As the Soviet Union refused to use world prices as an objective standard, Soviet accounting was unable to reveal which transactions were profitable or which made a loss. The Soviets tried to calculate the 'profitability' of trade by assessing the difference between trade prices and domestic prices, and the 'cost per unit of production', defined as the ratio of costs to domestic prices. But since domestic prices were also set in an arbitrary fashion, and were often heavily subsidized because the prices of consumer goods were not allowed to rise, this ratio was meaningless, too. In such a quagmire, no factory or anyone else involved in the exports had any incentive to improve the quality of their products. All they wanted was to fulfil the quotas set by the planners in the industry or region. They did not comply with the requests of foreign trade officials in Moscow because the only orders that counted were those of their immediate superiors.

Even though no convertible currencies were used, trade officials still needed to calculate the transaction in some kind of unit. They created an entity called foreign trade roubles. Between 1950 and 1961, 4 roubles equalled the dollar, but afterwards it was arbitrarily decreed that the rate should be merely 1.1 roubles to the dollar. From there, Soviet planners and trade officials had to convert foreign trade roubles into normal roubles, again using a randomly chosen exchange rate.

Each of the centrally planned economies used at least three different exchange rates for the dollar—a tourist rate, an official rate and a commercial exchange rate. Hungary, for instance, set 11.74 forint to the dollar for tourists, 30 forint at the official rate and 60 forint at the commercial exchange rate. The officials responsible for the state trading monopolies could not officially use the dollar rate, which led to tortuous computations. Trade prices in the Soviet bloc were based on world prices quoted in London or Zurich (in Swiss francs) but were then recalculated according to complex formulas to ensure they diverged from the prices prevailing on capitalist markets.[8]

In other words, officials still had to use world market prices as their guideline but could not adjust their plans to respond to price signals. This meant that commodities like oil were generally under-priced (especially after 1972, when global oil prices quadrupled), while Soviet-made machinery was generally overpriced because it was treated as if it were comparable in quality to Western-made machinery.

Communist trade officials did negotiate transactions based on artificial prices, but they knew that a better buying or selling price was to be found on the world market. The East European satellites enjoyed the best opportunities to trade with the West, and they tailored their negotiating positions to the opportunities offered by the distorted prices. They bought raw materials and energy from the USSR, which they paid for with exports of machinery. This meant that the Soviet Union ended up mostly exporting oil and gas at subsidized prices to buy overpriced manufactures in return. Contrary to its intentions, the Soviet Union therefore ended up subsidizing its satellites.

Every year, the burden became more and more costly as the prices of energy and raw materials rose, especially in the 1970s as inflation took hold. Research in the archives shows that the satellites deliberately 'planned their trade in order to maximize the Soviet trade subsidy, rather than to specialize efficiently or to exploit comparative advantage', as Stone concludes in his study. The Hungarians reckoned the subsidy was worth 1 billion dollars at the time. The Poles figured out the way to make money was to import cheap Russian oil so they could then export their own Polish coal for hard currency.[9]

Satellite countries could also use the Soviet Union as a fallback. 'The Czechs, more than the rest, would habitually try to sell their manufactured goods in the Soviet Union when they found them impossible to sell competitively to capitalist countries', Stone says. They knew that they could sell almost any industrial product they wished to the Soviets, so they withheld the best goods for export to the West.

In the Soviet Union's final two decades, Moscow launched four major programmes with the East Europeans, each involving the participation of thousands of officials and the diversion of billions of roubles in order to make the system work better. Every major initiative failed to incentivize enterprises to make better products or to revise the terms of trade in favour of the Soviet Union. One grand initiative was the Comprehensive Programme for Socialist Economic Integration, agreed in 1971 after prolonged wrangling. Another was the negotiation of the 1978 Long-Term Target Programmes designed to expand trade, and a final effort was the Comprehensive Programme for Scientific and Technical Progress, intended to boost innovation and improve the quality of products.

Even as the Soviet Union tried to modernize, the East Europeans fought to retain outmoded products and to resist upgrading technology. That's because resistance to change was built into the system by the nature of the incentives. At one point, when the Soviets complained about the quality of Czech shoe exports, the Czechs offered to invest in making better shoes—provided that the quotas were set in terms of value rather than pairs of shoes. Higher-quality shoes would earn a higher price, but the amounts would fall. The Soviets rejected the offer because their trade plans were fixed in terms of quantity rather than quality. In the Soviet system, everything could only be measured by numbers or by weight.

The Soviet bloc countries could agree among themselves that there were shortages of certain products and that it would be desirable to expand their production, but when it was time to draw up a plan, each country lobbied to produce the overpriced items. Then when it was time to implement the plan, each conveniently neglected to produce the subsidized, loss-making goods.

At one stage amid all this protracted wrangling, the Poles presented a paper proposing to switch to a system of currency-based trading. The proposal stipulated that the fundamental obstacle to socialist integration was that all the member countries had incompatible price systems. Besides these individual price systems, the CMEA had an independent system of calculating foreign trade prices, and the rest of the world used yet another system that only influenced the first two indirectly. It was impossible to compare the prices of individual goods in different countries, because the currencies of the member countries were not convertible in any meaningful sense. Each country issued a variety of exchange rates to calculate the economic effects of trade and insulated its enterprises from the effects of foreign trade prices by putting them on the state budget or by employing an array of taxes and subsidies. It also added that the system meant that 'enterprises are not interested in expanding the turnover of foreign trade, since they perceive no economic benefit in doing so'.[10]

The report proposed that the CMEA countries establish a system of 'real exchange rates' with the new international currency managed by establishing an International Bank for Economic Cooperation. This new currency would be established to settle accounts in international trade, and each country would contribute to its reserves by providing stocks of 'first-priority goods' or basic raw materials.

The Poles also recommended that the CMEA countries unify the principles they used to set domestic prices and revise their price structures to make them gradually converge. An index of domestic prices would be used to set exchange rates. They also proposed a gradual transition to convertible currencies.

Naturally, all these ideas were rejected. The Bulgarians said: 'We are opposed to liberalization carried out on the model of the capitalist states.' The East Germans said the changes were unnecessary because the planned economy focused resources on the most important objectives. The Soviet Union under Leonid Brezhnev and the reformist premier Alexei Kosygin listened sympathetically but instead opted for more planning and improved financial accounting. Not until Gorbachev came to power in the 1980s would the Soviets begin to move in this direction. His government tried to reform prices, to allow enterprises to trade directly with each other and to calculate trade in hard currency. But by this point it was too late. Within a few years, the Soviet Union had been dissolved—and all the world's goods would be calculated in dollars.[11]

After Khrushchev was replaced, state subsidies for consumer goods grew and grew until they became another hidden hole in the budget. The cost of stabilizing retail prices went from 4 per cent of its 1965 budget to 20 per cent of the budget by the 1980s, equal to 12 per cent of the Soviet Union's GDP.[12]

A financial system that had failed so abysmally for the Soviet Union's domestic economy proved just as impossible when transferred to the world stage. All that international trade did was to put the USSR in a bigger economic hole.

13

FAKE STATISTICS AND SOVIET
DEFENCE SPENDING

In the Cold War, Western leaders needed their spy chiefs to tell them the answers to two pressing questions: how big was the Soviet economy? And how powerful was its military? In the 1970s, Western intelligence agencies had several pieces of good fortune. Several Soviet émigrés told them the real answers, and their information was then confirmed by a top-ranking defector from the KGB. Yet Western leaders and their spy chiefs could not believe what they were hearing. It ran counter to their notion of the Soviet Union as a vast, successful economic power that had no trouble throwing its military might around the world.

The CIA did concede that the prodigious growth rates the Soviet Union enjoyed during the 1950s had slowed down in the late 1960s. It detected mounting evidence of economic difficulties in the 1970s, positing that the Soviet growth rate had halved and the volume of investment dropped off sharply. As we now know, there never was a period of high growth in the 1950s. In the winter of 1946–7, the USSR experienced a severe famine during which up to 2 million died in Ukraine and many more may have died in other parts of the country.[1] When Stalin died in 1953, things were so bad that Beria was desperate to change everything he could. The Soviet Union's massive military machine was an immense burden, but the archives show no one in charge could find out what it cost—it was simply unknowable given the nature of the economy.

Western leaders therefore had to decide on their own defence budgets and formulate strategic policies based on what MI6 or the CIA told them. Winston Churchill famously described Russia as a 'riddle wrapped in a mystery inside an enigma'. Depending on what they wanted to believe about the Soviet Union, they could choose détente, confrontation or war. Whenever Western leaders went to war, as they did with China, Korea and Vietnam, or tried to match Moscow's build-up of missiles and nuclear warheads in the early 1980s, they had to face down vociferous public opposition. There were mass demonstrations and peace marches led by organizations such as the Campaign for Nuclear Disarmament (CND), which urged unilateral disarmament. All these peace movements shared the same message: America was a belligerent global hegemon destabilizing world peace through its aggressive and massive military spending.

Moscow not only sponsored these peace movements but from the 1960s onwards Soviet leaders made life difficult for the West by repeatedly proposing balanced cutbacks in military spending. They reported cuts in their own military spending to make such proposals seem more convincing. Even neutral countries often assumed that the two superpowers were as bad as each other and that both devoted roughly the same share of their GDP to the military.

A few weeks after the launch of Sputnik in 1957, the RAND Corporation released a report of an important presidential commission. The report, 'Deterrence and Survival in the Nuclear Age', warned of a dangerous 'missile gap'. It concluded that the Soviet Union was spending more on its military than the United States, along with the expectation, covered earlier, that the Soviet economy would grow faster and overtake the United States by 1993. It alleged that their machine tool production was already twice the size of the United States'. It also said that the United States was clearly inferior to the Soviet Union in strategic missile development and that the Soviets would have more than 200 intercontinental ballistic missiles (ICBMs) by 1961, whereas the Americans might not have any. Its chief author, H. Rowan Gaither, was a founder of the RAND Corporation and drew heavily on the work of its key experts, Abram Bergson, Alexander Gerschenkron, Norman Kaplan and graduate students drawn from the Russian Research Center at Harvard.[2]

The report's predictions were impossible to challenge because it remained secret until 1973. Since the United States had no human intelligence sources in the USSR, it relied heavily on the statistical evidence deduced by Bergson. The report chimed in nicely with the beliefs of the experts at RAND and among economists who held that a Soviet command economy worked better because it directed a highly centralized management system.

Parts of the report were leaked, however, and the ensuing outrage proved extremely influential. Eisenhower's CIA director, Allen Dulles, claimed in a 1958 speech that the United States was confronted with 'the most serious challenge' it had ever faced in peacetime. 'If the Soviet industrial growth rate persists at 8 or 9 percent per annum over the next decade the gap between our two economies by 1970 will be dangerously narrowed unless our own industrial growth rate is substantially increased from the present pace.' In Moscow, Khrushchev repeatedly predicted that by around 1970 the USSR would overtake the United States in per capita production, and in 1961 the goal of surpassing America by the end of the decade was even included in the official Party programme.[3]

However, President Eisenhower found the report to be excessively pessimistic, and he rejected the commission's findings. American U-2 spy plane overflights had failed to confirm the existence of an expedited Russian programme in missile development or indeed any missile gap. No evidence emerged to confirm the supposed existence of hundreds or thousands of missiles hidden away in the tundra. Yet during the 1960 presidential campaign, Senator John F. Kennedy used the missile gap to attack the Eisenhower administration and win the election. In 1963, the RAND researchers went on to issue claims that Russia was engaged in deliberate, systematic and sustained strategic deception.[4]

Yet once established, the belief in this missile gap never disappeared. The Gaither Report confirmed the worst fears about the Soviets' supposed economic and technological power. The

Soviets were of course keen to show off their military might every year at the annual military parade celebrating the anniversary of the October Revolution, but it was the West that embraced the lie that all these weapons were the fruit of a dynamic economy. This false belief led to the conclusion that the Soviet Union could not be defeated. In 1967, NATO adopted the so-called Harmel Report, which called for détente and started the search for ways to co-exist with Soviet power. The USSR was henceforth to be regarded as a potential partner in a new European order.[5]

Even in the Reagan administration, most experts and advisors around Secretary of State George Shultz doubted it was possible to stop the Soviet Union. In August 1982, Shultz hosted a seminar of twenty senior academics and high-ranking members of the administration to discuss the future of relations with Moscow. According to National Security Advisor Robert McFarlane, the general consensus was that the Kremlin had enough resources to go on forever. When Henry Rowen, chairman of the National Intelligence Council, addressed the meeting and said, 'Gentlemen, it is not necessary that Communism continue forever', the response was general laughter. However, the Reagan administration eventually came up with a plan to outspend the Soviet Union and drive it into bankruptcy by announcing the ambitious Star Wars missile defence programme. By developing the means to shoot down every missile, the United States would end the 'missile gap' and destroy the 3 to 1 advantage in missiles that the Soviet Union possessed.[6]

Conspiracy theories flourished during the Cold War. It is possible that both the United States and the USSR deliberately exaggerated each other's military capability and their respective malicious intent in order to justify massive investment in R&D and the production and acquisition of weapons. Some still believe estimates of Soviet military spending were manipulated in order both to benefit the 'military–industrial complex' and to undermine détente. Others saw the Soviets skilfully weaving a web of deceit, exaggerating their military power and technology. Perhaps they did this because they also counted on the Americans responding by boosting their defence spending, which in turn could be used to justify even greater outlays by the Soviet defence industry.

The Soviet Union released almost no information about its military or defence budget. In the Stalin era, the only figure given was in 1932, when the USSR reported to the League of Nations that defence spending was 130 million roubles, or less than 4 per cent of the total state budget. The true figure was 400 million, nearly 11 per cent of the budget. During the Cold War, Moscow released a single line in the state budget, and for long periods this remained frozen. No one knew what it included or excluded, or how the rouble figure could be adjusted to dollars in order to make comparisons with the defence spending of America and its NATO allies.[7]

Western leaders desperately needed to know how big the Soviet military was and whether it was growing or shrinking. NATO generals wanted to determine the quantities and dispositions of tanks and bombers, artillery pieces and battleships, but they also needed to assess the research and development costs for new weapons, manpower costs and the burden of paying for veterans' pensions. Since the two sides were seemingly committed to an escalating arms race and a battle for global influence, both generals and politicians needed to understand the overall size of the economy and the share taken by all matters related to defence.

In this intelligence war, accountancy mattered more than eyes on the ground. None of the secret codes, exploding fountain pens, the fast cars or the seduction of glamorous double agents could tell a prime minister or a president what they needed to know. That the Soviets cooked the books was certain, but there was no top-secret document to purloin. Instead, nine-to-five analysts and economists plucked out some percentage or statistic or adjusted their slide rules to make up graph tables and charts. They created economic models and argued with each other in obscure journals and conferences and wrote intelligence reports based on extrapolated data. In the end, they were all hopelessly wrong, although they were wrong in different ways.

One school of thought held that the official Soviet budget figures did mean something although not the whole truth. Others thought that with a bit of imagination a balance sheet for the Soviet military–industrial complex could be created by studying Soviet prices. Or you could work backwards by looking at what the same items would cost if they were made in America.

For a quarter of a century, the Soviet Union maintained that the defence budget was under 6 per cent of the state budget and less than 3 per cent of the Soviet economy. In 1980, this was put at 17.1 billion roubles, equal to what the Soviet population spent on sugar and sweets in government stores. That same year, the United States spent $168 billion on its military or 6 per cent of its GDP. Under Bergson's influence, the CIA largely accepted the Soviet budgetary figures and regularly reported that Soviet defence spending was 6 per cent of the state budget. Conventional wisdom held that the defence burden was low and remained so since its economy was expanding rapidly.[8]

This was especially believed outside the United States. The Stockholm-based International Peace Research Institute generally accepted Soviet figures and therefore always provided the lowest Western estimate. The London-based Institute of Strategic Studies rejected the official budget figure but also dismissed any high estimates of Soviet spending. When the validity of the CIA's work came into question in the late 1960s, the US military's Defense Intelligence Agency (DIA) began to do its own research and came up with the highest figures.[9]

The CIA, however, produced the estimates most widely used by NATO members, partly because it had the largest team working on Soviet military expenditures and partly because it worked closely with all the top academic authorities in the field. By 1955, it had a team of fifty-five full-time staff devoted to studying Soviet defence spending plus even larger resources in the RAND Corporation. The first step was to produce an inventory of the Soviet military. In the early years of the Cold War, this involved gathering information by parachuting in agents or flying weather balloons, or taking photographs with the high-flying U2 reconnaissance aircraft. As technology evolved, the United States replaced the reconnaissance planes with satellite surveillance. When the CIA had built up these detailed estimates of Moscow's inventory of military hardware, it then tried to put a value on each unit.

By the 1980s, they had collected rouble procurement prices for 100 different items that then had to be converted back to constant 1970 rouble prices. CIA analysts also constructed a model of each branch of the Soviet economy and then tried to assess the quantity and value of each item produced. To calculate the cost of producing a Soviet fighter plane, the CIA worked out the value of the labour and the cost of the aluminium and other inputs. Even calculating the rouble price was by no means easy. From time to time, rouble prices were adjusted, making it difficult to make comparisons over time. Then one had to take account of various factors by making assumptions about labour productivity, logistics, subsidies and most of all about inflation. Officially, the Soviet Union had neither inflation nor unemployment, and domestic prices and wages rarely changed.

Estimates of the rouble costs of the Soviet military–industrial complex were useful, but American leaders needed to be able to compare US and Soviet defence spending in dollar terms. Since the rouble was not convertible, they estimated the conversion rate based on what each currency could buy—how many British thermal units of coal, for example. This process was trickier than it sounds. The known costs to produce an American tank did not take into account the respective quality of that tank and one made in the Soviet Union. Nor could labour costs be compared. Further, there was no standard way of comparing a nation's total outlay on defence. Could Soviet wages and pensions be compared to those in the United States? Even mundane items like a ton of potatoes are hard to compare: there are hundreds of different kinds of potatoes for sale on the market on any given day, each with a different price. A complex piece of technology like a jet fighter posed exponentially greater challenges.

Finally, the CIA had to assess the relative burden that defence spending placed on the overall economy of the USSR, and this meant assessing the relative size of the two economies. Clearly, during the Second World War, both countries spent massively on defence and in the 1950s scaled down defence spending. US spending then rose to 10 per cent of GDP during the Vietnam War and in the 1970s declined to around 6 per cent. It was hard to make a comparable estimate of the size of the Soviet economy, despite CIA claims that its economy was at least half the size of the US economy.

In the early years of Soviet studies, Bergson had disputed Jasny's claim that from the 1930s onwards, the Soviet Union had been spending a disproportionate amount on the military at the expense of domestic consumption. Yet in the early 1960s, William T. Lee, an analyst at the CIA, had devised a different estimating system that made use of Soviet statistics and showed an even higher proportion of military spending. In 1964, Lee left the CIA over disagreements about his method. Disputing the CIA estimates, he later joined the DIA.[10]

Until the mid-1970s, the CIA reported that Soviet defence spending was increasing by 4 or 5 per cent a year, but this did not impose a great strain because it also believed that its economy was growing at the same rate. It estimated the 1965 per capita GDP of the USSR at 37 per cent of US GDP. Then in 1970 it put it at 45 per cent, in 1975 at 49 per cent and in 1980 at 46 per cent. It also estimated 1980 per capita Soviet GDP at $6,500 a year compared to $14,000 a year for the United States.

Yet there was never a period in Soviet history when the Party did not devote as much resources as it could to the military. From 1917 onwards, it was always a military dictatorship. Soviet military spending was always huge and rose before, during and after détente. In the 26 March 1992 issue of *Izvestia*, Russian writer Anatoly Rakitov complained:

> Over the last six decades, 80 to 90 percent of our national resources—raw material, technical, financial, and intellectual—have been used to create the military–industrial complex. Essentially, the military–industrial complex has absorbed everything that is good and dynamic that Russia has to offer, including its basic economic capacity and its best technology, materials, and specialists. Consequently, the military–industrial complex is virtually synonymous with our economy.

In the early 1990s, Gorbachev recognized that the Soviet economy was the most military-dominated in the world. The Soviet defence industry employed about 14.4 million soldiers and civilians in hundreds of plants and dozens of closed towns and protected areas. Every year, they produced about 1,700 tanks, 5,700 armoured personnel carriers and 1,750 field guns. The Soviets produced 2.3 times as many tanks as the United States, 8.7 times as many APCs, 11.5 times as many field guns, three times as many nuclear submarines, 1.5 times as many destroyers, fifteen times as many ICBMs, six times as many medium-range missiles. The military–industrial complex roughly accounted for about 80 per cent of the Soviet Union's total industrial output. The vast industrial investment and spending that the RAND Corporation experts and the CIA analysts thought would propel the USSR past the United States was largely military spending.[11]

During the Cold War, the Americans had remarkably few human intelligence sources inside the Soviet Union to help them with their estimates. One lucky break came when Nikolai F. Artamonov, the youngest destroyer captain in the Soviet Navy, defected with his Polish lover, Ewa Gora, and escaped to Sweden by commandeering a naval launch. Artamonov was given a new name, Nicholas Shadrin, and brought to the United States, where he gained a PhD in engineering. He also worked for the Office of Naval Intelligence and brought with him, or later obtained (no one is sure), a Soviet book that revealed the real rouble costs of building Soviet destroyers. Shadrin translated this for the DIA. The costs were quite different from those calculated by the CIA. It suggested too that the Soviet defence industries were far less efficient than had been imagined. In 1975, Shadrin was persuaded to work as a double agent, and on a mission in Vienna he was kidnapped and died after being drugged and stuffed into the car of his KGB captors.

That same year, another Soviet émigré arrived, this time an economist who claimed to have reviewed the actual defence budget figures when he visited the Soviet Central Statistics Administration. His specific job was to integrate the secret Soviet military budget with the rest of the five-year plan. He told disbelieving Americans that defence expenditures were far higher than in official accounts. However, the CIA was so reluctant to accept this that he was made to take lie detector tests. When he failed them, the director of the DIA, Lieutenant General Daniel O. Graham (who under President Reagan would become one of the men behind the Star Wars programme), decided the CIA had botched the tests by making the man too nervous. Graham interviewed the man himself and decided he was telling the truth. He persuaded the CIA to polygraph him again, this time using questions he had prepared, and he passed.

The following year, in 1976, the CIA's estimates of military spending doubled to 11 or 12 per cent from 5 to 6 per cent of Soviet GNP. Next, the CIA got hold of a secret recording in which Soviet leader Leonid Brezhnev boasted that military spending was 15 per cent of Soviet GDP. The CIA reluctantly increased its estimate to 14 per cent, although the DIA argued that this was still far too low. They thought the figure was closer to 30 per cent.

The DIA's projections were supported by the work of a prominent Soviet economist, Igor Yakovlevich Birman, who arrived in the United States in 1974. During détente, Soviet Jews were allowed to apply for permission to leave the Soviet Union, although it was a difficult and unpleasant process. Birman was lucky—it took him just three months to get out. A clever, humorous and often abrasive man who favoured a large beard, he had steadily risen up the ladder. After graduating from the Moscow Statistical Institute in 1949, he received a doctorate in economics in 1960 and then worked in various factories before becoming an economist in the construction and lumber industries. He became a member of the Soviet Academy of Sciences' council on mathematical economics, and in the late 1960s he joined the Commission on Economic Reform set up by Soviet Premier Alexei Kosygin.[12]

Since Stalin's death, the Soviet state had invested huge amounts in Soviet agriculture, especially through projects like Khrushchev's virgin lands scheme. These had been wasted as surely as the massive investments in industry. Labour productivity was deteriorating badly, partly due to the lack of incentives and poor technology. For example, the Soviet Union produced a pitiful 27.5 tons of paper and cardboard from 1,000 cubic meters of timber while Finland got 155 tons and Sweden 144, more than five times as much. The Kosygin reforms were launched in 1965 after Khrushchev was ousted. In the absence of market forces and the feedback from consumers to help guide investment, the Soviets tried other means such as quality targets. Instead of planning quotas based on crude physical quantities, the planners created around 100 quality targets that factories had to meet, but this produced poor results thanks to the general corruption in reporting results, known as *tufta*.[13]

Under Kosygin, the Soviets also placed their hopes on a system that replicated the working of the market using shadow prices to create a replica market. This system was pioneered by Leonid Vitaliyevich Kantorovich, a Russian mathematician who in 1939 had been given the task of optimizing production in the plywood industry. His 'optimization' method was used to help with military planning during the Second World War. Later this so-called linear programming method was used in the West to calculate the optimum routes for airlines and to schedule crews. Birman was one of the leading advocates of optimization and wrote the most popular book on the subject. By 1959, he was head of linear programming at the research institute on the economics of construction materials and then ran the department on long-range optimal planning for the lumber industry in Moscow.[14]

Optimization involved creating mathematical models for supply and demand. By using computer software, they hoped to coordinate planning and calculate the optimum price for everything. The Soviets hoped that one day every factory would be linked by computers and the economy could be set to run automatically according to the plan. The computers would calculate the optimum price for everything, and the factories would respond.

Birman's team created a model for the timber industry, fed the data into the computer and a month later got the results. It said that they needed to cut all the forests near Moscow, ship the timber thousands of kilometres east to have it processed and then ship it back to be sold and consumed. Unfortunately, as Birman discovered, any such system was doomed to fail for the simple reason that in order for the programs to work, they needed to be fed reliable data. If the data was faulty, then all the calculations would be wrong. It was a case of rubbish in, rubbish out. As the statistics reported to the centre were always falsified, the planning system could never work, irrespective of whether it was done by humans or computers.[15]

In 1968, Birman, disappointed and disillusioned, decided he should explain why the system would never work to a closed meeting of senior officials at Gosplan, the state planning agency. For this, he was berated for making 'anti-Party statements'. He was advised that if he apologized, then the matter would be forgotten, but he refused because he felt he had done nothing wrong. In 1970, he was given an official reprimand and expelled from the Communist Party. He realized there was little point in trying to continue his career. By the time Birman left the Soviet Union, Kosygin had lost influence and the country more or less abandoned any serious effort at reforms.

After Birman arrived in America, he was shocked to find that he had gone from being a dissident in the USSR to being a dissident in the United States. When he met Samuelson, Galbraith, Bergson and various Soviet experts, he was taken aback by the degree of their naivety and how little they understood. He imagined himself a real live Roman in toga and sandals who suddenly appeared in front of Latin scholars. 'He does not know what has been written by these scholars, and written wrongly, but soon finds out that the concepts and conclusions, reached with great effort, were quite misguided and sometimes utterly wrong', he wrote.[16]

The ignorance worked both ways. Friends back in Russia couldn't believe the sheer abundance and choice of consumer goods that Birman and his family encountered in just the local supermarket. Birman managed to find a new product on every visit. Relatives were particularly astonished that he could buy cottage cheese mixed with pineapple chunks.[17]

'Throughout the Soviet period statistics were deliberately distorted both at the top and lower levels', Birman told the disbelieving Americans. Birman soon came to realize that the CIA experts did not grasp that all the investment that the Soviet government injected into the economy as it tried to boost the supply of food and consumer goods was wasted. Although it came to believe that the Soviet economy was slowing in the 1970s, it still clung to the belief that the 1950s and '60s had been decades of high growth and prosperity. Yet Birman was convinced that this was never the case, and that by the start of the 1970s the Soviet economy was contracting.[18]

The true situation was hidden by statistics, which obscured the subsidies for consumer goods and disguised pent-up inflation. Birman pointed out that the official state budget of the Soviet Union had showed a surplus every year since 1944. This was simply not believable. Birman also argued that the Russian government was running a dangerous budget deficit. Although that fact was camouflaged in its official data, the deficits were having a destructive effect on the value of the population's money holdings. As Birman knew from his own experience, there was no point in working hard if there was no way of spending the money.[19]

One of the essential points that Birman grasped, and Bergson did not, is that money still played an important role in the Soviet economy. Very little hard data was made available on the flow of money, but Birman thought the American academics could learn a lot by doing a few calculations. Ever since the early 1930s, when Stalin decided to retain the use of the rouble, two kinds of money had been used. In the state planning system, transactions were recorded in money, but no money was actually used. All Soviet enterprises and institutions held an account at an allocated branch of the government banking system. The accounts automatically debited and credited as transactions were made. The money flowed passively according to the requirements of the plan. It therefore followed a transaction but did not provide its normal role of providing an incentive for a supplier to deliver goods or services. It was the plan that allocated money so that enterprise and institution could not spend the money credited to its account. It was not therefore money in any normal sense.

A second kind of money in circulation was the printed paper roubles used to pay wages, to buy agricultural goods, pay taxes and conduct all kinds of small cash purchases of consumer goods. In theory, a planned economy allowed planners to control wage payments and match them to the supply of retail goods. After the 1950s, most people received around 800 roubles per month in wages, but the state rarely raised the prices of any goods. When in June 1962, the state raised food prices, especially for butter and meat, by 25–30 per cent, there were strikes and riots. In Novocherkassk, the military opened fire on rioters, killing twenty-two people. The 1970 protests against price hikes in Gdansk, Poland, were suppressed with the same brutality and left hundreds dead. After Khrushchev was replaced, the Soviet Union began to steadily increase wages but not prices, so the cost of stabilizing retail prices went from 4 per cent of the 1965 budget to 20 per cent of the budget by the 1980s, equal to 12 per cent of the Soviet Union's GDP.[20]

Birman explained that the Soviet figures had been doctored to hide an increase in cash in circulation. Although the Soviet Union released almost no monetary data, it did publish data of savings and deposits in a section headed 'Growth in the Standard of Living of the Population'. Birman perused the savings deposits, cash savings, bonds and deposits in Gosbank (the Soviet central bank) and called this 'internal debt'. In 1960, this ratio was 19 per cent, growing by 1970 to 43 per cent and to 66 per cent of the economy by 1976. His conservative estimate was that at the end of 1975, households held 50 billion roubles in cash. Soviet households had no incentive to accumulate savings, deposits or cash because they did not need insurance against illness or unemployment. Nor could they invest this money, so why were they saving so much?[21]

Birman concluded that consumers could not find any way to spend their money. In other words, the escalation in savings showed the lack of increase in consumer goods. The government tried all kinds of methods to soak up this money, such as by organizing patriotic savings campaigns and by forced bond sales, but the cash savings kept on piling up. In short, the system did not produce enough goods and outlawed most kinds of services. The unsatisfied demand for these goods and services could better be described as repressed inflation. Inflation was supposed to be a Western malaise, a monetary phenomenon that could not exist in a socialist economy where money played no role. In simple terms, people were being paid with money that could not buy anything, which meant it was practically worthless. Therefore, they had no incentive to work harder.

Birman further argued that the system would never create more consumer goods and services because so much was spent on the military. Hence at some stage painful political decisions had to be made. In lieu of a sharp increase in the price of consumer goods to match supply and demand, the government would have to confiscate or 'freeze' a substantial part of the savings of the population. This was usually carried out in the guise of a currency reform under which each citizen was permitted to exchange only a strictly limited amount of old currency for new tender. Plus, Birman said, a simultaneous economic reform would involve a radical adjustment of prices and wages. 'This will inevitably lead to discontent among the population which cannot even be compared with the dissatisfaction of a small group of [dissident] Moscow intellectuals', Birman said. And he pointed out that there could still be a revolution in the USSR, even without a revolutionary party. The longer the day of reckoning was put off, the more drastic and unpopular the reform would be. Lastly, he argued that any reform would require a major rebalancing of the economy, including drastic cutbacks to military spending. Birman concluded that the best strategy for the United States would be to ramp up the arms race and bankrupt the Soviet Union into submission.[22]

Birman's thinking was completely unacceptable to the Bergson school, which made great efforts to prevent his opinions from being heard either in conferences or specialist journals. Their first meetings were amicable, but when the Bergson school realized that Birman found their notions quite risible, relations became chilly and then downright bitter. Birman found he could only publish books in Britain because no American publisher dared touch them. Unable to get published and excluded from any academic post or think tank, he set up a journal called *Russia*.[23]

After Reagan won a landslide victory over Jimmy Carter in 1980, Birman began to find a more receptive audience for his views. Reagan was not interested in détente or in tolerating Soviet gains in the Third World. In February 1981, he brought in a new director of the CIA, William Casey, who called for fresh intelligence estimates of the Soviet Union and a different strategy that targeted its weaknesses. Neither President Reagan nor Casey believed the previous CIA reports on Soviet GDP or its assertion that the Soviet Union was spending 12 or even 14 per cent on the military. Instead of looking at Soviet statistics, Reagan and Casey asked what the USSR was really like and what GDP level was consistent with the observations of those who had lived there. Casey hired Herb Meyer, who had written on the problems of the Soviet economy, as a special assistant. Meyer sent memos saying that the USSR was 'terribly vulnerable economically … It should be a matter of high national policy to play to these vulnerabilities.' As Reagan put it in his autobiography, the Soviet economy was in such bad shape 'that if the Western countries got together and cut off credits to it, we could bring it to its knees'. Casey would eventually conclude that the Soviet economy was one-sixth the size of the US economy rather than one half. He suspected that actual Soviet military spending in 1980 was about 33 per cent of its economy rather than 12 per cent. However, many people around the world were unconvinced, and not just in the CIA. Reagan was popularly demonized as a crazy cowboy trying to destabilize the world.[24]

Finally finding a receptive audience for his views, Birman began to gain access to the mainstream media. On 27 October 1980, his first piece in the *Washington Post* argued that the CIA's current picture of the Soviet economy was far too optimistic. The Soviet economy was in a state of 'crisis', Birman declared, and he claimed Russian living standards were 'a fourth or even a fifth the American level'. He wrote that Soviet GNP was nowhere near 55–60 per cent of US GNP, as the CIA claimed, but more like one-fifth of the US economy. To keep up with US military expenditure, the Soviets had to invest such a large percentage of their GNP that if such spending were sustained, the Soviet economy would collapse:

> For the Western observer ... it is almost impossible to imagine what ... the Soviet rulers set aside for war preparations. Precisely this enabled them to have tremendous military strength with a weak economy. This misunderstanding, the root of which is transferring Western impressions to Soviet reality, is the basis of [overestimating] ... CIA economists, believing in a modest share of military expenditures, unavoidably had to believe also in the very big overall size of the Soviet economy.[25]

After the article appeared, he was invited by Defense Department futurist Andrew W. Marshall to give briefings at the Pentagon, and for the next ten years he was awarded annual research grants as an outside contractor. Marshall, who later went by the moniker Yagoda, ran a think tank in the Pentagon called the Office of Net Assessment, which specialized in crafting innovative and contrarian strategies.

In addition, Birman horrified the Bergson/CIA camp by touting the importance of intuitive thinking. In one conference, he explained why reasoning, simple logic and 'anecdotal economics' often make the most sense:

Finally, let me submit another very simple consideration. American agriculture produces more than does the Soviet. Though our population is smaller, we eat much better and export food, whereas the USSR imports it. Nevertheless, let's assume the two agricultures' sizes are equal. American agriculture is something like 3 percent of GNP. In regard to Soviet agriculture, it is not so clear; estimates vary. According to the CIA, in 1976, Soviet agriculture produced 16.7 percent of GNP. From this you may easily conclude that the total Soviet GNP was at most five and half times less than [that is, about 18 per cent of] the American.

Americans, he said, spent about 17 per cent of their income on food, while residents of the Soviet Union spent about half. In 1985, Birman told an international conference:

If the Soviet Union continues to raise production of goods and services as it has done over the past 23 years, it will catch up with the United States' 1976 level in 62 years in fruit, 74 years in meat, 142 years in housing, 176 years in automobiles, 188 years in telephones and 298 years in roads.[26]

Yet the CIA's belief in the strength and durability of the Soviet economy remained unshakeable. In the 1980s, the CIA lowered its estimates but insisted that the Soviet economy was growing at 2 per cent a year and per capita consumption was about one-third of the US level. In 1987, a CIA memorandum stated that the Soviet economy was 'vested with great crude strength on a strong resource base and remains a viable system capable of producing large quantities of goods and services annually, especially for industrial and military use'. It also noted: 'The Soviet economy has made solid gains since 1960 ... but its growth has slowed, especially in the last decade.' However, it still predicted annual growth of 2–3 per cent in the coming three years.[27]

Birman tried without success to influence the CIA. In 1984, he wrote to Robert Gates, then a senior CIA analyst and later the CIA's director, asking for a meeting to discuss the Soviet economy, but this was declined. He was instead interviewed by junior CIA officials.

'I was alone in the world, saying the huge CIA is wrong', Birman told journalist Ronald Kessler in an interview for his 1992 book *Inside the CIA*. 'The wonderful American press has criticized the CIA for spy operations, but never for their analysis. I did. I knew I was alone, and if I say the truth, nobody would believe me.'[28]

In the early 1980s, British intelligence scored an impressive coup when it recruited the KGB bureau chief in London, Oleg Gordievsky. After he returned to Moscow, he came under suspicion and had to be smuggled out of the USSR. Back in London, he was thoroughly debriefed but, as he related many years later in *The Commanding Heights*, a PBS documentary, his interrogators struggled to believe what he told them about the state of the economy: 'When I was a British agent inside the KGB, the British intelligence service didn't have time to ask me about the economy, because they were interested about strategic problems. The arms-control questions were so overwhelming, the West neglected the important foundation of the argument: the economy.'[29]

He told his handlers that the Soviet Union devoted more than a third of its struggling economy to the military:

> And the analyst said, no, I can't put such a huge figure down because nobody would believe it. Later, economists realized that the Soviet Union had been spending at least 50 percent on the military ... The Communist administration reported that the economy was growing. It was not the case. The economy started to go down all the time, and the deficit was covered only with the help of the oil prices. And the extra money made it possible to claim that they were successful. And they were deceiving the world.

Gordievsky's information was shared with President Reagan. By 1986, Reagan was also being told by Henry Rowen, chairman of the National Intelligence Council, and Charles Wolf Jr, dean of the RAND School of Graduate Studies, that the Soviet economy was in worse shape than the CIA was saying. 'Your advisers have seriously underestimated the difficulties of the Soviet economy', Rowen told Reagan. 'We are in a much stronger bargaining position.'

By this time, Gorbachev had been in power for a year and was pushing forward a package of reforms called *perestroika*. This caused the CIA's belief in the Soviet Union's strength to grow rather than diminish. So in 1985 Birman published another article in which he sought to convince readers that the Soviet Union was locked in a deep spiral from which there was no escape. He predicted the USSR was destined to collapse because Gorbachev's reforms could never succeed. Further, he said that the new leadership would have no choice but to undertake a drastic cut in military expenditure and radical reforms of industry and agriculture. In 1988, Birman wrote another article in which he again predicted the 'collapse of the Soviet economy' and the regime. By collapse, he meant 'a situation of negative growth rates, with the economic situation worsening rapidly'. In his view, there 'is no real possibility for rapid improvements in the situation, even if Gorbachev decides on real radical reforms, i.e. the introduction of private property'.

By that point, the Soviet Union was in the grip of Gorbachev's *glasnost*. The new openness meant that it divulged the existence of large and rising budget deficits, corroborating what Birman and others had been saying. In 1989, it was suddenly announced that the official Soviet defence budget was three times higher than any before and even so this did not cover all R&D and procurement. By 1991, it was revised upwards again from 75 billion roubles to 140–50 billion roubles. In a fascinating chapter of *Soviet Defense Spending: A History of CIA Estimates 1950–1990*, authors Noel E. Firth and James H. Noren pose the question: did the Soviets know what they spent on defence? 'There is a good reason to believe that the Soviets did not know and could not know the real cost of Soviet Military Programs', conclude the two CIA economists.

They note that in 1990 Gorbachev said that defence spending reached 19 per cent of state expenditure in the 1981–5 plan at 94 billion roubles per year. Yegor Ligachev, a protégé and later a rival to Gorbachev, said the same year that defence accounted for about 18–20 per cent of national income. In 1991, Soviet Foreign Minister Eduard Shevardnadze wrote that Soviet military spending as a percentage of GDP was two and half times more than the military's share of the US economy. Around the same time, several other senior Soviet officials such as Yuri Ryzhov thought the defence burden was not 70 odd billion but more like 200 billion. General V.

N. Lobov, chief of the general staff, said in 1990 that it was a third of GNP. Even Politburo members had to rely on incomplete and unverified evidence. None of these figures could adequately separate defence from civilian spending. They could not count the elusive subsidies granted to suppliers, the costs of services provided free or at big discounts to the military by local governments or all kinds of off-budget financing. 'It is highly uncertain that defence spending series in nominal prices can be compiled from Soviet sources', the authors conclude.[30]

Even after the fall of the Soviet Union, no one can say for sure who in the Kremlin knew the true figure. Possibly four men did: the Party's general secretary, prime minister, defence minister and chief of the general staff. According to Gorbachev, it was: 'Two or three.'[31] Perhaps the truth is that no Soviet leader knew the answer because it was unknowable, just as Mises predicted back in 1920. Marx and Lenin had thought that running an economy was a simple matter of book-keeping that anyone could be trained to do. Yet ultimately, it was the impossibility of book-keeping that was to doom the Soviet Union. It was to doom the other communist countries too, including the other giant, China. As Western intellectuals became disenchanted with Russian communism, many transferred their hopes to China despite this fact, or perhaps because there were even fewer statistics to consider. Or perhaps because Chinese peasant culture was more open to communism. Yet the same problems that bedevilled the Bolsheviks soon produced the same results. It turned out that culture or history was not as important as some believed.

14

HOW AMERICAN EXPERTS MISUNDERSTOOD
MAO'S CHINA

The previous chapters look at the consequences of the failure to understand the Soviet Union. After 1945, it turned out that it was just as important for the United States to understand China as it was the Soviet Union. The United States became involved in immensely costly wars with the Chinese communists first on the mainland, then with proxy wars in Korea, Vietnam, Cambodia and Laos, as well as insurgencies all across South East Asia. The Americans ought to have been far better placed to understand China than Russia because before 1949 so many had lived in China to trade, invest, educate, proselytize and advise. Yet for decades, the CIA, helped by academic experts at Harvard and other prestigious universities, provided American leaders with a completely misleading picture of its economy and the priorities of its leaders. Much the same errors continue to be repeated in the educational materials used in schools and repeated by the numerous Confucian Institutes established in schools and universities and are amplified by Chinese who repeat what they are taught in their own schools.

The textbooks should make clear that Mao Zedong set out to replicate all the policies of Stalin and to recreate a totalitarian state intent on world revolution. He pursued policies that he knew—or must have known—would cause economic disaster and immense suffering as they had in Russia. Like Stalin, Mao poured vast resources into the military–industrial sector, which had at least as large a share of the economy as we saw in the USSR. Mao never had any intention of redistributing land for the peasants to keep as their private property. It was always clear he intended to follow Lenin's and Stalin's policies of destroying the small peasant economy in favour of the urban proletariat. Yet most textbooks deliver a picture of an agrarian reformer dedicated to improving the lot of the Chinese peasantry and a narrative of political campaigns, purges and meetings largely explained by using Chinese Communist Party propaganda jargon. The political convulsions like the Cultural Revolution were all about destroying the opposition to Mao's policies in the 1950s, and then destroying his enemies who blamed him for creating a forewarned disaster.

We also need to better understand why Western experts, the CIA and its precursor, the OSS, failed to predict the communist victory in 1949 that brought Mao to power. Why it failed to predict that Mao would commit 3 million troops to the Korean War at the cost of nearly 50,000 American lives.[1] Why it underestimated how committed China was to the eventual victory of the Vietnamese communists, starting as early as 1954 when Chinese generals masterminded the Vietnamese victory at Dien Bien Phu. The CIA somehow did not uncover the 40 million deaths during the largest famine in history, otherwise known as the Great Leap Forward in 1958–62. Had Americans grasped the truth about the great famine, they might have encouraged Chiang Kai-shek's proposal to invade the mainland in 1961, and it might very well have succeeded. It misunderstood the internal Party battles that led to the Cultural Revolution and the split with the Soviet Union. Many other events took it by surprise: the attack on India, the assault on Taiwan and the whole course of the war in Vietnam. If the truth about the Mao's disastrous mismanagement of the economy had been known, perhaps President Nixon would never have travelled to China to parley with the dying Mao and recognize China as a great power.

The extent of these misunderstandings became better known when in 2004 the CIA released its top-secret intelligence reports on China's economic performance during Mao's twenty-seven-year long rule. The CIA transferred its faith in the efficacy of Stalinist central planning to Maoist China. In 1959, the CIA's intelligence officers estimated that in the first five-year plan (1953–7), China's economy grew by 7 to 8 per cent a year. This rate would be faster than either West Germany or Japan. It also said that in 1958—the first year of the catastrophic Great Leap Forward—there was a 10 per cent increase in agriculture, possibly as much as 20 per cent, and industrial production had doubled.[2]

Although it received reports describing the Great Leap Forward as a catastrophic failure and accepted that many millions were suffering from severe malnutrition, the United States did not conclude that millions had starved to death. This mistake was made following an internal debate among CIA officers over the reliability of testimony from the numerous refugees who arrived in Hong Kong (where the CIA had a station) and reported mass starvation deaths.[3]

As with the Soviet Union, the CIA preferred the Bergson methodology to the testimony of eyewitnesses, who were deemed unreliable. So one CIA report claimed that GNP had increased by 8 per cent in 1960, the worst year of the famine. In 1961, the CIA reported that 'widespread famine does not appear to be at hand' but that there had been no increase in GNP. A 1962 CIA report blamed the disaster on adverse weather, faulty management, ill-conceived programmes. It reported that in 1961 GNP fell by 10 per cent, yet the population had increased by 60 million. A CIA report in 1963 estimated that economic growth had resumed at the level of the first five-year plan of around 7–8 per cent a year.[4]

Then the CIA estimated that in 1965–70 the economy was growing at 6 per cent annually and that 'food production has kept ahead of population growth, a remarkable achievement'. In the early 1970s, the CIA believed that industrial production was expanding at 10 per cent a year.[5]

As with the Soviet Union, the CIA grossly underestimated the burden that defence spending put on the Chinese economy. In 1972, the CIA guessed that it equalled 10 per cent of GNP, roughly what it thought the USSR was spending. Yet, although the figures are uncertain even now, China was probably devoting even more to the military than the USSR: possibly as much as 40 or 50 per cent of its total expenditure. It was an unsustainable burden, and much of the investment was wasted in useless projects with little or no returns.

In the late 1970s, China had built up the largest armoury in the world with 10,000 battle tanks, 5,000 military aircraft and the world's largest fleet. Aircraft production peaked in 1974 when 540 military aircraft were made in one year. The manpower committed to fighting wars was enormous. China sustained a million casualties during the Korean War. The People's Liberation Army sent over 400,000 troops to fight in Vietnam, more than the Americans. It supported major wars and insurgencies in Malaysia, Burma, Indonesia, the Philippines, Cambodia and elsewhere, committing both scarce foreign exchange and manpower.[6]

The heaviest burden was the vast military spending programme constructing what was known as the third line, a series of military–industrial factories located in remote areas in the interior designed to ensure victory in a nuclear war with Moscow. The first were the defences along the coast and the preparations for an invasion of Taiwan. The second line was in Manchuria, with the third line as an ambitious programme to build or relocate some 29,000 factories in the undeveloped interior, at a cost estimated at US $54 billion. From the mid-1960s to the mid-1970s, nearly half of China's budget went into third line construction alone. It was a gigantic effort for a country with an industrial economy much smaller than the Soviet Union's, which lacked both the gold reserves the Bolsheviks inherited and the oil and gas exports that sustained the Soviets from the 1960s onwards.

The CIA could draw on the testimony of refugees who arrived in Hong Kong, the intelligence from its allies in Taiwan and a reservoir of expertise from academics who spent many years in China. Yet it preferred to put its faith in the vague statistical data that China produced. To this day, China has not stopped propagating the myth of the 1950s as a golden period when the country was liberated and restored to prosperity. It still claims that during the first five-year plan, 1953–8, industrial production grew by 19 per cent a year and workers' income by 9 per cent a year. A Wikipedia entry claims:

Gross output value from industry and agriculture rose from 30 percent in 1949 to 56.5 percent in 1957, while that of heavy industry increased from 26.4 percent to 48.4 per cent. In 1957, grain production reached 195 billion kilograms and cotton output 32.8 million dan (1 dan = 50 kilograms), both surpassing the targets set in the Plan.[7]

In his book *The Tragedy of Liberation*, historian Frank Dikötter described the propaganda:

> The People's Republic widely advertised its success. It built up a glowing image with a profusion of statistics. Everything, apparently, was measurable in the New China, from the latest coal output and grain production to the number of square meters of housing built since liberation. Whatever the object of measurement, the trend was always upwards, even though the figures were sometimes rather vague. Percentages, for instance, were always favoured. Lump sums were not broken down. Categories were rarely defined, indices often came without items, and price base periods shifted erratically. Sometimes they vanished altogether. Cost and labour seemed irrelevant and were excluded from accounting. The ways in which the data was collected and the methods used to produce the official statistics were never published. Sceptical statisticians found huge discrepancies. But dreamers around the world were dazzled. In every domain, it seemed, the People's Republic was surging forward.[8]

These statistics were bolstered by the books and reports produced by the same sort of fellow travellers who had visited the Soviet Union in the 1930s. They were taken on exactly the same kinds of tours of model villages, prisons and factories in China.

The CIA does not seem to have used the methods of Bergson or Gerschenkron to analyse the Chinese economy in the same detail as the Soviet Union's. It accepted the Chinese claims and assumed that what worked in the Soviet Union should work just as well in China. In doing so, it ignored the work of a few sceptics like the American expert on Chinese agriculture John Lossing Buck, who had surveyed and studied Chinese agriculture before 1949. After seeing the published Chinese figures, he realized that by postulating too low a figure for grain yields before 1949, China had produced a 'series of production data which record increases that are primarily statistical'. Even so, they could not disguise the fact that average grain harvests between 1949 and 1958 were below those of 1931–7 and that the peasants had been better off between 1929 and 1933 (years of great famine in northern China) when annual per capita grain production was higher.[9]

The Chinese Communist Party implemented only one five-year plan. After 1957, it did not follow any coherent plan and no real planning was possible. The National Office of Statistics was disbanded in 1958. Once the famine set in, the Chinese Communist Party stopped issuing any statistics at all. For twenty years, China did not publish or release any economic statistics, not even population statistics or meteorological data. In 1978, a Chinese leader would confess to a visiting dignitary that he had no idea how big the population was. After 1980, the newly re-established State Statistical Bureau invented figures to fill in a twenty-five-year-long void. From 1959 onwards, Beijing largely stopped issuing invitations to foreign visitors, even fellow-traveller well-wishers, but the paucity of information did not stop the belief in the miracles being worked in China. A worldwide Maoist movement sprang up, devoted to eulogizing Maoist economic policies and seeking to replicate them across the Third World.

China started extending invitations again to selected groups of visitors in the wake of President Nixon's 1972 visit. These visits resulted in a new spate of books praising Maoist economics. The leading China expert at Harvard, Fairbank, released a book in 1974, *China Perceived*, in which he confidently asserted, 'valued in the Chinese peasant's terms, the revolution has been a magnificent achievement, a victory not only for Mao Zedong, but for several hundreds of millions of Chinese people'.[10]

After a visit to China, the economist J. K. Galbraith also became convinced that the country's agriculture worked well. As he wrote in his 1973 book, *A China Passage*:

> There can now be no serious doubt that China is devising a
> highly effective economic system. Frank Coe and Sol Adler

[who travelled with him] ... guess that the rate of expansion in Chinese industrial and agricultural output is now between 10 and 11 percent annually. This does not seem to me implausible.

Professor Dwight H. Perkins of the Harvard Kennedy School wrote in *Agricultural Development in China 1368–1968* that the communists' centralized control over the grain harvest had enabled them to cope with natural disasters:

> The impact of this change was clearly demonstrated in the poor harvests of 1959 through 1961. The 15 to 20 percent drop in grain production which probably occurred in the entire country would have meant in years past many millions of deaths in the areas most severely affected. Tight control, particularly an effective system of rationing, together with the past development of the railroads, meant that few if any starved outright. Instead the nutritional levels of the whole country were maintained, perhaps not with precise equality, but with a close approximation to it. As a result, the regime averted a major disaster.[11]

Behind all these entrenched attitudes lay a pervasive belief that Mao was not copying Stalin but was a genius who had invented a new path for economic development tailored to China's individual needs. Under Mao, state control of the rural economy was not a disaster but a blessing, as Professor Perkins concluded. It was virtually taboo in academia to link famines in Russia with those in China. The Chinese communists were seen as agrarian reformers who had come to power on the crest of a genuine peasant rebellion. It seemed impossible to conceive that Mao could be deliberately enslaving the peasant population to finance the build-up of an aggressive military–industrial machine. Several CIA reports did acknowledge setbacks in agriculture during the Great Leap Forward, fears arising from pressure to keep up food production to meet population growth and the later-acknowledged outsized spending on military procurement programmes. Yet no connection was drawn between the two.

One of the most influential voices was Fairbank. He had worked in the OSS, and while in China he had developed a healthy contempt for the nationalist government of Chiang Kai-shek and a corresponding sympathy for the communists. With the outbreak of 1960s campus radicalism and fervent enthusiasm for Ho Chi Minh in the anti-Vietnam War movement, however, Fairbank and his generation were outflanked by a new generation of academics and students for whom nothing less than unadulterated worship of Mao's China would do.

In the numerous books and biographies written about this period, one searches in vain for discussions of Stalin's or Lenin's influence on Mao's policies. We don't know if he disagreed with anything that Stalin said. There's no evidence that Mao ever had any original insights or even any interest in economic matters beyond copying Stalin in everything. Unlike many of his colleagues, he never studied in the Soviet Union and only went there on two occasions, once in December 1949 when he spent two months in Moscow and again in 1957 on a shorter trip. On these trips, he is not known to have shown any curiosity about whether Soviet socialism actually worked or what truth lay behind Soviet statistics. It seems likely that Mao did not care what happened to the Chinese peasants as long as he could create a totalitarian military superpower.

We do know that once in power the Chinese Communist Party followed the template set by Lenin after 1917. In the first four years, it closed down all markets, imposed strict price controls and established buying and distribution monopolies. All other private commerce was outlawed, too. Shanghai's numerous commercial banks and its stock market were also shuttered. Private businessmen were targeted in a series of campaigns such as the Wu Fan or Five Antis Campaign. The Party abolished the grain market and all forms of private property and commerce. In 1958, it introduced Stalin's internal passport system across the country so no one could flee their homes and migrate to the cities in search of food. Urban residents were issued with grain ration tickets that they could only use locally. Foreign businesses were forced to leave and their property confiscated.

The government created a new currency, the renminbi (RMB), or People's Money, but it could not be used in foreign or domestic trade. Trade was conducted by barter agreements between different countries and between the provinces and municipalities. The nationalized state enterprises no longer used real money in transactions. As was also the case in the Soviet Union after 1930, the state-owned enterprises used cashless transfers through the banking system when purchases were made from each other. This was called the *jingji hesuan zhidu* (economic accounting system) in China. The monetary transfers passively followed the flow of goods within the state sector. Money, along with prices, became a mere accounting device.

Urban workers and state employees were paid nominal wages in RMB, but after 1955 most goods, including food and clothing, were distributed with ration tickets. The rationing system soon covered between 200 and 300 items, but it remained essentially an urban phenomenon. Cloth, cotton, matches, soap, candles, needles, thread, cooking oil, wood, paper, coal and other fuels, fish, meat, bean curd and so on could only be acquired with coupons. The soap ration was one bar per month, and in some places a ticket was necessary to obtain hot water or a bath. There was in any case little to buy in the state-run retail shops, and cash purchases often required an additional voucher. Much of the RMB was therefore saved, spent in the black market or periodically deducted in forced state bond savings.[12]

After 1955, many peasant cooperatives started issuing their own quasi-currencies in the form of 'vegetable tickets', 'cash circulation notes' and 'cooperative currency'. These money substitutes, like the grain ration tickets issued in the cities, had only a very limited circulation. Most of them could only be traded for goods or services inside the collective or work unit. As in the Soviet *kolkhoz*, the agricultural collectives, the state allowed farmers to hold monthly markets where people carried out trade and barter. Inside the collectives, the farmers could only obtain goods, including grain, that the local administration was willing or able to deliver.

Before 1949, China's most successful industry was cotton spinning and weaving. Yet Shanghai's cotton mills lost the freedom to import cotton and had to buy supplies from the government and sell their cloth at fixed prices. The output of cotton yarn and cloth would not recover for another twenty years. The factories became cooperatives, and companies were grouped into industry guilds that were controlled by executives appointed by the Communist Party. Each guild had to meet a tax quota set by the government. The head of each guild then asked each factory to deliver its own sub-quota. All the 5,000 cotton and textile factories were then merged and consolidated into 470 state companies and placed under central control. Many small factories were closed and the employees lost their jobs.

The workers were organized into new labour unions, and each branch was headed by the lowest-paid workers, who had the power to issue orders to their employers. The employers were subjected to detailed inspections of their accounts and then had to pay taxes retroactively. Foreign businessmen were not allowed to leave until they had handed over all their property; sometimes these negotiations dragged on for years.

China's foreign trade collapsed and was replaced by barter trade deals with other socialist countries. The closure of marketplaces and commercial exchanges put a huge sector of urban society out of work. Gone was the need for traders, middlemen, sales agents, hawkers, advertisers, shops and retailers and restaurants. The closure of small family-run businesses and factories left millions unemployed in the cities. The number of workers who lost their jobs as a direct consequence of the campaign against the bourgeoisie amounted to 80,000 in Shanghai, 10,000 in Jinan and 10,000 in the region around Suzhou. Further inland, in the city of Wuhan, once described as the Chicago of the East, 24,000 workers lost their jobs as trade dwindled to a mere 30 per cent of its earlier level. Railway transportation and tax collection came to a standstill. The whole city was reduced to desolation.

When Mao introduced Stalin's internal passport system to China, peasants could no longer travel to market towns without permission, or seek work outside the village in slack seasons. The emphasis on grain production in the collectives and the travel restrictions discouraged handicrafts like embroidery and woodcarving that had previously helped peasants supplement their incomes. All the small-scale private enterprises of village China withered, leaving the peasants dependent on what the state could supply from its factories.

The most damaging policy was the closure of grain markets after 1953, when the Party mandated compulsory grain procurement prices. These prices were deliberately set too low in order to subsidize investment in heavy industry. Many peasants refused to sell grain to the state because it was uneconomical. Cadres were dispatched to the villages to extract state procurement quotas by force and make the peasants sign promises to deliver still more grain. Such was the pressure exerted that local officials or peasants who failed to meet their quotas were beaten. Some even committed suicide when they could no longer feed their families.[13]

Mass starvation started in parts of China right after 1949 as the Party and army forcibly seized grain to feed itself. In Jilin province, the Party seized over 40 per cent of the harvest to feed the army fighting in neighbouring Korea, leaving the peasants without enough to feed themselves. Many starved to death on rations of less than 15 kilos a month. In November 1951, Deng Xiaoping announced that farmers in south-west China would be asked to contribute an extra 400,000 tons of grain beyond the usual procurements. Six months later, 2 million people were reduced to starvation, with reports of cannibalism reaching the higher echelons of the leadership. In Yunnan, more than a million people were starving, and many of the victims stripped the bark off trees or ate mud.

In 1956, the first year of collectivization, grain yields alone fell by as much as 40 per cent. The authors of *Chinese Village, Socialist State* recorded that in Hebei province villagers recalled that year as a catastrophe exceeded in its toll of human life only by the great famine of 1943. The collectivization of farm animals led peasants to kill them and sell their meat. In Hebei province, the number of draft animals fell from 4.3 million to 3.3 million in that one year alone. By the following year, the first secretary of Henan, Pan Fusheng, was complaining that women were forced to yoke themselves to the plough with their wombs hanging down, such was the shortage of draft animals.[14]

In the spring, 3 million people in Shandong went hungry. Five million people were destitute in Henan, close to 7 million in Hubei and another 7 million in Anhui. In Guangdong, over a quarter of a million people went without food. In Shaanxi and Gansu, over 1.5 million people went hungry. In Guizhou and Sichuan, desperate farmers sold the seeds on which their next crop depended: this was the case with a quarter of the people in some villages in Nanchong county. The practice was also common in Hunan, Hubei and Jiangsu. In Shaoyang county, Hunan, starvation compelled farmers who used to be well off to sell everything they had. In many of these provinces, desperate parents even bartered their children.[15]

Once the grain market was closed across the country in 1953, people died in large numbers. Between 1953 and 1958, in Sichuan province alone an estimated 3 million people died from hunger and malnutrition. The peasants began to go on strike. Mao openly boasted, 'This is a war. We are opening fire on peasants with private property.'[16]

When the Great Leap Forward was launched in 1958, the Party abolished money entirely. Chen Boda, who was Mao's secretary and a key ideologue, established a new journal, the *Red Flag*. In the first edition of July 1958, he wrote that the leap into communes would open the road to communism. Communism meant the end of money. Food would be free. A few weeks later, the editor of Shanghai's *Liberation Daily*, Zhang Chunqiao, published another key article praising the public distribution of all goods and demanding the abolition of all wages.[17]

Mao endorsed both articles. He never quite endorsed the formal abolition of money, saying this would take time. The policy of abolishing all forms of money would later be raised by Chen Boda, Zhang Chunqiao and the other ultra-leftist ideologues during the Cultural Revolution (1966–76), notably in 1969 and 1975 when these men were at the pinnacle of power.

Yet in 1958, such a step was unnecessary because it became a crime to carry out private trade. China came closer than any society in modern history to abolishing both private property and markets. Everything became public property, so the ownership of anything, even a sweet potato or an ear of corn taken from a stalk in the field, could be treated as theft or sabotage. The punishment was often death or severe torture. Money and the commodity economy disappeared. The black market, which had flourished before 1958, especially in the cities—and revealed the huge gap between official and unofficial prices—could barely function.

Yet even in the face of the harsh punishments meted out for any commercial exchanges and labour camps flooded by over 10 million political prisoners, the propensity of human nature to 'truck, barter and exchange one thing for another' that Adam Smith observed could not be suppressed. Desperate peasants resorted to selling or trading their children and wives for food. Official documents also show that many were also arrested for selling or trading human flesh.[18]

The Chinese Communist Party attempted to put into practice the ideas of Marx and Lenin by creating a system of free distribution, labour certificates and communal living. Mao also anticipated the imminent end of the family. 'In socialism, private property still exists, factions still exist, families still exist. Families are the product of the last stage of primitive communism, and every last trace of them will be eliminated in the future', Mao said in a speech on 22 March 1958.[19]

With the establishment of the people's communes that year, all private property disappeared and people were paid in kind. People destroyed their cooking pots and utensils and ate in communal halls. They could eat as much as they wanted. In many communes, families lost their homes, and men and women lived in separate dormitories. In Henan province's communes, food was distributed in communal mess halls free of charge according to individual requirements. Everything was free, from clothes to haircuts. Under this supply system, the expenses of seven of the ten 'basic necessities of life' were borne by the commune: food, clothing, housing, childbirth, education, medical treatment and marriages and funerals. No one received any money.

Later, when the food supplies ran out, most communes adopted a different system. The members were awarded work points instead of cash with which they could claim goods in kind distributed by the commune. The local Party secretary would calculate the value of these accumulated points and then pay the peasant a share of the collective's output. The work points were effectively labour certificates based on the number of hours of manual labour an individual performed.

A prominent Chinese economist, Sun Yefang, argued in 1959 that money should merely be regarded as a 'labour certificate' (*laodong quan*): 'It is a certificate indicating how much labour a worker has provided for society, and on the basis of the system of distribution according to labour it shows the worker's "right" to a portion of the consumer goods in the state's warehouses', he wrote. In a labour-certificate economy, the state commandeered masses of people into performing long hours of hard labour on public works—digging canals, tunnels, dykes and dams—irrespective of the economic value of their work.

In *Red Flag*, Minister of Finance Li Xiannian insisted that the communes were absolutely forbidden to print and issue any disguised forms of money. They could print and issue meal tickets, hairdressers' and washroom tickets. However, these were merely vouchers and must be a strictly differentiated form of currency. He said their use must be limited and that they must not circulate outside the communes.

In 1958, the Party tried to replicate the people's communes in urban China. They started building new housing with communal mess kitchens and apartments without individual kitchens. The programme to abolish wages, wage differentials and military ranks was well under way. However, when city-dwellers began to starve, too, the programme to create urban communes was abandoned. Instead, tens of millions living in the cities were relocated to the countryside to be nearer food supplies.

The Communist Party seemed to have adopted Preobrazhensky's policy of 'primitive capital accumulation'. The first five-year plan was deliberately designed to squeeze the peasants in order to funnel investment into heavy industry and defence. It was supported by a major barter deal negotiated with the Soviet Union. China swopped agricultural products for Soviet help in constructing 151 large-scale industrial projects, most of which were military–industrial complexes. China's industrialization programme was therefore largely designed to support its military spending, not to improve living standards. Military spending was soon accounting for more than half the published budget and would reach 63 per cent by 1958. It is not clear how much of its GNP went to the military, but it was very likely well over 30 per cent.[20]

Here the lessons of Joseph Stalin were learned too well. His war against his own peasants would be replicated in the most populous nation in the world with the same fatal results.

15

CHINA'S GREAT FAMINE AND THE SOCIALIST CALCULATION PROBLEM

In the middle of the greatest famine in history, Chairman Mao wasn't sure if anyone really was starving. There was not much food but plenty of boastful claims. Mao was told that in 1958 the national grain harvest had risen from 185 million tons to 430 million, even an incredible 500 million tons. To discover the truth, he travelled all the way back to his home village in Shaoshan, Hunan province, to ask his kith and kin: was it true that there was nothing to eat? He thought that at least his own relatives would tell him the truth. Up and down the country, Party officials had been boasting of record harvests, but some of Mao's deputies were privately telling him not to believe these lies. The most famous critic was Marshal Peng Dehuai, the military chief whom Mao later had tortured and killed.

As the Great Leap unfolded, the Party leaders were kept informed by reports collected by local officials and sent up upwards through the bureaucratic pyramid. The lies got bigger the higher they went, fuelled by the 'wind of exaggeration'. The *People's Daily* went as far as to start a debate on how China should cope with its food surplus. In response, the quotas set on high became greater and greater. The absence of meaningful statistical data or market prices left both Party members and the public in the dark. It enabled the Party leadership to operate in total secrecy and hide the huge diversion of resources into the military. Yet at the same time, the planners could not know whether their actions, such as the merging of private factories into huge state enterprises, actually resulted in higher levels of productivity. They had no way of assessing the returns from the investments in heavy industry made possible by the enormous sacrifices of the peasants.

This shows that even before the launch of the Great Leap Forward, Chinese leaders were making decisions in a statistical fog. The economy was faring far worse than their statistics showed. Had they known the truth, other leaders might have persuaded Mao to hold off from launching a programme so disastrous that it came close to destroying the regime.

Without market prices, the state became totally dependent on the flow of information from its local officials in order to issue directives to plant more of this crop or the other, to tax more, or less, to invest more in irrigation, or in storage and so on. Yet the successive waves of terror campaigns had created a climate of fear that made reporting reliable information impossible. No one had been safe from arbitrary execution in the rolling campaigns that Mao launched throughout the 1950s. The victims were often chosen to meet arbitrary quotas, as percentages of the population of provinces and cities. The purge that took place just before the Great Leap, the 1957 Anti-Rightist Campaign, sent half a million people—mostly the educated—into labour camps. Anyone suspected of disloyalty could follow them at any moment. Naturally, everyone in a position of authority felt safe only by telling Mao what he wanted to hear, a fact that must have been obvious to all concerned. But knowing that information is wrong is not the same as finding a way to obtain the right data or interpret it correctly.

The Chinese leadership received plenty of reports packed with statistics but had no way of knowing what any of them meant. They couldn't compare data from one year with another because the figures were so crude and the definitions so vague. The data was all in quantities, but even commodities like corn or rice grain came in a wide variety of forms and types. So many factors determined its value. For example, as the state had only limited silos available to store the grain harvest, much of it was spoilt.

No one along the chain of command had any authority to make their own decisions in response to local conditions. They could only fulfil the targets set by the centre. Consequently, everyone in a country of 600 million depended on the decisions made by a handful of leaders in Beijing. But these men couldn't assess the gravity of the food shortages or make reliable forecasts about the future. This led to an absurd situation—China's leadership concluded that the only way they could find anything out was by conducting their own personal research. They did this by heading to the countryside to talk to relatives in their home villages. As many of them hailed, like Mao, from Hunan province, often dubbed the cradle of the Party, the leaders disputed the issues by references to what they had seen or heard in villages in the same county of Xiangtan.

Mao stayed for two nights and talked and ate with his relatives, who, like his father, were all peasants. The Shaoshan peasants all hinted that they were going hungry and admitted that they didn't like the collective kitchens in the new people's communes. None of them dared tell Mao what was really happening: all over Hunan province, people were starving to death because the fantastic harvests were an illusion. Mao's policies were an utter failure.

When Liu Shaoqi, China's second most powerful leader, decided he had to see for himself and went back to his home village in Xiangtan, local leaders went to extraordinary lengths to deceive him. Along the road leading to Liu's hometown, starving peasants had torn the bark off trees to eat, so officials plastered the tree trunks with yellow mud and straw to conceal the scars. As the *People's Daily* reported in an article published in December 1989, 'the grassroots Party organ interfered in everything to cover up the death toll'. Liu only managed to discover the truth in the village where he had been born when some villagers dared to tell him that twenty of their number had starved to death, including a nephew of Liu's, and that a dozen more had fled. Later in the Cultural Revolution, Mao took his revenge and had Liu arrested, tortured and murdered.[1]

In fact, there was no way of knowing the real size of the harvest since the State Statistical Bureau had been dismantled and its local office replaced by 'good news reporting stations'. The propaganda machine churned out one triumphant claim after another. China had outstripped the United States in wheat and cotton production, it had beaten Japan in per unit yields of rice and had bettered the United States in cotton yields.

Everywhere Mao went, Party officials told him of astounding successes: fields no longer produced 330 lbs of grain—the average before the Great Leap Forward—but 49,500 lbs or even 53,000 lbs per 0.17 acres. Deng Xiaoping was equally optimistic. He expected per capita grain distribution in 1958 to be 1,375 lbs on the strength of a peasant's assurance that by using Mao's agricultural methods he had produced 77,000 lbs per 0.17 acres on an experimental field. Deng calculated that at this rate yields would rise to 231,000 lbs per 0.17 acres and would by 1962 stand at 2.5 tons. 'We can all have as much as we want', he concluded.[2]

In Anhui province, to take one example, the Great Leap Forward began with claims of extraordinary success. In the county of Fengyang, one so-called sputnik field supposedly grew a national record of 62.5 tons of tobacco on just 0.17 acres of land. Fantastic pressure was exerted at every level to meet the quotas that the provincial leader Zeng Xisheng had set. Local Party secretaries were kept locked up in rooms for weeks until they agreed to meet their grain quotas and other targets. They in turn put their deputies through the same ordeal. So it went, from prefecture to county, from commune to brigade, from production team right down to the individual peasant.[3]

If a peasant didn't agree to double or treble or quadruple his harvest, the production team leader would beat him until he gave in. Nobody believed these targets could be reached, but cadres reported that they had been. The lies went back up the pyramid, and with each repetition, the lies became more and more fantastic. All over the province, grain yields, which were at best 726 lbs per 0.17 acres, were inflated to an astonishing 33,000 lbs (14.9 metric tons).[4]

Poor, impoverished Anhui claimed to be flush with a fantastic bonanza, and Zeng began to deliver large amounts of grain to other parts of the country and even abroad. In 1959 alone, Anhui exported 200,000 tons, although its grain harvest had shrunk by 4 million tons from the record 10 million tons harvested in 1958. In 1959, the state demanded that the peasants of Anhui hand over 2.5 million tons, that is, 40 per cent of the harvest.[5]

In the county of Fengyang, the previous year had been bad enough. In 1958, the county had harvested 89,000 tons but reported 178,500 tons to cover up a sharp decline in output. Some of this grain was not even harvested but rotted in the fields because too many peasants were out making steel or building dams. After the peasants deducted what they needed to eat and keep for seed, a surplus of only 5,800 tons was left to deliver to the state—but the grain levy was fixed at 35,000 tons on the basis of the false harvest reported. The missing 29,200 tons had to be extracted by force. In 1959, the county authorities lost all touch with reality. The county reported that 199,000 tons were harvested, a little higher than the reported figure for 1958, but in fact the harvest had further declined from 89,000 to 54,000 tons. Of this, the state demanded 29,464 tons.[6]

In 1958 and 1959, Fengyang officials lied not just about grain production but also about the amount of arable land sown, the area of virgin land ploughed, the number of irrigation works created and practically everything else. They said they had raised 166,000 pigs when the true figure was only 43,000. One production team claimed it had grown 19.6 acres of rapeseed when it had grown none at all. The brigade chief thought this lie was too modest and informed his superior that the team had grown 100 acres.[7]

The folly of pursuing targets set by quantity was demonstrated by China's efforts to increase steel production. Mao envisaged a doubling or trebling of steel output within a year. The entire country, from peasants in remote villages on the Tibetan plateau to top Party officials in Zhongnanhai in Beijing, set up smelters in 1958 and 1959 to create 'steel' in backyard furnaces. Everyone had to meet a quota by handing over their metal possessions. People handed in bicycles, railings, iron bedsteads, door knobs, their pots and pans and cooking grates. And to fire the furnaces, huge numbers of trees were cut down. In the countryside, people worked day and night fuelling these furnaces. While they did so, they could eat as much as they wanted out of the communes' collective food stores. The lumps of useless metal that emerged were supposed to be used in the mechanization of agriculture.

In the first half of 1960, Mao and his supporters called for another great leap forward, including a giant jump in steel production. Mao ordered the mobilization of 70 million people to achieve a target of 22 million tons of steel, a ludicrous goal since only 8 million tons had been produced in 1957 and 11 million tons claimed in 1958. He grandly proposed raising total output to 100 million tons within ten years.[8]

The fantastic claims about miracle harvests and record steel output were impossible to believe, but the leaders of China couldn't be sure if officials were merely exaggerating real successes. Mao firmly believed the latter, so at the height of the famine he ordered peasants to plant less food. He thought that any shortages of grain existed only because the middle peasants and former landlord peasants were craftily hiding it.

Those who supported Mao's absurd fantasies not only saved their skins but rose to the highest positions. Zhao Ziyang, who became general secretary of the Chinese Communist Party in 1987, was a senior official in Guangdong during the famine. In 1959, he set out on an inspection tour of Xuwen county, from which he concluded that the peasants were hungry only because grain was being hoarded. So he launched 'anti-grain concealment' drives to ferret out the grain hoarders. Afterwards, he sent Mao a report that the peasants were lying about food shortages and that 'rightists' and grasping *kulaks* were conspiring to hide grain in order to demand further supplies from the state. Mao was delighted to hear this.

The Party secretary in Mao's birthplace in Xiangtan, Hunan, was Hua Guofeng, a thirty-eight-year-old from Shanxi who refuted the claims of the provincial Party leader, Zhou Xiaozhou, that there was widespread hunger in Hunan. Afterwards, Hua wrote an article in the provincial Party newspaper headlined 'Victory Belongs to Those People Who Raise High the Red Flag of the Great Leap Forward'. He personally supervised the brutal persecution of Marshal Peng Dehuai's family, who lived in the same Xiangtan district. Hua became Mao's successor after his death in 1976.

On another occasion, Mao did not bother going back to his home village but sent Hu Yaobang, who had been born in the same district and was head of the Party's Youth League. Hu Yaobang found out that most of the province's population was starving to death and returned to Beijing to deliver his report to Mao. Yet Hu's courage failed him.

As he explained twenty years later when he had been elevated to general secretary of the Chinese Communist Party, 'I did not dare tell the Chairman the truth. If I had done so this would have spelt the end of me. I would have ended up like Peng Dehuai.'[9]

Mao regarded the peasants as an army of free labour, which he treated much as Stalin did his Gulag slave force. Vast numbers were compelled to work long, back-breaking hours terracing steep mountainsides to create more arable land or building giant engineering projects. By the early 1970s, most were being fed semi-starvation rations that largely consisted of chips of dried sweet potatoes. Many were worked to death on ill-conceived endeavours that Mao saw as a way of emulating or outdoing Stalin's achievements.

For instance, the Red Flag Canal in Henan province was the Chinese answer to the White Sea Canal—and just as useless. In order to re-route a river and divert water to a poor drought-stricken region in Linxian county, tens of thousands of peasants spent years constructing a water channel through mountains and along steep hillsides using the most primitive tools. Unaided by engineers or any machinery, the peasants built 134 tunnels and 150 aqueducts and moved enough earth to build a road 42,480 miles long, enough to go nearly twice around the equator. The Party insisted on building a stretch of the canal along the side of a steep cliff so it hangs suspended in the air. It is a remarkable sight that awes the many visitors it attracts; indeed, its only practical use is as a tourist attraction.[10]

Terrible punishments were meted out to those working in labour gangs on these huge reservoir and irrigation projects. Of the 60,000 workers sent to work on one dam project in Gushi county in the same province, 10,700 perished from exhaustion, hunger, cold or beatings, according to official figures. A Party document from Anhui province describes what happened in Fengyang county:

> Peasants were forced to work extra hours at the construction site of the hydro-electric power station. The cadres, including the county Party Secretary and deputy magistrate, treated the peasants harshly. If the peasants did not work, they were not given food. Some sick peasants were sent back home and died on the way. ... In the construction site of the reservoir, a prison was

set up where 70 peasants were imprisoned, of whom 28 died. There were many methods of torture, including being forced to stand, being tied up by ropes, or suspended by ropes. One of the worst methods was to thread iron wire through people's ears.[11]

The vast majority of the thousands of dams and water conservancy schemes built with huge inputs of manual labour proved to be useless. They were not properly designed and made with mud and stone. The Shimatan and Banqiao dams at Zhumadian in Henan province broke apart in 1975, unleashing flash floods that killed hundreds of thousands of people. Elsewhere, reservoir dams quickly silted up like the Sanmenxia hydroelectric scheme on the Yellow River.

The peasant labour force was also dispatched to frontier regions to cut down forests, drain marches, dig mines and farm marginal steppe lands. In his book *Laogai: The Chinese Gulag*, Harry Wu, who spent nineteen years in the camps, estimates that during the Great Leap Forward, the number of political prisoners in the camps peaked at close to 10 million. Many camps had annual death rates of 20 or 30 per cent during the height of the famine years. Mao biographer Jung Chang claims that during Mao's rule 27 million died in Chinese prisons and labour camps—equal to the total number who passed through the Soviet Gulag camps.[12]

As with Stalin, the Chinese leadership placed no value on the lives of the peasants. Instead, they took a special pride in reporting primitive manual labour measured in hours. As in the Soviet Union, a high proportion of the Chinese Gulag came from the educated urban classes. As a result, for decades China suffered from a shortage of qualified personnel in a range of different fields. Rather than a statistical method to calculate the value of any individual's work or the returns from the investment of so much crude labour, the basic unit remained a day's manual labour and the half a kilo of grain sufficient to sustain human life for a day.

Within a few years of Mao's death in 1976, the state reluctantly abandoned his policies. It recognized that terracing mountains by hand had been a worthless investment. The attempts to turn steppe lands into farmland had created an environmental disaster. Cutting down forests had caused a massive amount of soil erosion, leading rivers and reservoirs to silt up. The Gulag labour camps were mostly closed down and the inmates sent home. Most of the factories built in the interior had to be closed or relocated. Many had been built in caves or underground to protect from a nuclear attack, and these proved to be investments that never produced products of any value. Military engineering programmes like one to build nuclear-powered submarines had to be abandoned. Tens of millions of people were allowed to return home, but they returned to cities where barely any new housing had been built for decades, let alone railways, roads or power stations.

After 1979, the Party did not make a clean break with the past or formally acknowledge what had gone wrong. It could not admit that its revolutionary programme had been a mistake without undermining its legitimacy. It moved towards creating a market economy in fits and starts that were obscured under ambiguous slogans like 'economic reform', 'socialism with Chinese characteristics', the 'socialist market economy' and so on. As it broke up the people's communes and opened rural markets, it embraced a form of Bukharin's NEP; Deng Xiaoping borrowed his edict, telling the peasants that to 'get rich is glorious'. Chinese food production rose rapidly, and the surplus rural labour was put to work in foreign-invested export-processing enterprises. Beijing slashed military spending and enabled the overhang of unspent wages to be spent on imported consumer goods.[13]

Yet even after decades of reforms, it is still hard to create a clear picture of the economy or to know how much malinvestment goes on in the Chinese economy. The many state-owned enterprises, supported by an inexhaustible amount of state credit, are never allowed to go bankrupt. After 1979, China established a dual pricing system, creating both market and state prices, and a convertible and non-convertible currency, the foreign exchange certificates (since abandoned) and the renminbi. It established a confusing hybrid statistical system that measured output value based on notional prices. Only in 1992 did it say it would adopt the UN System of National Accounts and discard the Soviet system. As of 2022, it has yet to establish a fully convertible currency.

The result is that it is very hard to form a clear picture of China's GNP, or to compare one year with another, or one period to the next. Or indeed to compare China's performance with that of other countries. Chinese leaders continue to deplore the fact that they govern in a statistical fog, relying on statistics that are no better than propaganda. In 2007, China's future Premier Li Keqiang said that China's GDP figures are 'man-made' and 'therefore unreliable', according to US diplomatic cables released by WikiLeaks.[14]

One country where it was possible to compare directly how the two systems worked was Germany. Thanks to the fog of false statistics, it was for a while possible to believe that the industrious Germans succeeded in making both capitalism and socialism work.

16

THE EAST GERMAN ECONOMIC MIRACLE
THAT NEVER WAS

Two peculiar developments took place in Germany after the Second World War that ought never to have happened. The first is that against all expectations, West Germany became the largest and most successful economy on the continent. It was the only country to embrace the ideas of Mises and the Austrian school. In 1948, it freed itself from all price and wage controls and created a miracle economy. Second, the West Germans somehow convinced themselves that their East German counterparts were running an economy that was nearly as successful, even though it was run on entirely contrary ideas largely borrowed from Stalin. The illusions about the GDR led the West Germans to push a policy of détente and engagement that involved large-scale financial transfers and subsidies. This inadvertently resulted in West Germany propping up the failing East German economy from the 1970s onwards. As a consequence, the GDR became, other than Albania, the only Eastern bloc state that never experimented with any kind of reform.

The West German economic and intelligence experts who reported on the GDR needed to hold two contradictory views simultaneously. They knew that many East Germans were desperate to flee to the West and those that did painted a dire picture of life in

East Germany. At the same time, they took at face value the glowing but bogus economic statistics that the GDR put out and therefore concluded that both East Germany and the whole Soviet bloc were here to stay. Hence, it became a top foreign policy objective not to bring down East Germany but to avoid a third global conflict breaking out on German soil.

Although the West Germans were better placed than anyone to observe what was going on across the Berlin Wall, they never came near to deploying the sort of intelligence-gathering resources that the CIA did. The Germans, like other members of NATO such as France and Italy, relied on what the Americans told them about the Soviet Union and its allies. Only the British had a relatively large intelligence budget. As a result, the Bergson view of the Soviet Union's success and by extension the economic performance of the other socialist countries was left unchallenged in Western Europe.

European complacency about the intelligence they were getting from Washington was only matched by an acute anxiety about the perils of a nuclear war erupting on European soil. People feared that the Soviet Union and America could start a new war that would devastate Europe.

Many European politicians and opinion formers had their own reasons for not enquiring too deeply into the methodology behind the CIA's estimates of the Soviet economy. After 1945, many believed that Stalin's five-year economic plans had transformed a backward nation and created such industrial strength that it could equip the Red Army's juggernaut and enable it to come back and destroy the invincible Wehrmacht fighting machine. The Soviet Union had clearly borne the brunt of the fighting, destroying far more German divisions than the other allies. Those successes were augmented in the post-war years when in quick succession Russia achieved striking technological successes—it tested a nuclear bomb, launched the Sputnik satellite and put the first man into space.

After 1945, it seemed inevitable that the Soviet Union would remain a military colossus bestriding a ruined continent, if only because it could draw on such dynamic economic strength. The European politicians who set about rebuilding their devastated economies mostly decided to adopt elements of the USSR's central planning. The experience of the 1930s convinced even the leaders of some Christian democratic parties that capitalism had failed and the future lay in state intervention. Post-war France launched its first four-year plan in 1946, followed by a second plan covering 1954–7. Italy adopted similar economic planning, although not with quite the same enthusiasm. In Britain, the Labour Party swept to power and seized control of most parts of the economy, nationalizing the commanding heights and starting a long period of state control over prices and wages. Although it eschewed five-year plans, it established a highly centralized and planned economy.

The revival of West European economies was often credited to the Marshall Plan, a Keynesian splurge of government lending designed by US Secretary of State George Marshall. The United States gave around $13 billion ($153 billion in 2022 prices) to European nations. Germany received its fair share, around 11 per cent, but not as much as Britain (26 per cent) or France (18 per cent). Yet over time, Germany pulled dramatically ahead of its neighbours.

Of course, it is true that Germany had always been the largest industrial economy before the First World War and probably had the strongest economy during the 1930s. And it is also true that all European countries experienced dramatic improvements in living standards, especially in the 1960s. The French talk of *Les trente glorieuses* ('the glorious thirty') when referring to the thirty years from 1945 to 1975. Across the Channel, British Prime Minister Harold Macmillan claimed in a famous 1957 speech that 'most of our people have never had it so good'. Yet the German economy's phoenix-like resurrection was so remarkable that it became known as the 'German Economic Miracle' or *Wirtschaftswunder*.

Even so, its growth occurred during an era when European intellectuals, even when they conceded that human rights issues behind the Iron Curtain were troubling, rarely doubted the Soviet Union's achievements in economic management. The French and Italians had very large and influential communist parties that waged a militant campaign against those opposed to communism. Intellectuals and academics who decried the enthusiasm for Stalinism found themselves attacked and isolated. Even after Stalin was unmasked, luminaries like Jean-Paul Sartre and Simone de Beauvoir quickly shifted to an unrestrained glorification of Chairman Mao's China.

In Germany, the environment and circumstances were quite different from France or Italy. None of the victors wished to see the re-emergence of a strong Germany, and they were happy to see it divided. The West German state was created as a federal republic, the Bundesrepublik Deutschland or Federal Republic of Germany, with a weak centre. An obscure provincial town, Bonn, was chosen as its capital. The leading German Communist Party (KPD) members who survived the Nazis naturally went to live in East Germany. The West Germans eventually outlawed the KPD in 1956. Furthering this harder line, 6 to 8 million ethnic Germans had been driven from their homes by the Red Army and had to be resettled in West Germany. These new citizens were less susceptible to promises by the hard left.

The West Germans also had more pressing concerns than ideology. Many German cities and factories had been bombed to rubble. The war had destroyed 20 per cent of the housing stock. Food production had collapsed, reduced to half of what it had been before the war. During the first few years, the victors insisted that heavy industry be cut to half what it was before 1938; they destroyed or dismantled 1,500 listed manufacturing plants. The Soviets stripped Germany of many major industrial plants and shipped them back to the Soviet Union—the Kugel-Fischer ball bearing plant at Schweinfurt, the Daimler-Benz underground aircraft plant at Obrigheim, the Desching shipyards at Bremen-Weser and so on. In particular, the victors insisted that the steel industry be dismantled, and its capacity was reduced to a quarter of the pre-war level.[1]

On top of these losses, the West German state was saddled with annual reparations and restitution payments well in excess of $1 billion, and each year it had to pay 7.2 billion DM ($2.4 billion) for the cost of the Allied military occupation. It also had to shoulder the enormous burden of housing and employing those homeless Germans driven out of Eastern Europe. West Germany did enjoy a few advantages compared to, say, Britain, in that it had much lower defence spending and it was not burdened by a crippling war debt.

After Germany's surrender, the Allies kept in place all the price controls, rationing system and currency established by the Nazis, as well as labour conscription. By 1947, the Reichsmark was almost worthless, the shops were empty and everyone made purchases on the black market. Few people turned up for work and instead spent their time travelling to the countryside and trying to barter whatever they had for food. In view of the shortages, both the SPD (the German Social Democratic Party) and the American and British military chiefs wanted to continue with the rationing and keep price controls. They also imposed heavy taxes, a 65 per cent corporate tax and income taxes of up to 95 per cent.

By this time, the price controls had been in place for twelve years and the rationing system for nine years. No one could raise the price on any particular good without the express permission of the occupying military commander, which in the US Zone was General Lucius D. Clay. Everyone naturally feared an explosion of unrest that might play into the hands of the Nazis or even the communists.

The situation was strikingly similar to that in 1918. After Germany's first defeat, the lifting of wartime price controls after years of shortages had led to an explosion of prices, a worthless currency and rampant inflation that turned to hyperinflation when the central bank responded by printing more money. Unlike 1918, any politicians linked to the communists or National-Socialist parties were debarred from playing any role. On the contrary, the military commanders had to find Germans who had clean hands. If they were to be placed in positions of trust, it was best that they could show a record of opposition to the Nazis.

The Western Allies managed to find one such economist, Ludwig Erhard. He came to the Allies' attention because he had written a memorandum in 1942 proposing a programme to create a post-war market economy that assumed that Germany would lose. He belonged to a small school of dissident economists based in the University of Freiburg led by Wilhelm Ropke, Walter Eucken and Franz Oppenheimer, who kept their distance from the Nazis. They were neo-liberals or Ordoliberals, as they were called in Germany, and they opposed central planning and price controls. Their ideas drew heavily on the work of Mises and other members of the Austrian school. Erhard had joined the staff of the Nürnberg Business School in 1928 and by 1942 became its director. The Nazis removed him from this position after he refused to join the party. Erhard spent the remaining war years as a consultant to business enterprises.

After 1945, Erhard was given the job of dealing with the industries around Nürnberg (Nuremburg). Then he was tasked with the job of economics minister in the Bavarian state government. After losing this post in 1947, Erhard was named to key positions in the council set up jointly by the British and American occupation authorities to coordinate economic activities in their zones. Erhard recommended a quick reform of the currency system and an end to price controls. When the Soviets withdrew from the Allied Control Authority, General Clay, along with his French and British counterparts, was free to start the currency reform. On Sunday, 20 June 1948, the amount of currency in circulation was cut by over 90 per cent and a new legal currency, the Deutsche Mark, was introduced.[2]

Between June and August 1948, Erhard lifted price controls on vegetables, fruits, eggs and almost all manufactured goods. He substantially relaxed, or suspended entirely, the enforcement of other price ceilings. According to some accounts, Erhard pushed the price reforms through without first obtaining General Clay's consent. Over the strong objections of its Social Democratic members, Germany's Bizonal Economic Council adopted a law that gave Erhard the authority to eliminate price controls. At the same time, the government, following Erhard's advice, sharply cut personal and corporate tax rates.

The German economy responded immediately to the new currency and the market prices. The shops were soon full of goods. People went back to work. Unemployment fell rapidly. Industrial production shot up by 53 per cent in 1948, by 48 per cent the next year and by a further 25 per cent in 1950. Small companies began to flourish, giving birth to West Germany's famous *Mittelstand*, an economy driven by small and medium-sized family companies rather than large state-directed corporations. The Germans went a step further, enacting tough anti-cartel legislation to restrict big business growth. In the next stage, these enterprises began to export to neighbouring countries. Only later would giant corporations be reformed and play a large role in the economy.

This time, the sudden lifting of price controls did not result in hyperinflation. A similar thing had happened when Hjalmar Schacht, as president of the Reichsbank, had introduced the new Rentenmark in 1923 and ended that spiral of hyperinflation. In 1948, the Germans were also lucky to benefit from the Marshall Plan, which provided the hard currency that enabled authorities to finance imports of raw materials and provide them to producers at stable prices.

Mises, while delighted with Erhard's success, criticized the Marshall Plan, saying in 1951 that 'the American subsidies made it possible for [Europe's] governments to conceal partially the disastrous effects of the various socialist measures they have adopted'. Later, Mises would also fall out with the economists of the Freiburg school, whom he felt had strayed too far to the left by pursuing a social welfare state.[3]

Erhard himself went from strength to strength, becoming first minister of economic affairs and then chancellor of West Germany in 1963–6. Many historians and economists do not believe that Germany's economic rebirth had much to do with Austrian economics. Yet nothing quite like this economic miracle happened anywhere else in Europe.

Britain, for example, strangled its economy with a complicated system of state controls over both exports and imports and maintained rationing of even basic food stuffs until 1954. Various governments pursued wage and price policies for thirty-five years, until Margaret Thatcher came to power in 1979. Successive governments also attacked small and medium-sized firms, forcing them to close down or merge into large state-owned or state-controlled corporations. Harsh inheritance taxes made it impossible to hand on family enterprises. The government created a state planning ministry, called the National Economic Development Council, which invested in new plants located around the country in order to redistribute industry. With the commanding heights of the economy in the hands of the state, public sector trade unions enjoyed great political power and influence, and Britain became notorious for its industrial strife. Unlike in Germany, where small, independent companies enjoyed the support of local governments and banks, Britain imposed punitive taxes on the incomes of individuals and firms.

In France, the basic price control legislation of 1945 remained in force, with modifications, throughout the 1950s and '60s, and the government was able to impose controls at any time. The 1950s were characterized by alternating periods of liberalization and stiffening of price controls. In the first four-year plan, the government intervened to develop the coal, electricity, steel, cement, transport and agricultural machinery industries. These were either nationalized or threatened with nationalization. The French forced small firms to merge into large publicly controlled enterprises, and their workforces were often controlled by the French Communist Party, which in turned was controlled and financed by huge subsidies from Moscow.

Much the same happened in Italy, and other economies in Europe struggled to find their way. Hungary, for instance, experienced the worst bout of hyperinflation in history. The 25 billion pengö in circulation in July 1945 rose to 1.646 trillion by January 1946, to 65 quadrillion (million billions) by May 1946 and to 47 septillion (trillion trillions) by July 1946. At the height of the inflation, prices were rising at a daily rate of 200 per cent. By then, the government had stopped collecting taxes altogether because even a single day's delay wiped out the value of the money the government collected. By 1949, the monetary collapse had been overtaken by events because the Moscow-backed Hungarian Socialist Workers' Party had taken over the government completely. All over Eastern Europe, Moscow-backed parties established systems of single-party rule.

Other explanations can be devised for West Germany's success. One is falling back on national stereotypes: the Germans are by nature industrious, efficient and disciplined and so were bound to do better. This argument was undone, though, because Germany was divided, making it the equivalent of a controlled experiment in economics. One part was transformed by Erhard's price liberalization, and the other by the adoption of the Stalinist model. As we now know, West Germany powered far ahead, but for decades the West believed that the East Germans were just as industrious and efficient.

In the 1950s, CIA estimates stated that the West German economy grew at an average of 7 per cent a year while East Germany's grew at 6.5 per cent. In the 1960s, the CIA claimed that East Germany was even growing faster than West Germany—4.7 to 3.3 per cent. The intelligence agency's belief that the East Germans were out-performing the West Germans extended throughout the post-war period. In 1986, the CIA claimed that on a per capita basis, the East Germans had been more productive than the West Germans. The CIA later recognized that while the East German economy was not doing so well in the 1980s, the East Germans were nearly as productive as the West Germans. The *Handbook of Economic Statistics* published by the Directorate of Intelligence claimed that West German per capita GDP was only 32 per cent greater than East Germany.[4]

These projections were cruelly exposed after 1989. Not only was the East German state bankrupt, but none of its enterprises could produce any goods that were competitive in the international market. They had to be closed down, and when sold off, they fetched very little. It has since been estimated that East Germany's productivity was a lowly quarter of West Germany's, although it is impossible to know the truth about East Germany's economic performance for the same reasons that finances were so murky in the Soviet, Chinese and all the other planned economies. East German statistics were routinely falsified by toadies so that even their leaders struggled to understand how badly the country was doing.

German academic Peter von der Lippe gives some examples in a paper, 'The Political Role of Official Statistics in the Former GDR (East Germany)'. At one point, the East German statistics bureau confidently told the Central Committee that the GDR's per capita national income had outstripped the United Kingdom and Italy in terms of both labour productivity *and* prosperity. Even in 1985, it was claiming that labour productivity was better than Japan's. Von der Lippe's paper also reveals how routinely the East Germans falsified the trade statistics that they reported to international bodies like the UN. The East Germans claimed large trade surpluses when in reality they were running huge trade deficits. Even when they were not intentionally falsified, East German trade data was fundamentally meaningless because it was measured in the Valuta Mark, the hard currency mark, whose value in relation to the internal mark was a mystery and whose exchange rate with the value of the Deutsche Mark was set arbitrarily.

Since CIA analysts generally accepted these bogus exchange rates, this led to an inflated estimate of the size of the East German economy and its competitiveness. West German research institutes such as the DIW (Deutsches Institute für Wirtschaftsforschung) adopted the same uncritical course, as did the West German intelligence service, the BND (Bundesnachrichtendienst), which from 1969 onwards used statistics supplied by East Germany as the basis for all its reports. It should be noted that other Comecon countries were overvalued too. In 1988, the CIA thought that the per capita output of Czechoslovakia was 78 per cent of the Netherlands, for example.[5]

The difference between East and West Germany should have been obvious for a simple reason. When those in East Germany noticed how much better life was in the West, they began leaving in ever larger numbers. When the Iron Curtain was still going up, this was easy enough to do. Any East German just had to make their way to Berlin and walk over. The harsh Sovietization of the economy and the general repression led to a popular uprising in 1953 that was only put down by Soviet tanks. The loss of hope led more to flee their homes until East Germany had no choice but to erect the Berlin Wall. By the time it went up in 1961, 3.5 million East Germans had voted with their feet and left the country.

From the late 1960s onwards, the East German government and its flailing economy began to rely ever more heavily on financial transfers, hidden subsidies and direct transfers from the West Germans. The same socialist failures drove other Eastern Europeans to revolt. The East German uprising was followed three years later by another in Hungary, and then in 1968 came the suppression of the Prague Spring. Yet experts and analysts in Germany believed that all these protests had to stem from the lack of human rights and political freedoms in the Soviet bloc. The answer was therefore détente, an effort to encourage political liberalization. Such attempts at placating their weakened enemies would prolong the suffering of their eastern neighbours for several more decades.

17

FAKE STATISTICS LED TO DÉTENTE

The most damaging consequence of Bergson misunderstanding Soviet economic data was the false credibility it gave to détente, a policy that needlessly prolonged the life of the Soviet Union and its East European satellites for two decades.

Based on the misunderstanding of Soviet bloc economies, the Americans and their NATO allies became convinced that communism was here to stay for two reasons: it created an economic system that, as Bergson's statistics showed, was manifestly successful at raising living standards. Secondly, most Europeans came to believe that once a Leninist dictatorship was established, it was unlikely to be overthrown. So, in the interests of peace and security, the logical step was to seek an accommodation with the Soviet bloc. In practice, this meant buying Soviet oil and gas and selling it desperately needed grain at subsidized prices and granting extensive loans and trade concessions to East European countries. This aid arrived in the late 1960s and early '70s, just in time to stave off fresh uprisings in Eastern Europe and convince Soviet leaders they could afford to step up military spending.

Détente came in two flavours. The American kind was led by Republican President Richard Nixon and his national security advisor, Henry Kissinger. This process involved high-level summits, arms-reduction treaties and bilateral trade deals with Moscow, along with a secret high-level engagement with the near senile Chairman Mao. The European variety was a left-wing phenomenon not welcomed by the Americans. It was led by West Germany's Social Democratic party leader, Willy Brandt, and was called Ostpolitik. Egon Bahr, Brandt's chief advisor, described it as 'change through rapprochement' (*Wandel durch Annaehrung*), but it later became known under the snappier phrase *Wandel durch Handel*—or change through exchange—meaning trade.[1]

By the late 1970s, détente was under attack from the right, and it was abandoned by President Reagan, who believed that the Soviet Union could be defeated. When he went to Berlin, he called on Gorbachev to 'tear down this Wall'. When it did come down in 1989, some claimed that Ostpolitik engagement had undermined East Germany from within. Although the right did not agree, the strategy of *Wandel durch Handel* has since been tried with China and various rogue regimes ranging from North Korea to Iran but without success.

In essence, the American and German flavours of détente were quite similar. Exhausted by the burden of fighting costly wars in Korea and then in Vietnam, and by the massive effort to bridge the 'missile gap' with the Soviet Union, Americans were ready to try a different tack. The Germans had their own motives for engagement with the East: to atone for the horrors inflicted by Hitler's invasion and occupation. Simultaneously, they sought a reconciliation with their Eastern neighbours in order to find a path to re-unify the country.

When European leaders formulated their policies towards the Soviet bloc, they relied heavily on the intelligence reports provided by the United States, especially the CIA. Britain had the best independent assessments, although there was an unusual degree of cooperation between the American and British intelligence services. The British were the only allies who had an office in the CIA headquarters at Langley. During the last years of the Cold War, the annual budget for the British secret services reached 1 billion dollars, far short of the 28 billion dollars the US spent. It employed under 10,000 staff, and MI6, the overseas intelligence arm, employed 2,000 people, a sizeable number but a fraction of the resources that the CIA could command. It had a network of agents behind the Iron

Curtain but soon lost them when their identities were betrayed by various double agents.[2]

British leaders were advised by the Joint Intelligence Committee, which brought together all available intelligence from different sources. British academia, the foreign office and the military, however, never really questioned the Bergson/CIA view of the Soviet economy. The focus was on opposing the military threat and supporting the Americans.

Across the Channel, French presidents like Charles de Gaulle, Georges Pompidou and François Mitterrand largely relied on the opinions of their ambassadors in Moscow. After the Second World War, the small French intelligence service worked under American influence, but after the 1962 Cuban Missile Crisis, President de Gaulle ordered the newly formed intelligence body, the Service de Documentation Extérieure et de Contre-Espionnage (SDECE), to stop cooperating with the CIA. He thought the Americans were exaggerating the Soviet threat. In turn, the Americans believed the French government was riddled with communist agents. After Mitterrand was elected in 1981, he included French communists in his government. The SDECE never employed more than a dozen people to cover the Soviet Union. When Pierre Marion became its head in 1981, it did not have a single agent in the USSR. Instead, he said it relied on its station in Warsaw and what the Americans shared. 'I generally accepted the CIA's views about what was happening in the USSR', Marion said.[3]

The Italians also lacked sources to make their own assessments of what was going on behind the Iron Curtain and followed the American lead. Moreover, the CIA was heavily involved in financing the Italian intelligence services, partly because the Italian Communist Party, the largest in Western Europe, was heavily funded by Moscow. Because Italy was a key NATO ally, the CIA were alarmed, first by the extensive influence of the Party and later by the rise of the Red Brigades, one of the ultra-left terrorist organizations that sprang up in the 1970s. Between 1945 and 1948, the United States dispensed 75 million USD to Italian intelligence services, while the Soviets subsidized the Italian Communist Party to the tune of around 1 billion USD.[4]

The Germans were the best placed to make independent observations about Eastern Europe, given their close ties with East

Germany. Yet the BND also relied heavily on the CIA and failed to predict the end of East Germany and the collapse of the Soviet Union. Hans-Georg Wieck, the BND president in the second half of the 1980s, said: 'We worked with the CIA and got from them processed information about the USSR.' After the Wall came down, it turned out that almost all the BND agents in East Germany were double agents feeding back false information. Even more humiliating, the Stasi had infiltrated West German government agencies and had spies working everywhere in the chancellor's offices. The Stasi ran a huge intelligence machine with larger budgets and more staff than any of its West European counterparts. Yet it too failed to anticipate the events that ultimately doomed it.[5]

When Erhard was German chancellor in the early 1960s, however, he recognized the economic weakness of the Soviet Union. He offered Khrushchev loans worth 25 billion USD in exchange for political freedom in Eastern Europe. Nothing came of the deal because Khrushchev was removed from power in 1964. However, West Germany started the business of buying East German political prisoners for hard currency. These deals were negotiated by Jürgen Stange, a lawyer based in West Berlin. At first, the going price was 800 DM per prisoner, and it rose to 1,000 DM the following year. By the early 1970s, the price had jumped to 40,000 DM per head, and in 1977 it reached 95,847 DM. Tens of thousands were able to leave East Germany in this way.[6]

Much of the hard currency was transferred to a special bank account personally controlled by the East German leader, Erich Honecker. It was used to finance the import of consumer goods, mostly for the East German elite, such as the import of French Citroën cars for the families of top officials. Honecker also used the money to cover the cost of the state's thirtieth anniversary celebrations in 1979. By the end of the Cold War, the West Germans had transferred some 3.5 billion DM. Although this was never mentioned, it was similar to the Nazis' trade in Jewish lives before 1939. The regime held its own citizens to ransom when they tried to flee and then sought to blackmail overseas Jewish communities.[7]

East Germany not only extracted money from its West German counterpart; it also benefitted from getting rid of trouble-makers, which improved domestic political stability. It encouraged other communist states to follow suit. North Korea also tried a policy of family reunions in the 1970s as it took out foreign loans. China allowed family members to leave if their overseas relatives made donations. When in the 1970s the Soviet Union was seeking Western loans, it agreed to allow Jewish emigration.

The worse the East German economy performed, the more dependent it became on extracting ever greater amounts of cash. The West Germans started making payments for the reunification of families, including children separated from their parents by the building of the Wall, and for visits by East Germans to see their families. Welcome money was paid to every East German visitor, which totalled 2 billion DM over the twenty years from 1970 to 1989. The accompanying visa fees and compulsory exchange of currencies at favourable exchange rates were worth another 5 billion DM, not to mention lump sum payments to cover the real or alleged postal costs of sending presents from West to East. The total value of all these direct and indirect transfers to private citizens amounted to an estimated 30–40 billion DM.[8]

Even more important for the East German economy were the trade concessions. West Germany allowed duty-free access for East German goods and an interest-free overdraft facility, the so-called Swing Credit. Commercial bank loans were also made, such as the 1 billion DM loan in the summer of 1983 and another 950 million DM in the summer of 1984.

It is likely that the West Germans provided a staggering sum of 50 billion DM from 1972 to 1989, creating a crippling level of economic dependency. Yet somehow, the West Germans failed to grasp how bankrupt the East German economy was. Even so, by 1989 the East German leadership was told that its net debts were 49 billion Valuta Marks, a figure calculated on an arbitrary exchange rate. The real final net debt was more like $20 billion. A memorandum to the East German Politburo predicted that the net debt could soar to 57 billion Valuta Marks by the end of 1990.[9]

In the end, the GDR collapsed because it could not service its growing hard currency debts, which amounted to over 40 billion DM. In October 1989, a paper prepared for the Politburo, named the Schurer-Papier after its principal author, explained that the country needed to increase its export surplus from around 2 billion DM in 1990 to over 11 billion DM by 1995, which was next to impossible. The truth was that East Germany's export performance was composed of the re-export of Soviet oil. It imported the oil at 'friendship prices' and re-exported it at world market prices. That was all very well until the Soviet Union's economic problems deepened and in 1981 it halted the transfer of cheap oil. East Germany could no longer rely on the arbitrage profit from the difference in internal and external prices.

The Ostpolitik engagement policy was intended to bring about gradual change in the East German regime. Actions such as diplomatic recognition of the GDR was supposed to boost its status and make the East German Communist Party feel less fearful of dissent and reform. An aggressive posture by the West encouraged, or even forced, the communist leaders in the Eastern bloc to adopt an equally aggressive posture, not only towards the West but also towards their own people. Instead of softening these regimes, it hardened them. 'Increasing tension strengthens [East German leader] Ulbricht and deepens the division', as Egon Bahr, one of its architects, said in a speech made in Tutzing in 1963. If overthrowing a communist regime was impractical—as the crushing of popular uprisings in East Germany in 1953, Hungary in 1956, and Czechoslovakia in 1968 seemed to show—then perversely it might be better to support these regimes. In practical terms, the loans and transfers artificially raised living standards in the East, without which there would have been even more unrest, more repression and more human rights abuses. This led many on the left into the morally dubious position of refusing to support East European dissidents who were risking their lives to fight for more political freedom—that one could best help dissidents in East Germany by not helping them, as writer Timothy Garton Ash put it.[10]

When the Polish Solidarity movement emerged in 1980, Western political leaders and intellectuals were unsure whether they wanted to support it because it would jeopardize détente. So Mitterrand, a keen supporter of détente, was against supporting Lech Wałęsa. Reagan, by contrast, had no qualms in backing him.

Ostpolitik must be judged a failure because it never led to any changes in East Germany. It remained a hard-line communist regime to the end. Indeed, it could be argued that it ensured that it was almost the only East European state that never dabbled in any kind of economic reform. The West German subsidies ensured that it could afford to avoid making any concessions. It had enough money to subsidize food prices, housing and consumer goods for citizens. The investments made with the money borrowed from the West never produced any meaningful returns. Perhaps, one could say that at least it made the East German elite aware that its economic system would not work no matter how much money was poured into it.

Détente allowed the communist governments of Poland, Hungary, Romania, Yugoslavia and others to take out hard currency loans and import Western technology. By 1980, Hungary owed $9 billion and Romania owed $13 billion, Poland $56 billion, but the capital was misspent. Without real prices to guide state planners, it could not properly be invested in projects that would provide real returns. So the debts could not be serviced. Romania's leader, Nicolae Ceaușescu, caused immense hardship to his own people by trying to repay that debt by exporting most of the country's agricultural and industrial output. It led to punitive food rationing and endless blackouts. Later, the population took revenge by executing Ceaușescu and his wife.[11]

As a book by Yegor Gaidar, Russian economist and reformer, points out, the Soviet Union eventually found itself in the same boat. The US–Soviet détente of the 1970s had only staved off the day of reckoning. As Gaidar writes in *The Story of Grain*, the USSR was doomed by its inability to feed itself, which followed from the extension of Stalinist agricultural policies towards Eastern Europe. When the small farmers in the agriculturally wealthy countries like Poland, Hungary, Bulgaria and Romania were forced out, food production fell quickly. The factors were not so much the loss of ownership and the collectivization of farming but the pricing policies. In the Soviet Union, the price of bread was lower than the cost of the wheat used to produce it. On collective farms, it was cheaper to feed the animals with bread than grain, because the bread cost less.[12]

After Stalin's death, Khrushchev had tried to tackle the food shortage by stepping up investment in agriculture and opening up more land in Central Asia to farming, the so-called Virgin Lands scheme. Khrushchev promised to overtake America in grain production. The grain harvest reached a record in 1956, but after 1959 harvests began to decline and could never keep up with the demand from the growing population moving to the cities. In the following quarter of a century, the urban population grew by 80 million, and it expected a better living standard, including a richer diet.[13]

By 1963, Khrushchev was obliged to write to the other leaders of the Soviet bloc and notify them that he could no longer supply them with grain. Next, the Soviets began importing grain. In 1972, Moscow had to buy 15 million tons of grain, spending a third of the country's gold reserves to do so. The Soviet Union's weakness placed it at the mercy of the Western powers. It had to gain their consent to buy the grain, and later it needed their cooperation in order either to pay for it with exports or by taking out loans. So in the atmosphere of détente, the Soviet Union signed an agreement with the United States to buy \$136 million of wheat and \$126 million of drilling equipment. In return, Brezhnev agreed to help President Nixon by pushing North Vietnam into negotiations that were supposed to bring an end to the Vietnam War.[14]

Moscow had to keep coming back to the West for more grain. There were seven bad harvests from 1979 onwards. Grain imports nearly doubled in a decade from 15 to 28 million tons. In 1981, imports totalled 30 million tons, and in 1984 the Soviet Union needed 28 million tons solely of wheat.[15]

The Russian Revolution had partly been started by a bread shortage, and the Party was concerned to make sure always to supply enough bread. When in 1962 workers in the city of Novocherkassk found out that the government had suddenly raised food prices by 30 per cent, they took to the streets and troops opened fire, killing or wounding over 100 people. After that, Moscow was too scared to hike the price of bread. By 1985, Gorbachev found himself in an impossible position: the food shortages kept worsening, but he had no mandate to take the kinds of steps necessary to boost output by raising prices and restoring private farming.

He could import more food, but only if oil prices remained high. His predecessors had benefitted from the oil and gas export revenues following the discovery of the huge deposits in Western Siberia. Oil production shot up twelvefold in the 1970s, benefitting not only the Soviet Union but also its allies everywhere. Oil prices quadrupled after the 1973 Yom Kippur War and the resultant oil embargo. This allowed Brezhnev to change direction, stepping up arms spending such as by building a huge fleet and by financing all kinds of 'adventurism' in the Third World.

The Soviet Union then began building a huge gas pipeline all the way to Western Europe. To do this, it needed drills, pipes and know-how, as well as Western bank loans to pay for these imports. Under détente, the Americans and Europeans, notably the Germans, were ready to help. By 1979, the Americans had lost faith in détente. Russia hadn't really helped in Vietnam. Instead it had funded the onward march of communist regimes around the world. Then, in December 1979, came the final straw. Moscow sent its forces into Afghanistan.

President Reagan came to power with a new ambition: to bring down the Soviet Union. In September 1985, the Saudi oil minister, Sheikh Ahmed Yamani, changed the price of oil by quadrupling exports, causing international prices to collapse. The Soviet Union immediately lost revenues of around $20 billion a year. Gorbachev was now confronted with unpalatable choices: drastically cut food imports by the same amount or go to the West and bargain for loans. In any case, he was forced to start demanding payment in hard currency for the oil and gas delivered at friendship prices to his allies in Eastern Europe. They in turn were forced into the same corner. If the Soviet Union or its allies had been able to manufacture goods that would sell on the international market, they could have survived. Or if they were able to produce a surplus of agricultural goods. Instead, Moscow and its allies faced a Hobson's choice: either undertake radical price reforms, or reintroduce tough food rationing. Either way, Gorbachev risked provoking massive unrest that would bring down the state. Or he could have radically cut the massive military budget, but the military–industrial complex was so politically powerful this was not possible either.

Instead, Gorbachev talked about reforms but undertook very little of substance. He borrowed heavily between 1985 and 1988, because the Soviet Union was judged a good credit risk, but the money was soon gone. As Gorbachev became more reliant on Western support, he became more reluctant to authorize any crackdown against political opposition. He could not allow an East Bloc ally to impose martial law the way the Poles had done in December 1981 when confronted by Solidarity. His Western creditors would cut him off.

When its economy began to stall completely in 1989, the Soviet Union tried to persuade a consortium of 300 banks to provide a large loan. Gorbachev thought he needed 100 billion dollars to prop up his economy and soon realized that such vast sums could only be obtained in exchange for making huge geopolitical concessions. As people in Poland, East Germany and elsewhere grasped that Gorbachev could not send in the tanks as had been done so often in the past, they took to the streets. The bankrupt governments of East Germany, Poland and the rest could do nothing on their own.

Hungary found itself in such a grave financial position that when East Germans began flooding into the country in August 1989, its foreign minister, Gyula Horn, secretly flew to Bonn. He asked for 1 billion DM in exchange for opening the frontiers. Soon after, East Germany collapsed. He got half that sum.[16]

The Soviet Union bargained away East Germany in exchange for badly needed cash and supplies of meat and grain. In September 1989, Gorbachev haggled with West German leader Helmut Kohl and secured 12 billion DM plus a further 3 billion to cover the cost of the 350,000-strong Soviet garrison in East Germany. In October, Honecker resigned after Moscow refused to intervene and stop the exodus. In November, the Wall opened. In January 1990, at Gorbachev's request, Chancellor Kohl provided the Soviet Union with more aid as negotiations opened over the question of German unification. Kohl provided about 220 million DM in food subsidies, 160,000 tons of meat and a loan of 5 billion DM. The total amount West Germany ultimately paid to the Kremlin for reunification is unknown, although it's usually estimated at between 50 and 80 billion DM or $31–50 billion. Ironically, this was roughly the sum that Erhard had wanted to offer Khrushchev back in 1963, allowing for inflation.

The drama in Germany turned out to be the opening act before the Soviet Union itself disintegrated. Gorbachev and his advisors simply couldn't raise enough money or import enough food to solve the country's economic shortages. The faith in détente only came to an end when the Soviet Union went bankrupt.

18

HOW MISES' IDEAS CHANGED EASTERN EUROPE AND RUSSIA

The Russian Revolution began amid bread riots and ended pretty much the same way seventy-four years later. In late 1990, there was almost no food left to buy in the shops in major cities. The grain shortage had become acute. Gorbachev's foreign policy advisor, Anatoly Chernyaev, recalls in his diaries how in March 1991 he warned: 'If [the grain] cannot be obtained somewhere, famine may come by June ... Moscow has probably never seen anything like that throughout its history—even in its hungriest years.'[1]

Everyone, even the elite, had to queue for hours to buy bread or milk. By 1991, the Soviet Union had $66 billion in foreign debts and had gone bust. The state had sold off all its gold reserves, and only $100 million was left in the foreign currency reserves. According to Gaidar, the document that effectively brought down the curtain on the Soviet Union was a letter from the Vnesheconombank, the Soviet foreign trade bank, which in November 1991 informed the Soviet leadership they had not a cent in its coffers. No foreign bank or state was prepared to lend Gorbachev the vast sums required to keep the Soviet Union afloat.

When Gorbachev came to power in 1985, the situation did not seem threatening. The Soviet Union had foreign currency debts of only

$14.2 billion. Gosplan told him that it expected economic growth of 2.5–2.8 per cent a year through to the end of the century. These estimates were based on the usual false data, so when Gorbachev discussed economic reform with his colleagues, the governing idea was to adjust a few things so that the old command economy would work better. He did not consider radical price reforms because he feared that allowing food prices to rise quickly would lead to riots.

After the Berlin Wall opened in November 1989, Gorbachev tried to juggle three policies: borrowing money abroad to pay for food imports, restoring the economy with (four) half-hearted economic reform plans and cutting back the size of the military–industrial complex. In May 1990, he embraced a more radical '500 day' reform programme, which in reality was a mere rehash of a 1989 reform package. Within a year, Gorbachev had retreated from these price reforms, but the damage had been done. These various programmes had weakened the rigid controls over the Soviet republics and over the state enterprises. Factory managers freed from the discipline of central planning began raising prices and wages on their own initiative. The fifteen union republics increasingly stopped sending their tax revenues to Moscow. As inflation took hold, the chronic shortages of basic goods were exacerbated by hoarding. People's rouble savings became worth less and less. Amid the crisis of confidence, an estimated $20 billion secretly left the country. By the end of 1991, the Soviet Union had debts of $56.5 billion that it could no longer service.

The Soviet Union found itself in a position resembling that of the defeated nations of both the First and the Second World Wars. It had a war economy, a worthless currency, price controls, food shortages and political and ethnic unrest. Of course, there were major differences: no cities in ruins, no defeated army and no refugees. It was entirely an economic defeat and no less humiliating for that. In August 1991, a group of communist hard-liners had tried to stop the inevitable by placing Gorbachev under house arrest in an attempted coup, but the effort failed when it became apparent that they had no means to salvage the failing economy. Sending in tanks was simply not an answer to the shortages of food. The plotters gave up in the end because they had no fresh ideas on how to reverse a collapse that had gone beyond the point of no return. Whereas in 1918 and 1945, most countries had sought solutions in centralized state control of the economy, whether it was democratic socialism or Leninist dictatorship, this time round the result was very different. The challenges were met by leaders who nakedly embraced the ideas of the Austrian school.

The initiative was seized by a few economists, mostly in their thirties, who had read Mises and grasped that freeing prices was the key to reform. They believed this should not be done gradually. The worse the situation, the more radical the reforms must be. The crash programme of price reform became known as 'shock therapy'.

In some ways, countries like Russia and Poland had no alternative. Everyone understood that no one had the will or the desire to impose strict rationing under the force of a severe dictatorship followed by a return to central planning. No one wanted to follow China's example, which in 1989 sent in tanks to massacre student protestors, followed by purges and a perma-freeze of political and personal freedoms.

The economists knew that any all-out privatization and price liberalization by the first post-Soviet government was a kamikaze mission. The immediate result would be mass unemployment and sky-high inflation for which they would be blamed. Still, they opted for it in the belief that the pain would be short-lived.

The Russian reforms undertaken by Boris Yeltsin followed the ideas of a youthful team headed by Yegor Gaidar. Immediately after Gorbachev resigned, Yeltsin plunged into price reform. On 2 January 1992, he freed 90 per cent of all wholesale and retail prices from state control. Prices immediately rocketed ten- to twelvefold, and inflation soared to 600 per cent a year. Overnight, Russians found their life-long rouble savings were worthless. Yeltsin had made the thirty-five-year old economist his prime minister, but with the growing unrest Gaidar knew his days were numbered. Yeltsin fired him in December. He took it with equanimity. As he explained on Russian television: 'It is well known that the first government that starts a price liberalization almost always has to resign. There is nothing terrible in this fact by itself, because it is obvious that something has to be done and somebody has to pay a political price for this.'

Gaidar had already seen what had happened in Poland and was therefore confident that prices would soon stabilize. The change-over was more difficult for the Polish reformers, but they had had much longer to prepare a plan. The leading Polish economist behind the first post-communist government led by Solidarity leader Lech Wałęsa was Leszek Balcerowicz. He had started preparing reforms back in 1980 during the roundtable negotiations between Solidarity and the Polish communist government. The Solidarity movement created a huge demand for reform proposals, and a team around Balcerowicz worked on them for two years. Then came the declaration of martial law. Balcerowicz had graduated from the foreign trade faculty of the Central School of Planning and Statistics in Warsaw, perhaps the most liberal economics department in the Warsaw Pact, where he had a chance to study Western textbooks on international economics. Then he went to America for further studies at St. John's University in New York before returning home to work for his doctorate. As he recalled many years later in *The Great Rebirth: Lessons from the Victory of Capitalism over Communism*:

> In the early 1980s, I studied the debate on the efficiency of socialism (the socialist calculation debate). I was struck by the naiveté of the 'socialist side', represented by Oskar Lange et al., and the reasonableness of the anti-socialist camp, represented by Ludwig von Mises and Friedrich Hayek. I fully shared von Mises's ironic prediction that the effective reform of socialism entails a return to capitalism. Also in the 1980s, I became very interested in 'growth miracles', especially in South Korea and Taiwan, and I studied the relevant literature. The popular view was that a special kind of state intervention was behind the phenomenal catching-up of these and other countries. I, however, came to the conclusion that the true reason was an unusual accumulation of growth fundamentals, such as predominantly private ownership, a higher rate of saving and investment, low fiscal burdens, and an export orientation.[2]

He also went to West Germany in 1988, and after studying Ludwig Erhard's 1948 reforms, he concluded that his reforms would have to be even more comprehensive. 'Under the war economy of

Germany capitalism was only suspended, whereas socialism entailed the destruction of its institutions.' In the spring of 1989, he wrote a paper outlining radical policy recommendations for Poland. 'I had no idea that a few months later I would be in charge of Poland's stabilization and transformation program', he later said. Until then, he had never been in charge of anything larger than a seminar. Three days into the job, he discovered that the situation was worse than he had expected—the previous government had spent the hard currency savings in the state banks.[3]

All along, he and his colleagues had assumed that the one-party state would endure along with the Soviet Union. When Solidarity won the June 1989 elections, he became minister of finance and deputy premier. The price reform started in September 1989. The new government slashed state subsidies to heavy industries including coal, electricity and petroleum. Around 1.1 million workers at state-owned firms lost their jobs and 20 per cent became unemployed. The economy shrank by nearly 10 per cent, and inflation peaked at 640 per cent. Growth returned in 1992, and more than 600,000 private companies were set up, creating about 1.5 million jobs. Change was especially drastic in the countryside. In the ten years until 2000, Poland enjoyed the highest annual growth rates of any post-communist economy. GDP doubled between 1989 and 2013.[4]

The Russians also learned from Czechoslovakia's privatization programme. Reformers there had started thinking about changes in the 1960s, which culminated in the Prague Spring of 1968. Although in the crackdown that followed, the Czechs and Slovaks lived under a very rigid government, they continued to read the works of Mises and Hayek and other members of the Austrian school. The communist regime resigned in November 1989, just after the fall of the Berlin Wall, in the face of a relatively brief series of student-led protests. Demonstrators gathered and 'jingled' their keys to show they wanted to open the door to change. It was called the Velvet Revolution. On 29 December, the dissident playwright Václav Havel became president, and national elections followed in June 1990. The first finance minister, Václav Klaus, and one of the chief founders of the victorious centre-right party Civic Forum, immediately argued for radical reforms.

Like Balcerowicz, Klaus had studied economics, especially foreign trade, and had the chance to continue his studies abroad, first in Italy and then the United States. He described how in the period leading to the 1968 Prague Spring, intellectuals

> discovered the famous dispute about socialism, the so-called socialist calculation debate, between the Austrian economists Ludwig von Mises and F. A. Hayek on one side and the socialists Oskar Lange and Abba P. Lerner on the other, during the 1930s. This debate gave us many powerful arguments about the impossibility of economic calculation under socialism and about the futility of the idea of playing at markets instead of introducing a real market.
>
> The real revelation came when we came across Hayek's article, 'The Use of Knowledge in Society', originally published in 1945. You may ask how it was possible to get access to such articles in a totalitarian communist regime. Yet, it was possible. We scholars couldn't get our hands on the *Wall Street Journal*, *Newsweek*, or *Time*, but in the libraries of academic institutions we could get the *American Economic Review* and similar journals. They were sufficiently scientific as to be incomprehensible for the communist censors. Even now, I give this article to my students as the best introduction to rational economic thinking. The impossibility of centralizing dispersed knowledge is one of the most important ideas in economic science, comparable to the classic formulations of Adam Smith.[5]

Underground studies of Hayek's *The Road to Serfdom*, which was illegally and unofficially translated in the 1960s, was considered, he said, 'as a decisive and final rejection of all kinds of totalitarianism, collectivism, and interventionism and as an authoritative defence of liberty'.

The dismantling of the communist system of state controls followed much the same course as in Poland and elsewhere. GDP fell drastically in the first three years but then started to grow again in 1993. The country split into two—the Czech Republic and Slovakia—on 1 January 1993, so the statistics are a little confusing, but overall the two countries showed the same pattern of growth.

The Czechs avoided the kind of hyperinflation seen in Russia and Poland, and the annual rate never exceeded 10 per cent. What was distinctive about the Czech way of reform was the recognition of the urgency of immediately and smoothly establishing a private sector. Almost uniquely among communist countries, Czechoslovakia had almost no private sector because after the crushing of the Prague Spring in 1968 there had been no attempt at any reforms. Its situation was therefore quite different from, say, Hungary, Poland or Yugoslavia.

As Klaus explained:

> We had many reasons to believe that the speed of privatisation was an asset, not a liability. We did not want to leave the suddenly 'parentless' firms uncontrolled. Nor did we want them to become objects of spontaneous privatization by former managers appointed by the communist rulers. We were not interested in the size of the privatization proceeds, because our goals were different. Our aim was structural change—to privatize the whole economy.[6]

Unlike in Britain, the main goal was not to raise revenue for the state by selling off a few big firms but to quickly change the economic system and transfer the ownership of thousands of firms. There was no way of finding a market value for these firms because there was no market operating. As with East German firms, their products would probably not be going to find buyers in an open marketplace. Apart from a few firms sold directly to foreign or Czech buyers, the rest were disposed of by using a special voucher or coupon privatization method. The state-owned companies were turned into joint-stock companies. Next, Czech citizens over eighteen bought so-called voucher booklets that were sold for a price equivalent to the average weekly salary. These gave 8.5 million citizens a form of investment capital, which they used to buy and sell company shares. As Klaus recalls:

> Then we started a very sophisticated buying and selling process of shares for vouchers, which was fully computerized. It was one of the biggest computerized games in the history of mankind.

Eight million people participated. In the first round of buying we discovered excess demand for some shares, and an excess supply for some others. Then came the second round where we changed the prices. It took four rounds to find an equilibrium. It was done twice in a total time frame of three years.[7]

The voucher privatization method was used for less than a quarter of all the firms privatized. In the end, privatization funds held two-thirds of all the shares and individuals held the rest. By and large, the Czechs felt they had achieved their goal of a quick and fundamental change of the system that set them on the path to political and democratic stability plus economic growth. Klaus believed that any country had to embark on simultaneous privatization and liberalization of prices and foreign trade, market exchange rates and the end of all subsidies. Others argued that it was better to carry out gradual change, an optimal sequencing of reform measures, which required planning, preparation and the establishment of new institutions.

In Moscow, Gaidar and the rest of the team around Yeltsin studied what the Poles had achieved and what the Czechs were doing. The Russians knew they had to make the most of this extraordinary period of politics to push through the privatization of state-owned firms. They borrowed the voucher idea from Prague, but instead of selling the vouchers they were given to the public freely.

Unlike Gorbachev, Yeltsin in 1991 grasped that the situation required extraordinary measures, and he was prepared to do the unthinkable. Yet there is little to suggest that Yeltsin himself studied the Austrian economists or knew much about markets and prices. While Thatcher and Reagan had read books by Hayek, Friedman and Mises, the top Russian reformers seem not to have explored economic theory. Yeltsin had to be persuaded by his advisor Gennadii Burbulis, a friend from his political base in Sverdlovsk. Burbulis urged Yeltsin to adopt the proposals drawn up by a small group of young economists in their mid-thirties led by Gaidar and Anatoly Chubais.[8]

'We had already formed a group of young economists in St. Petersburg in the 1980s. We studied the history of reforms—Lenin's New Economic Policy, and the reforms in Yugoslavia, Poland and Hungary. We also read the works of Western economists, which were banned at the time. If state security had known what we were doing, we would have paid a heavy price', Chubais said in an interview with *Der Spiegel* in 1997.[9]

Those in the study group included Alexei Kudrin, who would become finance minister; Sergei Ignatyev, later the head of the central bank; and liberal economist Vitaly Naishul, who proposed the concept of the privatization vouchers. However, even the members of this study group never imagined that they would one day be planning the complete destruction of the Soviet economy. Instead, they were mostly concerned with looking at ways to improve the management of state-run enterprises. The Russians were therefore quite unlike the economists in many East European countries, which over the past forty years had thought about the reforms tried at various times in Poland, Hungary, Czechoslovakia or Yugoslavia.

Chubais, who later supervised the privatization programme, was initially against the voucher system but later advocated rapid privatization, only in order to raise revenue, as had been done in Hungary. In the end, Yeltsin decided to seize the day. He would use his popularity to destroy the old system and break the power of the *nomenklatura*. If they waited, these vested interests would organize themselves and fight back. At the time, he also argued that it was a necessity because a de facto privatization was already taking place thanks to the reforms that Gorbachev had started. The existing directors took control of state enterprises and started running them for their own personal profit. For instance, the former Ministry of Natural Gas converted itself into the Gazprom Corporation. 'Privatization in Russia has been going on for a long time, but wildly, spontaneously, often in criminal fashion', Yeltsin declared in 1991. So now there had to be a legal and transparent distribution of state property.[10]

Chubais said in 1997:

In early 1992 there were only two possible scenarios. One was already in place: The director of a state-owned enterprise and a relative sign a lease for a plant with an option to purchase it. He pays rent for three months and then he buys the plant for a pittance. That was legal at the time. I saw hundreds of those kinds of contracts. There was only one way to stop this gradual privatization: distribute vouchers to all citizens.[11]

Chubais was put in charge of a committee to oversee the programme, which was officially initiated by a decree of President Boris Yeltsin on 19 August 1992. The committee worked out that the productive capacity of the Russian Federation was 1.2605 trillion roubles. Dividing this by the number of citizens, everybody was to get 8,467 roubles in the form of vouchers. Yet in the absence of a functioning marketplace, the committee or someone had to set a price for the value of any given enterprise or property. A shipyard in St Petersburg sold for 150 million roubles, while a children's store brought in 701 million roubles. The gigantic ZIL auto plant in Moscow was sold for 800,000 roubles. The Machinery Manufacturing Plant, the largest in the Soviet Union, and still the largest in Russia, employing 100,000 persons, was thought to be worth only 1.8 billion roubles, that is, just $2 million at the then prevailing exchange rate.[12]

The programme ran for two years, 1992–4, and roughly 150 million Russians picked up vouchers, which were made available at branches of the state banks. Yet as most people didn't really know the value of these shares, they quickly sold them for money rather than investing them. In Russia, workers and managers were given the option of acquiring a majority of the shares in their own firm, a concession that Chubais had felt obliged to make in order to get the law through the Russian Federal Assembly. The result was that 70 per cent of firms chose the insider buyout option, so the incumbent Party officials and managers usually ended up staying in control. This left the public feeling they had been deceived.

Chubais recalled:

> There were 400 privately licensed funds that had collected 40 million privatization checks, so-called vouchers. From those, we distributed a total of 144 million to the public. We thought that the funds were helping people to invest their vouchers wisely. The ordinary man on the street couldn't know, after all, whether gas, oil or machine production offered the best prospects. All 400 funds went bankrupt, and the vouchers of 40 million citizens became worthless. That's why 40 million Russians are convinced

that I am a scoundrel, a thief, a criminal or a CIA agent, who deserves to be shot, hanged or drawn and quartered.[13]

On the other hand, most of the assets did fall into private hands, and most commercial exchanges were thus conducted at market prices, even if a great deal of commerce had to take place as barter. With a market economy based on private ownership, Russia could then begin to attract the foreign investment it needed.

Yeltsin's programme had two serious shortcomings: he did not order a lustration, and he retained state controls over energy and raw materials, two vital sectors. Lustration means that any officials from a disgraced regime are barred from public posts. This precaution was taken in Hungary, the Czech Republic, Poland and other post-communist governments. In Russia, almost the opposite happened. Members of organizations like the Komsomol (the communist youth organization) and the KGB were able to use their connections to get permits and credits from the banks. The Yeltsin government established export taxes and quotas on the export of raw materials, which enabled a lucky few to pile up great profits by buying Russian commodities at the old domestic prices and exporting them at world market prices. 'The profit margin was often staggering', notes Michael Dobbs in his book *Down with Big Brother*.

The privatization of the oil sector was regulated by a presidential decree of November 1992. It created vertically integrated companies, joining some oil-producing enterprises and refineries into open-stock companies. Then, starting in 1994, the Yeltsin government began privatizing the former state oil companies. This time, the privatization method was a 'loans-for-shares' scheme in which the purpose was to raise money, some of which was earmarked for the 1996 presidential campaign. This was again run by Chubais, who disposed of the largest state industrial assets like Norilsk Nickel, Mechel, LUKoil, Sibneft, Surgutneftegas, Novolipetsk Steel and Yukos. These huge enterprises—some of them, like Norilsk Nickel, originally built with Gulag labour—were auctioned off for quite modest sums to people who could borrow money from commercial banks. It created a generation of so-called oligarchs like Boris Berezovsky, who bought oil giant Sibneft for $100 million, although it was soon worth $3 billion. Mikhail Khodorkovsky managed to obtain a 78 per cent share of ownership in Yukos, worth about $5 billion, for a mere $310 million. However, he later fell foul of Vladimir Putin and was sent to jail.[14]

Those Russian oligarchs who feared ending up in jail moved as much of their money abroad as possible. It all smacked of gross corruption and unfairness. Under the rule of Putin, the old communist elite entrenched themselves as vociferous opponents both to liberal capitalism and to Western values like free speech and democracy. They are determined to defend the history of Soviet Russia. At the same time, no one wants to reject private property and return to central planning and fixed state prices. Russians, rich and poor, are better off than they ever were under communism. Most enterprises are in private hands, and even the larger ones are managed better. Yet a general perception remains that Yeltsin's shock therapy was a failure.

Each of the Soviet bloc countries responded to the switch differently. Russia arguably faced the largest challenge. Communism had lasted much longer, and the pre-1914 market economy, such as it was, had been thoroughly destroyed. Private property was a crime, and market traders were criminals, so the shadow economy had been in the hands of a 'mafia' for a long time. The supply chains of Russian enterprises stretched across vast distances, and these were shattered when the Soviet Union broke up into disparate states. When Gorbachev resigned, many Russians struggled to obtain enough food, and many feared that anarchy or war was inevitable. Instead, the economic theories of Mises and his followers worked out better than one might have expected. The queues and shortages disappeared quite quickly, and the return of market prices allowed enterprises to thrive under private ownership. But could the attendant hardships of price reform and inflation have been avoided or mitigated?

Some scholars argue that that those countries that made the most complete break with communism have prospered far better than those who opted for more gradual, incremental reforms. Poland has clearly done much better than its neighbour Ukraine, although their economies were roughly the same size in 1989. Poland is richer, more stable and its citizens enjoy far more democratic freedoms. After voting to split from the Soviet Union in a 1991 referendum, Ukraine opted for gradual, piecemeal reforms. This led to a pattern of corruption and rent-seeking oligarchs and political instability, familiar in other countries that opted for gradualism. According to one estimate adjusted to purchasing power parity, the Polish economy grew by 6.61 per cent in 1990–6 while Ukraine's contracted by 58.55 per cent. By 2013, the difference was even starker. The Poles were three times as rich. According to World Bank figures, Polish per capita GDP was $21,100, while Ukraine's was estimated at $7,400. In 2015, a new Ukrainian government led by President Petro Poroshenko invited Leszek Balcerowicz to advise on accelerating economic reforms.[15]

China's record poses the biggest challenge to this theory. It stayed under Communist Party rule, along with only a handful of other hold-outs like Cuba, Vietnam and North Korea, but it vigorously pushed ahead with building what it confusingly called 'a socialist market economy'. After a relatively brief power struggle, a faction led by Deng Xiaoping seized power and after 1979 began to formalize a package of policies, the 'four modernizations', which Deng always insisted on referring to as 'reforms' rather than an admission that Maoist–Stalinism was a failure.

In some respects, these were strikingly similar to the policies that Igor Birman recommended for the Soviet Union. Deng ordered a huge and immediate cut to defence spending and the demobilization of millions of troops. Mao's vast military procurement orders were stopped, bringing work at many factories to a standstill. The equally vast Gulag (*laogai* in Chinese) economy was dismantled, and prisoners labouring in camps in the border regions were allowed home. Tens of millions of people returned to their homes in the coastal cities, and a re-urbanization of China began. Many factories built in the interior had to be relocated.

Deng also grasped that it was vital to improve food production and embraced—without acknowledging it—the policies of Nikolai Bukharin. He was helped by the fact that the retreat from socialism started almost immediately, and seemingly spontaneously, after the death of Chairman Mao Zedong in 1976. Peasants in Anhui province spontaneously began dividing up the fields between themselves and selling food surplus to state quotas on the market. This 'contract responsibility system' was a return to the policies adopted in 1961 to escape the famine of the Great Leap Forward. Peasants were contracted to grow a certain amount of grain for the state and were then free to sell anything else on the market. By 1984, the hated people's communes were formally dissolved. Peasants could now own private property, including homes, farm tools and livestock, but not the land they farmed. The salaried urban elite could find a way to spend their accumulated savings. China also started importing consumer goods, beginning with imports of black-and-white TV sets from South Korea, even though it did not recognize the country. The peasants began spending their cash on new homes, creating a demand for building materials and furniture. Rural enterprises that had stayed underground in the Mao era began to flourish.

All this enterprise took the Party by surprise, but it might never have stayed in power without it. China never had the option that the Soviet Union enjoyed of exporting oil and gas to pay for imports of grain and other essentials. Nor could it take out hard currency loans on any scale. It had almost no gold or foreign exchange reserves, but it had few foreign debts.[16] Its success in quickly boosting food production ensured that it was not so vulnerable to Western pressure when it faced a succession of domestic and international storms.

To attract foreign capital, China began pursuing a strategy of exploiting its surplus labour by putting it at the disposal of foreign businesses in special economic zones. These export processing zones were modelled on those already tried and tested in Taiwan and elsewhere. They in turn owed much to the foreign concessions that had flourished before 1937, when businesses could grow under special laws and tax regimes. Beijing hoped to attract the wealthy Shanghainese who had fled after 1949, losing most of their property. Although few of them dared return, gradually China did attract light industrial factories making apparel, shoes and electrical goods. This export processing business would eventually provide for half the country's exports and ease China's foreign exchange shortages.[17]

It is unclear if Deng initially knew how he was going to modernize China or how far he was going to stray from Marxism. Deng didn't talk about Mises, Hayek or Keynes, and like the other Party elders, he did not have any formal economic knowledge.

He famously said it did not matter if the cat was black or white as long as it caught mice. On the course of reforms, he said it was a case of 'feeling the stones to cross the river'. In 1979, China had few if any economists educated outside the communist world to advise the leadership. Instead, the leaders invited foreign economists to come and lecture, and they or their protégés went off to Japan and the tiger economies on study tours.

In particular, they invited economists from East European countries such as János Kornai from Hungary, Ota Šik from Czechoslovakia and others from Poland and Yugoslavia—all of whom could share their experiences of trying to break away from the Stalinist economic model and finding a 'third way'. Americans were also invited to lecture, including many who were or would be Nobel laureates: Milton Friedman, Gary Becker, Joseph Stiglitz and Lawrence Klein.

After 1979, the Chinese leaders were divided about how far they wanted to stray from central planning and state ownership. They were extremely nervous about the possibility of fuelling popular unrest among the young or testing the loyalty of officials returning to their jobs on state-owned enterprises after the 'chaos' of the Cultural Revolution. They sought advice from a handful of reform-minded Chinese economists such as Li Yining and Wu Jinglian and listened to a younger generation who were busy devouring all the economic books that had been forbidden in China for so many years. Li Yining was an advocate of the third way advocated by Oskar Lange and Abba Lerner. He believed that state prices could be adjusted to reflect shortages but later changed his mind and thought that Hayek and Mises were correct. Wu Jinglian had fewer reservations and wanted to push forward with privatization and price liberalization in one big step. His model was Ludwig Erhard in Germany.

Perhaps the most influential foreign voice in China at the time was the Hungarian economist János Kornai, who had broken with the Hungarian Party on moral grounds just before the 1956 Hungarian uprising. The Chinese translation of his short book, *The Economics of Shortage*, published in 1980, sold over 100,000 copies in

China. Kornai argued that the chronic shortages seen throughout the Eastern bloc were the consequences of systemic flaws rather than planning errors or the wrong prices. He was sceptical of efforts to create market socialism. Although he made little mention of the Austrian school, his ideas were very close to those of Mises. Kornai didn't think it was enough to remove centralized price controls because managers at state-owned firms did not really respond to price signals but to commands from above and to official quotas.

The outcome was a compromise. Instead of 'shock therapy', the Chinese Party chief, Hu Yaobang, adopted a dual price policy in 1984. State planners bought rice from the countryside at a fixed price and delivered it to urban consumers either with ration tickets or through sales at a fixed price. The state bought coal at a fixed price from state coal mines and delivered it to state power stations at a pre-determined price. At the same time, peasants sold grain at a market price, and locally run coal mines sold coal at free market prices. The price of essential goods was under tight control, but the so-called side-line goods, like fruit, vegetables, eggs and fish, could be bought or sold at free market prices. The idea was that the production of any item would gradually rise until it was safe to free the price. Even so, retail price inflation jumped 30 per cent in 1985.[18] Soon students took to the streets demanding political change, and their most effective line of attack was to say that the Party was hopelessly corrupt. The dual-track price policy enabled privileged Party members to make huge and easy profits by buying goods at state prices and selling them on the free market. They also failed to pay the peasants for their crop with money but instead issued IOUs. This was called *guandao*. Somewhat surprisingly, the students did not attack the Party for causing mass famines or murdering tens of millions.

The Party leaders were horrified by the prospect of unemployed youths and former Red Guards joining the students, followed closely by demobilized soldiers and embittered peasants. The following year, Hu was ousted from power and replaced by Zhao Ziyang, another reformer who wrestled with the problem of how to bring urgently needed change without triggering a destabilizing bout of high inflation. In 1988, he raised the issue in a two-hour meeting with Milton Friedman. Zhao explained that price reform was the biggest problem that he faced. He explained that the psychological tolerance of Chinese people towards inflation was very low. After twenty-six years of fixed prices, they found it 'intolerable'. China had also had its own experience of hyperinflation in 1947–9 that helped destroy trust in the government of Chiang Kai-shek and pave the way for the communist victory.

Friedman told Zhao that China should not adopt an expansionary monetary policy because it would weaken competition and encourage corruption and should instead adopt a tight monetary policy while freeing prices. Friedman seemed more concerned with propagating his belief that 'inflation is always and everywhere a monetary phenomenon' rather than helping Zhao find a way to free prices and stay in power. The East Europeans were probably of more help than the Americans, who, as Birman observed from his own experiences in America, still thought the Soviet Union was an economic giant and had no idea how it worked. Some like Galbraith had returned from visits to China in the mid-1970s highly impressed by what they saw and unable to grasp what an economic disaster Maoism had been or why it didn't work. As such, none of them seemed able to imagine the impossibly difficult policy choices the Chinese leaders faced.[19]

Zhao wanted to change from prices based on value to market prices, and he said China had no choice about this. He wanted to move quickly towards freeing all prices, to privatize state enterprises and introduce some form of political liberalization. Parts of his programme were rather vague, but his ideas had the backing of Deng Xiaoping. Zhao ordered a fresh round of price liberalization in 1988, and the prices of some staples including pork, sugar and eggs shot up by 60 per cent. Panic buying ensued after rumours of more price rises spread. The sudden death of Hu Yaobang was the trigger for fresh student democracy protests in the spring of 1989, leading to hunger strikes and a full-scale crisis so big that it looked as if the Party might lose power. The Party declared martial law, but some army officers and soldiers mutinied. Deng finally sent in the tanks on 4 June. Zhao was overthrown and kept under house arrest until his death.

After several years of recession while the Party blocked or reversed economic reforms, Deng led the charge and re-instituted

Zhao's reforms. There were fresh rounds of price liberalization and fresh bouts of double-digit inflation. The planning system was abandoned, and the huge industrial combines were broken up and given greater autonomy. In the 1990s, the state-owned enterprise sector experienced traumatic change not unlike that in the Soviet Union. Amid a morass of unpaid debts and liabilities, as many as 70 million people in the state sector lost their jobs, savings and often their pensions. China could not avoid the consequences of decades of malinvestment or the hidden unemployment in the state sector.[20]

However, the bankrupt companies were not officially allowed to declare bankruptcy, and the unemployed were not officially recognized as being unemployed. China rejected the path of voucher privatization and after 1989 emphatically rejected the idea that the 'commanding heights' of the economy should be privatized. Instead, the Party would remain firmly in control of all important enterprises. The state banks would continue to fund these enterprises with as many loans as they needed to modernize. The smaller enterprises were in fact quickly privatized without any kind of public disclosure. A few experiments in voucher privatization were tried but quietly abandoned.[21]

China opted for a policy that was the opposite of Yeltsin's. The latter wanted to privatize the larger enterprises in order to destroy the political base of the Soviet Communist Party and deprive it of the opportunity to regroup and strike back. Yeltsin had opposed the tanks sent by the coup plotters in 1991, notably by standing on one of them. In Beijing, the Party sent in the tanks to maintain itself in absolute power. So afterwards, it wanted to use the large state-owned enterprises and state banks to strengthen its hold over the country. It established stock markets but only to raise capital to keep the large state enterprises going and to keep them under Party control.

China is now held up as a successful example of a communist country that avoided shock therapy by embracing gradualism. Nobel laureate Joseph Stiglitz is one American economist who has advocated the Chinese way of reform and lauded its political stability. Yet despite being credited for thirty-five years of reforms that turned China into a huge economic powerhouse, the Communist Party still does not feel it has any political mandate to undertake political liberalization and would be unlikely to win an open election. Chinese leaders like Hu Jintao and Xi Jinping have repeatedly warned that corruption is a life and death issue for the Party. The result are purges and campaigns against corrupt officials but no real change.

The chief cause of corruption is the dual pricing policy that remained even after the 1989 shock. For over thirty years Beijing maintained price controls on rice, wheat, tobacco, cotton, salt, vegetable oil, silkworm cocoons, sugar, pharmaceuticals, water, electricity, natural gas, oil, land use rights and more besides. The right to import most of these products was restricted to holders of government licences. Exports of most light industrial manufactures like apparel and textiles and shoes were also restricted to licence holders.

All this means that sometimes the state was buying agricultural goods at prices far above those on world markets or selling oil or coal at prices well below those on international markets. Not surprisingly, many Party institutions, including the army and navy, devoted all their energies to smuggling activities. Party officials or their relatives could make a fortune by arbitraging between international and domestic prices. Each effort to promote reforms in a new area created fresh opportunities for corruption, which poisoned attitudes to the Party and fostered resentment. When the Party began to tackle the housing shortage, it allowed Party officials to buy land at a state-fixed purchase price only to sell the buildings at market prices. Peasants and urban residents were pushed out of their land or properties and given modest compensation while well-connected developers made staggering profits.

It is interesting to note how similar China and Russia have become since the events of 1989, although in only one of them is a Communist Party still in power. Both countries are undemocratic and run by oligopolies. The families of top Chinese Party leaders are multi-billionaires, although their identities are far less well known than the Russians. Both governments have also become committed to a huge military build-up and an expansionist and nationalistic ethos. The dramatic rise in living standards in China has come at a cost of individual political liberty. China still does not have a convertible currency or market prices for many staple products. It still grapples with heavy pollution. The official statistics are recognized as being fabricated and distorted, and many suspect the lack of transparent market prices has led to huge but still hidden malinvestment.

Countries like Poland that immediately abolished price controls have enjoyed twenty-five years of democracy and much higher living standards. However one may judge the relative merits of the policies followed by China, Russia, Poland or other socialist and post-socialist countries, one common trait emerged. Price reform proved to be the economic and political issue of overwhelming importance. There was no escaping the need to free prices in order to build a functioning market economy. That was the fatal flaw of socialism that Mises recognized in 1920. You could argue about many factors—private versus public ownership, or democracy versus dictatorship—but in the end the countries had to embrace price liberalization. Since 1989, no socialist government has returned to a system of state-controlled prices.

Mises has not been feted like the other 'Austrians' such as Hayek, Schumpeter and Friedman. Indeed, his name was largely forgotten in Europe for many years. Most economics textbooks treat his ideas as a relic of nineteenth-century liberalism. Or they note that Mises had been totally refuted by Lange in a by now obscure debate.

When Bergson died in 2003 at the age of eighty-nine, he was still being hailed as the world's one-time leading authority on the Soviet economy. In a glowing obituary in the *New York Times*, Samuelson is quoted as saying Bergson would be on anyone's shortlist for a Nobel Prize, or even two prizes.[22] One of his disciples, Padma Desai, noted without any intended irony: 'He correctly deduced that economic expansion in the Soviet Union was slowing during the cold war ... but some of his estimated comparisons of the Soviet economy and Western economies later proved slightly inaccurate.'[23]

As Samuelson put it in 2005:

Abram Bergson was a realist par excellence. He applied generous reasoned discounts to the statistical growth claims of the Stalinist and post-Stalinist statisticians. And yet, after the dozen post-Gorbachev years of communist dissolution, the emerging evidence suggests to me—and I think to 'Honest Abe'

234

as he was known at Harvard—that the Soviet system was even less productive in most sectors than the international almanacs had estimated. Why? Plain Machiavellian lying? No doubt there was some of that, as all our experts did recognize.

More important, I suggest after much reflection, is the fact that what are called 'prices' in a controlled society have little true relationship to relative scarcities and technical trade-off costs. From copious non-meaningful statistical inputs will have to come quite non-meaningful statistical estimates.[24]

This was the nearest that Samuelson ever got to acknowledging the mistakes and misjudgements that he and his friend had made for nearly forty years. On 10 September 1990, the left-wing economist Robert Heilbroner was blunter in an article written for the *New Yorker* called 'After Communism'. In it, he recounted the story of the refutation of Mises and how in graduate school he and his peers were taught that Lange had refuted Mises. Then he wrote: 'Mises was right.'[25]

Lange died in London in 1965 at the age of age of sixty-one and is barely remembered even in his native Poland. He left London and become a professor at the University of Michigan and in 1943 a naturalized US citizen. Then he accepted an invitation from Stalin to join the new post-war communist government in Poland. He became a deputy chairman of the Polish Council of State and one of four acting chairmen of the Council of State (head of state) in 1964. In his final years, Lange worked on cybernetics and the use of computers for economic planning. His ideas on a mixed economy were never put into practice and there is some irony in that it was the economic mismanagement of Poland's economy that led to the rise of Solidarity and the events that helped bring down the Soviet Union.

As an institution, the CIA was completely exonerated in a number of investigations undertaken after the collapse of the Soviet Union. Senator Daniel Moynihan failed to get the agency abolished. Its budget was not cut, and no one was sacked in disgrace. 'In my judgment, overall, the CIA performed admirably in meeting the challenges of assessing Soviet strengths and weaknesses', wrote former CIA director Robert Gates in the CIA's book *Analysis of the*

Soviet Union, 1947–1991, which was published in 1995. A number of books sympathetically described how Western intelligence agencies such as the CIA did their best to discover the truth and followed widely and internationally established best practice.[26]

Few of the numerous books detailing the history of the CIA, and its many debacles and transgressions around the world, ever dwell on its most serious fault—the failure to understand the nature of the Soviet economy. It was arguably America's greatest intelligence failure, but then again, the myth of the Soviet economy bamboozled many, many clever people around the world. As Mises would later complain, faith in socialism was akin to religious belief, so challenging it on logical grounds was an unrewarding task.[27]

The failure of communism should be studied much more than it is because in the end it is not about the role of money, or capitalism or the good or evil intentions of those involved in this story. It's about knowledge, how we get it and how we use it. We live in the information age, the knowledge economy, and talk constantly about data, statistics and number crunching. What really caused the CIA's errors, however, was not information but the creation of a belief system in which the high priests believed so strongly in their false data that they permitted no one to challenge it.

As Birman recalled:

> When we arrived from the Soviet Union in the 1970s, American academia greeted us with cold indifference at best and venom at worst. As émigrés who were willing to risk our lives and leave behind our families, our heritage and every scrap of material wealth, we were too biased. Our accounts were not to be trusted. Apparently, only Stalin is trusted among American intellectuals. In the two decades since the collapse of the Soviet system, nothing has changed in American Academia. People in these institutions of learning learn absolutely nothing, but to call them merely ignorant is a mistake.[28]

Some events we can predict with certainty. We know that on 28 July 2061, Halley's Comet will pass through our skies as it does every seventy-five years. We can predict the tides, the relative positions of the constellations, the planets and the moon. What we cannot predict are whether in 2061 the diamonds of Baroness Meyendorff will be worth a bag of flour or will be worth enough to buy a landed estate with its own flour mill.

Mises claimed that economics was about praxis rather than scientific laws—observing how human beings behave, something he called praxeology. It is not the catchiest epithet, and it may never catch on. Yet his ideas are still finding an audience. A Mises Institute in Alabama opened in 1982, with a Mises Institute Europe in Leuven, Belgium, in 2001 and another in Canada in 2010.

intelligence in that period – intelligence that insisted, in January 1953, that Stalin could not possibly be seriously ill (he died two months later) and that insisted, up to the day of Nikita Khrushchev's purge of Georgi Malenkov, that there was no power struggle in the Kremlin.

4. SIE 11-5-68, 1976 NIE 14-76, NIE 1981, SIE 11-9-63, NIE 1512-69.

5. Angus Maddison, 'Measuring the Performance of a Command Economy: An Assessment of the CIA Estimates for the USSR', *Review of Income and Wealth* 44(3) (September 1998), pp. 9, ... For China the CIA had much less information than for the USSR because of the collapse of the Chinese statistical system from 1960 to the mid 1970s. Their indexes did take a year presented in 1967 with only 10 indicators. In 1975 the number of indicators more than doubled, but for 7 of the 11 sectors of industrial production was measured output of a single commodity. The index was first presented in 1987, for the years 1949–85. By then coverage was improved but it was based on indicators for different commodities. The various weighted-sum-range fell, said, gross output, industrial production.

For China, the CIA made no serious effort to compare its level of performance with the USA. In JEC 1975 (pp. 92–4), they report dollar estimates for China without attribution, which were drawn from rouble estimates for 1955 by Hollister (1958), pp. 100–7, the CIA's own gross dollar estimates for China's GNP, which methods and bases they were made. JEC 1975 (p. 208) also provided dollar estimates, and on p. 230 explained that they were an update of the 1955 conferences. Their last effort in 1987 gave dollar estimates without any indication.

6. John Bradbury Jr and Mary Gill, 'Current and Future Challenges Facing Chinese Defence Industries', *China Quarterly* 146 (June 1996), p. 410.

7. 'Five-Year Plans of China', Wikipedia, last edited 10 May 2018, https://en.wikipedia.org/wiki/Five-year_plans_of_China.

8. Frank Dikötter, *The Tragedy of Liberation: A History of the Chinese Revolution 1945–1957*, Kindle edn, London: Bloomsbury, 2013, loc. 3223-4.

9. See John Lossing Buck, *Food and Agriculture in Communist China*, New York: Praeger for the Hoover Institution on War, Revolution, and Peace, Stanford University, 1966.

10. John K. Fairbank, *China Watch*, New York: Knopf, 1974.

11. Dwight H. Perkins, *Agricultural Development in China 1368–1968*, Chicago: Aldine, 1969.

12. Jasper Becker, *Hungry Ghosts: Mao's Secret Famine*, London: John Murray, 1996, pp. 108-11.

19

CHINA AND THE ROAD LESS TRAVELLED

When the Communist Party of China reflected on the causes of the traumatic events of 1989 when students inspired a popular uprising, it came to a surprising conclusion. The members of the democracy movement portrayed themselves as part of an anti-corruption protest. The aged Party leaders believed that in fact they intended to overthrow Communist Party rule and finally crushed the uprising by sending in tanks. Amid the soul searching that followed the sudden collapse the Soviet empire, the Chinese Communist Party concluded that the uprising in China was not just about a struggle for liberty, democracy or the rule of the law but was provoked by inflation. The Party had bungled price reform. Public anger had been roused, it argued, by lifting price controls in 1988, which unleashed a destabilizing bout of high inflation and panic buying. So the Chinese Communist Party concluded that the key to staying in power was to handle the future and unavoidable price adjustment in a better way. And that's what it did. Given a choice between shock therapy and gradual price reform, it now knew which path to take.[1]

On the way to a market economy, China took the road less travelled. While other countries lifted price controls, privatized property, introduced a new currency and endured a period of hyperinflation, China took small incremental steps spread out over thirty years or more—by 'feeling the stones across the river'. Indeed, by 2022 it has yet to complete the transition to a market economy—although this is something it disputes at the World Trade Organization—and has still not crossed the river.

There's no evidence that China's leadership ever wanted to reach the other side and become a market economy—it was never a stated policy—and it has certainly always denied wanting to become a multi-party democracy based on private property rights. Yet the country's transformation into an economic power still begs the question of why its gradual approach has proved so successful.

When contrasting the experience of two similar countries—Ukraine and Poland—the benefits of big bang reform over gradualism is obvious. Poland became much more prosperous. Further, a people's wealth is not just measured by economic statistics. Polish people enjoyed the security of being in a free democracy with the protection of individual and minority rights. Ukraine less so. The Chinese have not enjoyed such freedoms.

But Chinese leaders repeatedly claim that China cannot blindly copy other countries. It is unique and must therefore find its own path. There is a grain of truth in this. China was in a very different position in 1979 from many other socialist countries. It had little or no foreign debt, nor did it plan to borrow very much in the future. By and large, it did not rely on food imports. While the majority in the Soviet Union lived in cities, nearly everyone in China lived in the countryside, where they could grow and eat their own food. And after 1978 China demobilized many of its troops, slashed defence spending and cut subsidies to foreign allies. Swords were beaten into ploughshares as the state turned its attention to raising domestic living standards.

It is not admitted in any official texts, but much of China was far, far poorer than either the Soviet Union or Poland. During the 1970s, the rural population was so destitute, so visibly poor that the government closed off most of the country so foreigners would not witness their poverty. Many wore rags, subsisting in hovels on a diet based on little more than sweet potato chips, could not travel, and had no access to electricity or schooling. Most peasants lived in a virtually cashless world, earning 'work points' and a share of the communes' surplus grain production. They owned almost no private property. Chinese peasants almost never ate meat. When the government started building Shenzhen, the special economic zone next to Hong Kong, it recruited labour gangs from Sichuan who would work all day for nothing more than bed and board.

Without change, China could not feed, clothe or house this vast and growing rural population. Reforming the industrial sector was not so pressing. That its factories didn't export anything except textiles did not matter, and China could shelter them from international competition. There was a vast unsatisfied domestic demand for their products. But in Poland or even Russia, where most people worked in state enterprises, expected to eat meat every day and compared their living standards to those in Western Europe, this was not the case.

Chinese government statistics were strange. They focused almost entirely on achieving crude targets of grain production, excluding almost everything else. The first policy step was to raise grain procurement prices and allow peasants to grow extra grain to sell in the market. They could also sell all kinds of 'side line crops'—almost anything that wasn't bulk grain, cotton or vegetable oil.

Since the urban population had had nothing to buy for decades, they had saved their cash wages. Once the peasants could take their market garden produce to sell in the cities, they could spend their cash on once rare luxuries—chickens, fruit, fish, crabs, eggs, fresh greens, mushrooms, duck, goose or rabbit meat. They could also spend their savings on eating out in the family-run restaurants that suddenly sprang up—sometimes taking over the now redundant nuclear air raid shelters. Unlike other socialist and post-socialist states, no new currency was issued nor did hyperinflation wipe out their savings. The worst that happened was that the government forced them to buy low-interest treasury bonds.

Suddenly, the peasants had enough to eat and cash to spare. The first thing they did was to get some new clothes. The next thing was to build a new house, often with their own labour. The clothes (and shoes) were made in family-run workshops from cotton cloth or leather. The most famous hotspot of entrepreneurialism was

Wenzhou in Zhejiang province, China's button capital, which made and sold hundreds of different kinds of haberdashery. It was all bottom-up, small-scale enterprise, outside the planned economy. Like rain in a desert, the whole rural economy sprang to life, and its energy took the state completely by surprise—although this didn't stop it trying to claim the credit.

All this activity was inflationary—there was still too much money chasing too few goods—but it didn't show up in government statistics as excessive inflation. These products were never part of the planned economy, so they were never counted, and of course there were no price controls on them to lift. This did not stop the government sending inspectors to patrol urban markets to impose price caps. The real purpose seemed to be to mollify urban residents whose wages were not growing very fast and felt themselves getting poorer by comparison with the prospering peasants.

The new incentives were also successful in raising grain production, but the state kept strict price controls over rice and corn prices and indeed all basic items like cotton, wool, coal, vegetable oil, diesel, rice, corn, cabbages, salt, electricity, train and bus tickets, and so on. All these were rationed largely for the benefit of the urban population. Price rises were matched by wage hikes. China's economy of shortages also meant that many highly sought after consumer goods like bicycles were also rationed.

At this time, there was little inter-provincial trade. Under the Maoist economy, each province, and indeed each region, was supposed to be self-sufficient, and the only trade was by inter-provincial government barter deals. It took many years before normal trade started to flow between provinces (and even counties) because local governments did everything to stop it and often went so far as blocking roads. A region with a surplus in grain but a shortage of pork struggled to trade with another area with a surplus of pork but a demand for rice. Yet eventually the pressure of market forces proved too hard to resist. Goods began to move across provincial frontiers. As an internal market developed, prices across the country began to equalize. At the same time, the open-door policy led the government to adjust domestic prices to those on global markets whether it wanted to or not.

However, once even the limited market opening of the early 1980s began to ripple through the economy, the need to permit more change became ever more pressing. There were now two prices for everything—the state price and the market price—and those in privileged positions could quickly get rich by arbitrating between the two. Doing almost anything—like running a restaurant—required innumerable government permits, so bribery and corruption flourished. No anti-corruption campaign was able to curb this profiteering even though the Party tried to show its determination by executing a number of 'princelings'. China was like a forest with an underbrush of combustible dry tinder, built up over the years, that a single spark could ignite. The unfairness of it all was galling. Former Maoists who had persecuted anyone with a 'capitalist' background were now getting rich. Peasants who could barely write their names were getting rich too. And those who had served in the military or who were still believers in Maoism and opposed the market were also unhappy. Almost every family had suffered at some point during the thirty years of political persecution.

The Party leadership could retreat from the reforms or deal with the dual pricing policy but neither was easy to do. The initial reforms had been such a dramatic success that it was hard to retreat. Grain production doubled in just six years. The communes had been disbanded, private property returned to its owners, and the peasants had been granted leases on the fields. The return to specialization of labour enabled a proliferation of goods that had been unobtainable for years.

Yet the next step was perilous. China had to risk public anger by lifting price caps on tobacco, salt, grain, oil, cotton, diesel and other essential commodities. These essential products were not only in short supply but generated vital tax revenues for the central government and ensured social stability in cities where the potential for civil unrest was greatest. The government bought these key commodities at prices that were usually below the market price in order to subsidize the state-owned factories and the living standards of the urban population.

If prices went up, wages would have to go up too. The paper currency would be effectively devalued, and many factories could go bust. It made price liberalization in the industrial economy inescapable. Otherwise the dual pricing–corruption nexus would continue. The state-owned enterprise system—the backbone of the central planning system—would have to be abandoned. The privatization of most state assets must follow. In early 1988, the first experiments at privatizing factories by issuing shares was underway.

The battle between reformers and Maoists took different forms. There was the ideological battle. If the state liberalized prices and privatized its property, then why did China still need a Communist Party? Then there were strategic considerations: what would happen if there were panic-induced shortages of grain or oil? China did not have enough foreign exchange to import oil and grain. Like the USSR, it might then become vulnerable to American pressure. The Party feared its external and domestic opponents would join forces to overthrow the regime. The archives would be opened, and decades of crimes and lies would be exposed. Its leaders could be put on trial or forced to flee.

Whoever was in power, lifting price caps would inevitably bring about the complete restructuring of the economy. Many factories would have to shut down, and supply chains would be disrupted. The state sector employed over 100 million people. Many of them might suddenly lose their jobs. Debts would have to be written off. Pensions would not be paid. Foreign companies would take over many industries. The government could respond by printing money and flooding the economy with a paper currency, but this would only encourage bank runs and inflame the demand for gold, foreign exchange and other assets. The market value of the renminbi would collapse. Many people would want to leave the country and work abroad for better pay, especially those with qualifications.

A return to the centrally planned economy on the grounds that it had supposedly worked well in the 1950s when the first five-year plan was implemented didn't offer much of a solution. Most of the state-owned factories were now burdened by excess workers and huge pension liabilities. It was near impossible to fire anyone, and very tight bureaucratic control was exerted. You couldn't move a desk without formal approval. Their machinery was worn and out of date, and the factories were often located in the wrong place—

the interior of the country far from ports and the main domestic markets. Many had been put there to serve the military–industrial sector but had been left high and dry when all the defence orders had been cancelled.

The government led by Deng Xiaoping had closed most of the labour camps and sent the inmates home. They were followed by tens of millions of educated youth, the children of urban workers whom Mao had sent to the countryside. Along with them were an army of people sent to man the factories and military units in the 'third line' defence sector in case of a nuclear war. They all wanted to return to their native cities in the coastal belt. The population of the main cities swelled enormously, but there were no houses or schools for them. Little new housing or transport had been built for decades. All these people needed to find work, and their accumulated grievances and expectations made them a combustible mixture.

By 1988, many in the Party could see that only the private sector, in both cities and countryside, was capable of driving the economy and creating jobs for everyone. The rest of the economy existed only thanks to all kinds of subsidies for food, transport, fuel, housing and so on. In the absence of market prices, no one really knew what anything actually cost or what it was worth in this part of the economy.

Accounts in China were kept in the same way as in the Soviet bloc. They produced something called net material product, which excluded the service sector, most of the rural economy and the defence sector. Even without the inevitable and widespread falsification of statistics, it was useless as a planning tool. It was particularly unhelpful when it came to forecasting what would happen after subsidies were cut. Or what would happen if you kept raising government procurement prices for grain or cotton or vegetable oil.

In short, China's leaders took a plunge into the dark when in 1988 they decided to lift price controls on more daily commodities including salt, matches and sugar. It started a panic. Rumours spread that price caps would soon be lifted on everything. People rushed to hoard or panic buy all kinds of things, even toilet paper. They queued to withdraw money from banks and buy foreign goods or currencies.

When inflation took off, hurting urban incomes, the state reintroduced rationing of pork, sugar and eggs to try to calm the mood in the cities. In the countryside, the government kept raising procurement prices to try to close the gap with market prices. It kept paying out more and more money until it ran out of funds. Things got so bad that farmers were paid with near worthless IOUs, and in some counties cadres had to resort to forcible confiscation because farmers stopped delivering grain in return for state-fixed prices.[2]

When university students started protesting in the spring of 1989, their slogans were about government corruption, freedom and democracy, but everyone understood the significance of the political challenge to the Party—the students and their supporters wanted radical change, not gradualism. It was a protest against the gradual course of muddled thinking behind the Party's claims to be promoting a 'socialist market economy' or 'socialism with Chinese characteristics'. There is, of course, no way of knowing what a new, elected government might have done. One can only guess by looking at the post-communist governments of Eastern Europe and assume that a new government would in one fell swoop have freed all prices and privatized all state assets. Prices would have risen sharply before settling down after two years and aligning with those outside the country.

The leadership of the Chinese Communist Party defended its gradualism by declaring that the alternative was 'chaos' and a new famine. It claimed that because there was not enough arable land, any misstep might easily cause a famine. Some of the statistics it cited to bolster these claims were plainly wrong. Satellite analysis, for instance, showed that China had 50 per cent more arable land than recorded in official statistics. China always had the potential to grow plenty of food. We know that in the early 1990s, the state was accumulating so much extra grain and cotton that the state granaries had nowhere to store it and some was left outside to rot. By 1992, state grain companies had run up debts of 43 billion RMB while peasants were owed a further 33 billion RMB in IOUs. The state ended up with poor-quality rubbish that no one wanted to eat—usually a strange tasteless hybrid variety of rice—and the good quality rice was sold in the market. The state continued to run up surpluses and debts because it began procuring grain and other staple crops at prices above world market prices. It took ten years after Tiananmen for the state to make its third attempt to end the state grain monopoly. A grain futures market opened in Zhengzhou soon followed by a Cotton Exchange. The fifty-year-old state grain monopoly ended. Soon, the government was less worried about famine than it was about plenty—grain and cotton prices falling too quickly.

If a new government had immediately restored land ownership rights in the countryside instead of continuing the system of temporary leases, we can be sure that market forces would have ensured a swifter adjustment of prices, supply and demand, and a better allocation of resources. There would have been far less scope for corruption, and land ownership would have altered the entire political relationship between peasants and the state. They would have become fully fledged property-owning citizens. The record suggests it would have worked.

If one gives the Party credit for price liberalization, the rest of the story—half a century of state land ownership, price controls and subsidies—is one of unmitigated failure. On the one side, the record shows famine and persistent malnutrition and on the other remarkable growth. The official data cannot disguise the magnitude of the change. In the twenty years after 1978, China's grain production went up by 200 million tonnes; oil-bearing crops, sugar cane, sugar beet all quintupled; aquatic products went up tenfold; fruit tenfold; meat output was up nearly sevenfold.[3] Even these official statistics don't quite give the full scale of the vast improvement in consumption. Beer production, for instance, which uses a lot of grain, rose from next to nothing in 1978 to around 25 billion litres in this period. China is now the largest beer market in the world.

In the wake of the 1989 protests, the concerns of China's ruling class centred on the mood of the country's urban residents. They might riot again if food prices rose too quickly, especially if they were thrown out of work by the closure of their loss-making enterprises. The closure of many factories was unavoidable, but the authorities felt that it was better to delay the change in order to allow food output to rise. After Tiananmen, the government re-imposed many price controls and started a series of political campaigns exhorting each county and every province to grow this or that vegetable and bring prices down. Xinhua, the state news agency, gave almost daily updates on vegetable or pork prices. The government's battle to defeat rising prices by keeping inflation to tolerable levels was presented as a great success. But was it?

The government opted for a drawn-out reform of state enterprises rather than a swift and decisive privatization of state assets and the lifting of price controls. Employees in the state-owned factories, with their subsidized housing, transport and food, were considered a central pillar of Communist Party power. So after Tiananmen, the Party closed down many private enterprises and embarked on a long-term strategy to finance the state sector. The country re-opened stock markets, and most of the capital this raised went to state enterprises. State-owned banks also directed savings into subsidizing favoured state enterprises.

China's handling of this problem is often favourably contrasted with the 'chaos' that took place in post-Soviet Russia. However, the experience of both countries was rather similar in most respects. Most of the 300,000 Chinese state-owned enterprises went under or were merged into other state firms. The state sector employed roughly 100 million people, and by 2000, some 30 million had been laid off and a further 30 million would lose their jobs. In Shanghai, the centre of China's cotton spinning and textile industry since the 1920s, 400,000 textile workers lost their jobs. Altogether, a million of Shanghai's industrial workforce of 3.6 million lost their jobs. Around the country, the discarded workers relied on small and irregular handouts—often just 129 RMB or $15 a month (at 1998 exchange rates)—to survive. They effectively lost their pensions and savings since there was no national pension scheme. Each enterprise, even if it became defunct, was responsible for its own retired workers. By 1997, some 70 million workers in state-owned enterprises across the country were supporting the pensions of 24 million retired workers. This was partly financed by pulling down the factories and selling off the land for residential housing or retail developments. Yet it was far from clear who benefitted from the proceeds of the land sales. Further, the retired and laid off workers were given new housing when their old apartments were knocked down for redevelopment, but these were often in the periphery of their home cities or a distant suburb with lower land values.[4]

Some of the land sale proceeds had to go to reducing the vast pile of outstanding debts that the state-owned enterprises accumulated. The *Workers' Daily* once described them as a 'bottomless pit' with debts totalling 4 trillion yuan. As in post-Soviet Russia, the complex web of interdependent supply chains unravelled, leaving huge amounts of so-called triangular debts on the books of the state banks. Although China claimed to be managing a gradual transformation, this did not turn out to be possible in most parts of the country. Once the country permitted market prices, the system of planning and fixed prices quickly unravelled.[5]

Take Heilongjiang province, for example. Whole sectors like the coal and steel industries effectively went bankrupt. The crisis reached a nadir with the 1997 Asian Financial Crisis. The government felt obliged to close private coal mines, steel plants, power stations and so on in a desperate bid to prop up the rust belt factories. Two-thirds of the urban population were left unemployed in the 1990s and usually had to survive without pay.[6]

The situation in the Soviet Union and the Eastern bloc countries was no worse or better than in China. Around a third of the employees quickly lost their jobs in state-owned enterprises. In Russia, the rupture was awkward because many factories, like Russia's cotton spinning mills, were cut off from their raw cotton suppliers who were now located in newly independent states like Uzbekistan. However, getting a clear and comparative statistical picture is probably not possible because of the way employment statistics are drawn up. China, to give one example of the difficulties, never counted those who lost their jobs in state-owned enterprises as unemployed because although their employer may have stopped operating, these firms were not allowed to declare bankruptcy.[7]

Although the price reforms forced enterprises to shed workers everywhere, China proved more adept than others at quickly generating a wave of new enterprises. Even though few of those elder workers who had lost their 'iron rice bowl' found new jobs in these new enterprises, China successfully created an atmosphere of energy and confidence. Entirely new industries sprang into existence—consumer banking, telecommunications, computer manufacturing, computer software, mobile phones—as well as the proliferation of manufacturers churning out domestic appliances like air-conditioners, refrigerators, microwaves, TVs, DVD players, telephones and so on. Many new firms sprang up in sectors once dominated by state-owned enterprises like heavy industry and mining, transport, power generation, machine building, shipbuilding and other metal-bashing industries.

Huge numbers of Chinese—some 250 million—left home in search of work and usually found it. The outward migration from Eastern Europe after the fall of communism was much the same phenomenon. Millions left to find work in Western Europe and elsewhere. A tenth of the Polish workforce—over 2 million—moved abroad after the fall of communism, and many more moved to different areas within Poland.[8]

It was difficult to categorize Chinese firms as either private or public. The boundaries were rather fluid and blurry. Some were genuinely private, family-owned businesses. Others were owned by local governments or even military units or government ministries. Some were genuinely foreign-invested, but others were local businesses masquerading as foreign enterprises in order to qualify for tax holidays and other incentives. At one point, half of China's foreign investment came from the British Virgin Islands, which meant that no one could find out who exactly the ultimate owners were.[9]

The playing field was firmly tilted in favour of the newcomers and against the older state-owned enterprises. The newcomers paid less tax, employed peasant workers who didn't get pensions and other welfare costs, and they could start with newer equipment and better technology while the older state firms were saddled with debt and pension liabilities. The old enterprises quickly shed jobs, but the new enterprises were able to create new jobs even faster, although usually not in the same places. For example, the Chinese state statistical bureau claimed 78 million new jobs were created in urban areas between 2012 and 2019, overwhelmingly in small and medium-sized companies.[10]

What or who should get the credit and blame for this transformation? The drift of the government's propaganda narrative was generally to suggest the market was to blame for the job losses and that the government deserved the credit for job creation. There was always a changing cast of bad officials (usually from the north-east) who had to be punished for the former and good officials (usually in the south) congratulated for the latter. As in rural China, it was not so much government intervention that mattered but what it ceased doing. It stopped controlling and manipulating prices.

By 1992, there were price controls on only seventeen agricultural products compared to 110 at the beginning of the 1980s. Two-thirds of agricultural output was sold at market prices. Nearly 70 per cent of all consumer goods no longer had price controls, and price controls had been lifted from 58 per cent of industrial raw materials. By 2015, China's National Development and Reform Commission declared that the government now had a negative list system. This meant no controls over anything apart from just seven categories of products and services including natural gas, electricity, tap water and anaesthetics.[11]

During the 1990s, the price controls were increasingly ineffective and began to matter less and less. Take coal prices, for instance. Large state-owned mines delivered coal at fixed prices to government-owned power stations that delivered subsidized energy prices to favoured clients. Naturally, they all ran up large losses, but it was inevitable that over time the government had to close the gap between the market price set by non-state coal mines, and that domestic prices had to align with international prices.[12]

But that leaves unanswered the question of whether China really had been uniquely successful in delivering price reform without high inflation and political instability. The private sector (however that was defined) plus price liberalization brought an end to the economy of shortages. The economy flooded every sector with more goods—more clothes, furniture, bicycles, cars, television sets, dishwashers, air-conditioners and above all more housing. The prices of nearly everything kept falling, but plotting price inflation and wages over this thirty-year period is made impossible by the lack of a stable unit of account. The currency and the statistics have been too easily bent and distorted to be sure of anything. What we do know is that the Chinese Communist Party has never felt secure enough to relax the system of political repression and censorship after the Tiananmen protests of 1989. It's a telling indication that it never felt sure that it had slain the dragon of high inflation.

Unlike post-communist governments in Eastern Europe, the Chinese Communist Party was only staging a temporary retreat. It believed a strong state-owned industrial sector was central to its political survival. To achieve this goal, it embarked on a long-term strategy of squeezing out the private sector and building up four or five national champions that could dominate each sector. The favoured enterprises were able to raise large amounts of capital on the newly re-opened stock markets. The state ensured that their shares were never allowed to fall very far. It recapitalized the state banks and directed them to lend predominantly to the state-owned enterprises—to the detriment of the interests of savers and the private sector. The state also started huge infrastructure and house-building programmes that benefitted the firms in the heavy industry sector.

To further these policy objectives, the state manipulated the economy using capital controls, interest rates and exchange rates. It allowed the central bank to print money indiscriminately. This immediately introduced a new set of distortions into the economy. It replaced one kind of inflation with another. Inflation was no longer driven by a shortage of food or consumer goods but by printing too much money. Savers in search of higher returns than the dismal interest rates offered at the state-controlled banks created various kinds of asset bubbles—property in big cities, antiques, gold, jewellery, vintage wine and so on. Others found ways of smuggling their capital abroad to buy up foreign assets, especially in certain cities like Hong Kong, Singapore and Vancouver. It was easy too to take the cheap credit offered to the state-controlled companies and divert some of it into buying assets or companies either at home or abroad. The Anbang Insurance Company, for example, with assets of nearly 2 trillion RMB, embarked on a foreign spending spree that included the Waldorf Astoria in New York and other trophy assets. It ended in a fire sale and the arrest of its chairman, Wu Xiaohui, on charges of fraud and embezzlement.[13]

The second kind of distortion was the familiar kind of malinvestment. Under various giant stimulus programmes, the Chinese state directed vast sums into building ghost cities with 64 million empty apartments, networks of high-speed railways and railway stations (costing some $300 billion), grandiose municipal buildings, museums, opera houses, football teams and stadia, empty shopping malls, motorways to nowhere and other vanity projects. Among the most extravagant are those in the space and military sphere as well as overseas loans and infrastructure projects under the Belt and Road Initiative that might in total cost between $4 and $8 trillion. The state has also poured billions into a policy of trying to dominate new industries such as 5G networks, electric vehicles, and new batteries, often at the expense of providing more basic public services like pensions and health. The Chinese telecom giant Huawei was given subsidies of up to $75 billion to become the world's dominant supplier of mobile phones and networks, according to the *Wall Street Journal*.[14]

The Communist Party's leaders switched from supressing the price signals that revealed shortages to supressing price signals that flashed for malinvestment. The latter is always harder to grasp. The proof only comes out with a crash that reveals how much money has been wasted on poor investments, often long after the decision-makers have left the scene.

The malinvestment can also be seen as a consequence of the way the Chinese gather statistics. After 1980, the Chinese Communist Party reintroduced five-year plans and set itself the task of delivering an average of 8 per cent GDP growth in most plans. In this version of the command economy, each level of the Party apparatus was given targets and quotas. Officials therefore had a large incentive, if not an obligation, to distort their statistical reporting in order to show that the state plan was being followed.

But 8 per cent of what exactly? What was it counting? Setting a percentage increase on the previous year proved to be very problematic. The method by which China works out its GDP has changed so frequently that this becomes a very difficult, not to say nonsensical, challenge. For twenty-two years (1958–80), there was no statistical bureau, so any GDP figures can only be guessed.

Then after 1980 China reverted to the old Soviet statistical system and attempted to calculate its net material product. This is done by subtracting the value of all production costs (including the cost of material inputs, depreciation and labour in production) from the value of output produced in the material production sectors. It excludes most service sector activity. China only began to bring its methodology in line with the UN System of National Accounts in 2014. It adjusted its statistical methodology in 1998 and 2002, making year-on-year comparisons for the period from 1980 to 2014 tortuously difficult.

The state inevitably used the system to calculate the value of output based on the volume or tonnage of key products like coal, steel, grain and cement. In other words, officials wanted to make the kinds of things that the statistical bureau wanted to count, or found convenient to count, like tonnes of steel. But it is not easy to determine the value of a tonne of steel if you cannot use external market prices, and domestic market prices are distorted by price controls and a currency that is non-convertible. Even after the price controls were lifted, the value was expressed in renminbi, but the currency was subject to drastic devaluations. So this made it hard to chart the value of a commodity from year to year. In the decade up to 1995, the relative value of the renminbi fell from 2 RMB to 8 RMB for the dollar.

Foreign economists working for institutions like the World Bank then tried another route. They organized price purchasing parity surveys. Inevitably, these were handled or influenced by Chinese state officials. The government was always reluctant to allow outsiders to make independent statistical surveys. This method helped to show that the Chinese were not as poor as the RMB devaluations suggested, but it was not much use when it came to helping Chinese central planners plan an economy because the overall picture of inadequate or falsified statistics did not change. Chinese statistics remained an arm of the propaganda bureau.

Evidently, Chinese statistics under the net material product system were skewed in favour of primary and secondary industries. Naturally, this coincided with the Party's ambition to rebuild and indeed strengthen state-owned enterprises, which are (or were)

254

concentrated in these sectors. This suited local government officials because it was easier to report this sort of activity to the statistical bureau. They could hit two birds with one stone—boost the size of the local economy and strengthen the state-owned enterprise sector. This was all very well, but the tertiary or service sector is reckoned to make up 70 or even 80 per cent of a modern economy. The Soviet methodology was ill-equipped to measure the service sector. The explosive growth of private business and the service sector in the post-1978 economy went hand in hand. Without being able to adequately capture the value of the services and goods in the tertiary sector, it was impossible to guess at the size or growth rate of the Chinese economy. Official Chinese statistics, therefore, underplayed the importance of the service sector and exaggerated the significance of the primary and secondary sectors because these were easier to count.

The distorted image produced by Chinese statistics coupled with the Party's wish to promote state-owned enterprises over the private sector was reflected in the priorities of the state banks, which were reluctant to lend to private entrepreneurs, and the private companies could rarely list on the stock markets. Instead, they had to borrow on the kerbside market at rates of 20 per cent per annum. Those enterprises that did not quickly succeed were winnowed out. The state-sponsored enterprises could borrow at 3 per cent and were almost never allowed to go bankrupt. Inevitably, the result was a Chinese economy with a strong manufacturing base that flooded the world with manufactured goods.

Consequently, many suspect that the capital being invested in the state-owned enterprises is squandered and misallocated. In short, is it wise of the state to subsidize so much of its industry and to subsidize its exports? And to manipulate its exchange rate to further boost exports? Is it wise to keep printing money to finance so many extravagant public works projects in order to bolster the state-owned enterprises? How long can this go on without a crisis that will drag the rest of the world down with it?

Many worry about the ever-expanding size of China's debts in relation to its GDP. You can make a crack at reckoning up the loans and money in circulation. But what is the size of its GDP, and by how much is it growing—or indeed shrinking?

Finding answers to these questions is such a tough nut to crack that a small industry has sprung up around it. Some have tried to clear the statistical fog by examining internal freight or electricity consumption data, or property sales—believing that such things are less open to fraud and manipulation. Others have tried the mirror route—trying to extrapolate what is happening in China by looking at other countries' data on freight, shipping and exports. Some have taken to studying night time satellite images of China in order to work out the rate of activity. All of it reveals a widespread conviction that the official statistics are wrong, perhaps even very wrong. A reliable picture of economic activity can answer some questions but not answer the question of how much of China's growth is really malinvestment and how painful a crash will be when it comes.[15]

20

HOW NORTH KOREA TRIED TO
DEFY THE MARKET

If there is a state that proves Mises wrong, perhaps it is North Korea. Ever since Stalin put Kim Il Sung in charge of North Korea (or the Democratic People's Republic of North Korea—DPRK—to use its official name) after 1945, no other country has stayed more resolutely faithful to the Leninist/Stalinist economic model. Perhaps it has found a way to defeat the market and prosper.

Through three generations of Kim dynasty rule, North Korea has largely refused to change or reform. It remains an autarkic, centrally planned economy. The DPRK's economic system has survived every test thrown at it—invasion, war, recurrent famines and economic embargoes. Like Stalin, Kim Il Sung claimed that North Korea's first five-year economic plan (1957–61) was completed a year ahead of schedule. Output of steel and all kinds of other commodities increased by 700 per cent. And like China, it delivered a Great Leap Forward crash industrialization programme, called the *Chollima* campaign (a name taken from a mythological Korean flying horse). North Korea's command economy reportedly outperformed South Korea in the 1950s and 1960s by producing more steel, coal and grain on a per capita basis. It urbanized the population at a faster rate.

After the 1962 Cuban Missile Crisis, Kim Il Sung set about a 'military first' programme designed to turn the country into a military fortress. At the same time, it has performed technological marvels beyond the reach of many other states. It built its own nuclear industry, successfully tested nuclear weapons and developed long-range missiles. No enemy has dared attack it.

North Korea stopped issuing any meaningful statistics over fifty years ago. It has not published any official indicators or statistics since 1965, and after 1978 it stopped releasing any details of its grain harvests. From time to time, the government has released some data, but these are invariably cast in percentage increases of basic commodities. There is no reliable demographic information, and what information exists is probably propaganda, produced for UN organizations in bids to obtain aid.

The second economic plan (1961–7) had to be extended by three years because none of the targets for food production and other necessities had been met. The next plan also needed an extra year of 're-adjustment', and soon after 1978 a seven-year plan was adopted but abandoned two years later. Since then, North Korea hasn't announced any long-term plans, and outside observers have struggled to uncover enough scraps of information to paint a reliable picture of the economy. The UN agencies, the CIA and various South Korean institutions tasked with producing a picture of the North Korean economy have laboured to produce even comparative year-to-year GNP estimates.

So what is the true picture of what has happened in North Korea? Perhaps the government of this extremely closed and secretive state continues to gather useful economic statistics but has chosen to hide them from the outside world. It is more likely that in keeping with Mises' socialist calculation theory the regime has always operated in an informational fog. And that unable to gather any meaningful or reliable data, it has been unable to manage a planned economy but instead operates on the instructions of Kim Il Sung and his successors. Virtually everything is owned by the state, which in turn is de facto owned by the Kim family. There are no functioning shops to buy anything, since anything desirable or necessary is rationed. Officially, there is no room for private property rights or for market prices, although as we shall see later this is not always the case. There is a currency, the won, and in fact, there are at least four different versions of the won, plus many ration tickets that are another kind of currency. But none of these paper notes are a useful means of exchange because everything is owned and distributed by the state.

When Lenin introduced rationing in 1917, each person in the main cities was categorized according to their loyalty to the state. There were three main categories, and the more loyal a person was the more food they were entitled to. Many years later, the USSR abandoned the system, but North Korea continued using a rigid class system for seven decades. Initially, a quarter of the population was put in the 'loyal class', 55 per cent in the 'wavering class' and 20 per cent in the 'hostile class'. The *Songbun* system, as it is called, became hereditary, and the entire population was divided into at least fifty sub-categories. The rationing system was therefore the most elaborate ever devised.

Kim Il Sung's most far-reaching policy decision, made at the start of his reign, was to prove the most catastrophic. Korea had a reasonably successful farming sector by the standards of the time. The land had always been farmed by small tenant subsistence farmers. Under the Japanese occupation, only a few commercial farms were established, and most grain and other crops continued to be traded in the local markets. Enough was invested in the sector to create a surplus, which Japan imported to feed the imperial war machine. After the Japanese had left, rural Korea could have flourished.

Instead, Kim implemented the policies of Stalin and Mao but with excessive rigour compounded by the folly of his own impulsive instructions. The small farms were merged into state factory farms modelled on Russian collectives and the Chinese communes. North Korea's collectives depended on large inputs of chemical fertilizers instead of the traditional human or livestock manure. Every ton of rice required 2 tons of chemical fertilizer. Water was pumped from large-scale irrigation projects and required tractors (and diesel) to plough the fields instead of oxen. Seeds were planted very close together, contrary to established practice. North Korean peasants could grow food in tiny garden plots outside their houses, but these were even smaller than those permitted in Maoist China, and afterwards they were forbidden to sell any surplus food in urban areas.

The state bought all the grain, and private trading became a criminal activity. It confiscated what it wanted and issued the peasants with basic rations. Kim toured the country regularly inspecting fields and issuing on the spot guidance. Since his word was law, these edicts superseded the regulations issued by the central planning office. For example, he stopped the North Koreans planting cotton—the traditional fibre for clothing—and insisted they wore clothing made from chemical fibres. He thought growing cotton harked back to the time of the Japanese occupation when Koreans had to grow it for export. For unknown reasons, he took a dislike to millet, potatoes and sweet potatoes. These are low-status crops that were nevertheless suitable for growing on the many hills in Korea and across China's uplands provide food for hundreds of millions. On another occasion in 1979, he ordered peasants to plant runner beans, but only up against fences not in the fields. He thought the beans were a promising new source of protein.[1]

At first, the new factory farms lifted output, and the country was reportedly reaping 5 to 6 tonnes of grain per hectare. Ever more ambitious grain harvest targets were set. Then after 1978, Pyongyang stopped reporting details of its harvests, and there were reports of growing food shortages. Malnutrition became more and more widespread, although it was not noticed by visitors to Pyongyang because it was initially concentrated among those sectors of the population who were regarded as politically unreliable.

By the end of the 1980s, the yields had dropped to just 1 tonne per hectare. Some technical factors explain why the factory farms failed. The soil was quickly exhausted. The reservoirs silted up, which meant that its hydroelectric plants produced less and less electricity, so the irrigation schemes did not function. Without electricity, the state could not manufacture chemical fertilizer nor deliver it. The tractors did not work because there were increasing shortages of diesel fuel and spare parts. By the 1980s, shortages of basic foods became endemic, and in the early 1990s, a devastating famine cost millions of lives.

The irrational and arbitrary decisions of Kim Il Sung meant that the country was never adequately able to feed or clothe itself. Persistent failure did not prompt him to change his mind. For thirty years, Kim ignored the evidence and continued on the same course. North Korean agronomist Lee Min-bok believed the reason was simple. The supreme leader was constantly fed a diet of inflated statistics and outright lies to protect him from the truth and to protect those lower down from being punished for failing to meet their targets.

For instance, Kim Il Sung was informed in 1982 that the country had reaped a record harvest of 15 million tons when the actual harvest was half that.

Lee, whom I interviewed in 2003 after he fled to South Korea, described it like this:

> Everyone knew how to please the Great Leader—all you had to do was lie. So what people did was to cheat by making false reports. Say a party official had to meet a target of 100 tons of grain, and the real harvest was 70 tons, he would report that he had fulfilled the quota. When the inspectors from Pyongyang arrived, they would show them 100 tons in the barn by borrowing the missing 30 tons from a neighbouring district. When the inspectors arrived at the next district the favour would be repaid.

It's fair to assume that Kim Il Sung and his son and successor, Kim Jong Il, also knew how the system worked and realized there was a great deal of inflated figures and misleading flattery in the reports they received. So they were constantly travelling, visiting factories and farms in person to conduct their own research and then offering what is called in North Korea 'on the spot guidance'. At the entrance doors to many buildings are plaques above the lintels detailing the time and place of each visit by Kim Il Sung or his son, Kong Jong Il. Yet the in-person inspections still meant that it was impossible for them to know what the real situation was. Of course, no one would dare to say that the supposedly infallible 'Great Leader' was wrong to forbid planting cotton, or sweet potatoes. Moreover, the focus was always on crude quantities. Leaders of enterprises and collective farms are constantly exhorted to increase output and meet quotas set as crude quantities, tons of this or that, kwh of electricity and so on. Targets and quotas had to be met or surpassed. Even if the increases were real, they could be meaningless. After all, bulk quantities of grain, even if correctly counted, reveal nothing of their quality, the return on investment in producing it or how much is stolen or wasted before it gets to the recipient.

Around 1980, Kim Il Sung's son, Kim Jong Il, took over the reins of power as his father withdrew from active administration. It was exhausting being an absolute dictator. Every decision no matter how big or small was referred upwards for approval. The younger Kim found it hard too. For twenty years, he would routinely work through the night until 3 a.m. reading and replying to the hundreds of reports sent to his desk by every department in the state bureaucracy. Just one small office, the International Bureau, supplied up to forty documents a week. In 2000, Kim Jong Il told the South Korean media that he had developed the habit of sleeping just four hours a day.

As Kim Il Sung's word was treated as divine law, even his own son could hardly question his father's policies, nor his 'on the spot guidance' edicts. His hands were also tied by his own actions—Kim Jong Il spent his apprentice years in the propaganda department boosting the myth of his father's divine status and the reputation of his infallible genius. By 1980, he had erected 30,000 monuments and other images celebrating his father's wisdom and benevolence.

Change was only possible in the USSR after Stalin's death when senior officials like Beria and Khrushchev distanced themselves from Stalin. Beria may even have claimed to have murdered Stalin. Khrushchev denounced Stalin in his famous Secret Speech to the Twentieth Congress. China changed course when Deng Xiaoping, a senior figure whom Mao had sacked and exiled, was able to seize control after Mao's death and introduce a range of new policies.

As Kim Jong Il took over while his father was still alive, this sort of break was too much to expect. For fourteen years until his father's death, he lived in his shadow. His sole claim to legitimacy derived from his loyalty and devotion to his father's cult. He was thus never really well positioned to embark on a programme of radical change before or after his father's death. While his father was retired, Kim Jong Il appears to have done his best to hide from him the true extent of the country's economic weakness, and thus acknowledge that the policies didn't work. He also tried to resist Chinese pressure to embark on similar reforms and open up the country, which would also have caused his father to lose face. Instead, Kim Jong Il staked the country's future on ten ambitious megaprojects designed to end the perennial food shortages. These all turned out to be another set of malinvestments.

The largest of these ill-conceived projects was the West Sea Barrage project at Nampo, which was designed to reclaim tidal flats and create half a million acres of flat farmland. Another was a huge irrigation scheme that involved building a 5-mile-long barrage at the mouth of the Taedong River. Next, millions were mobilized to fell trees to clear steep hillsides to create an extra 740,000 acres of terraced cropland. Two huge industrial plants were built at Sunchon and Sariwon to produce more chemical fertilizer. All these efforts ended in failure. The hill terraces were quickly washed away. The Taechong dam and hyroelectric plant scheme failed when the irrigated land proved to be too salty; the same was also the case with the Nampo barrage. Neither the Sariwon nor the Sunchon plants went into full-scale operation during his lifetime. Food production continued to decline.

China and the United States exerted immense pressure on North Korea to change course. After Kim Il Sung died in 1994, Washington dangled alluring incentives—billions towards nuclear power stations—but Kim Jong Il turned down every opportunity to turn over a new leaf, establish a new relationship and open the economy to change. And after his own death, no change took place after *his* son, Kim Jong Un, took over.

The chief obstacle to change is surely the unchanging military ambitions of the Kim dynasty. Kim Il Sung believed that North Korea would be vulnerable if it became dependent on the outside world to supply essential food or fuel supplies. He insisted the railways should be entirely electrified so that even if oil imports were blocked, the military transportation could still function. The electricity would be supplied from domestic coal mines and its hydropower schemes.

The military had absolute priority in North Korea. Kim Il Sung took the country's most far-reaching policy decision in the early

1960s when he declared his 'military first' policy. Defence spending became the absolute top priority since, like Mao, he believed a global nuclear war was imminent.

The DPRK built up one of the world's largest armed forces. Military service became longer and longer so that many men were not discharged before they were thirty. Many of them spent years turning the country into an 'impregnable fortress', digging caves out of mountainsides to house military factories, depots and hospitals. It built 8,000, maybe 15,000 underground installations and hundreds of miles of tunnels. Some housed the astonishingly large numbers of tanks and artillery pieces the DPRK acquired, plus large numbers of aircraft and ships.[2]

Kim Il Sung was following Chairman Mao's path but without China's vast resources to draw upon. What did it cost? No one can put a dollar price on a North Korean tank, nor an artillery shell factory built in a cave, or even work out what the labour costs might be. When it comes to calculating the cost of building submarines or medium-range rockets, the task is even harder. The military–industrial complex became known as the 'second economy', and its requirements took precedence over everything else. It may even be larger than the rest of the economy. If one accepts that the USSR devoted a third of its economic spending to the military, then in North Korea it wouldn't be unreasonable to suppose that it required the resources of half the economy to sustain this effort.

There is no way of computing how military spending grew or shrank over the decades. Nor is it really clear what it was designed to achieve. In the 1950s, North Korea needed to withstand the type of bombing campaigns inflicted by UN forces during the Korean War. In the 1960s, it seemed to be designed to enable the DPRK to survive a global nuclear Armageddon. So its military had to be sheltered underground—just as Mao did in China. Surrounded by a hostile world, Kim's declared aim was to make his state completely self-sufficient in every possible way. Every region had to be completely self-sustaining and autonomous. In case it was cut off during a war, any given region could still keep functioning. This was a large part of the country's *Juche* philosophy.

A low-tech people's self-defence militia defending tunnels, bunkers and concrete fortifications makes sense for a poor country. It is a good strategy against an American enemy that could swiftly mount an overwhelming attack with aircraft, missiles and ultimately nuclear weapons.

Yet Kim also set about building up a mechanized invasion force designed to punch across the DMZ (Demilitarized Zone or de facto border) and race 300 miles south to Pusan. An aggressive Blitzkrieg-style invasion of the South would unify the country under the Kim family's rule. To sweep aside the American garrison and the South Korean defences, Kim set about assembling 8,000 artillery pieces, 2,000 tanks, plus thousands of aircraft and navy vessels.

To aid this liberation strike force, poised to attack with overwhelming force and speed at the right moment, Kim Il Sung had to devote additional resources to sowing confusion and disunity in the South, and to weaken the resolution of South Korea's allies to rush to its aid. The North Koreans probably looked at the successful example of North Vietnam. Although North Vietnam's army had been knocked back whenever it tried to invade the South with a conventional military attack, it did mastermind a fifth column-led war in the South by supplying and training the Vietcong. This undermined political stability in the South and weakened American public support.

The South Koreans never allowed such divisions to take hold, and an insurgency never took root. Most South Koreans had already experienced the horrors of North Korean invasion, and many had fled the North to start a new life in the South. They had no illusions about what North Korean communism meant.

Building a force of this order is a very costly undertaking even for a large and wealthy power. At a certain point, any sensible leader would have judged it to be an impossible task. By the early 1980s, North Korea was already enduring famine conditions, while in South Korea the economy was turning into an industrialized exporting powerhouse. In an age of microchips and satellites, North Korea's military hardware was rapidly becoming obsolete and outclassed. After the Berlin Wall fell and the Soviet Union broke up, the prospect of a conventional invasion of the South ever being a success had gone for good. Its remaining ally, China, was busy establishing commercial ties with the South and had no interest in allowing another Korean War.

So in 1984, the Kim family decided to join the small number of nuclear powers. With Soviet assistance, it set about building its own nuclear facilities and long-range missiles. Since then, the purpose of the nuclear weapons programme has been unclear—perhaps it shifted with time. It was sometimes a deterrent, a bargaining tool for diplomatic recognition, a tool to extort aid from the rest of the world, and lastly a new weapon to enable a successful invasion of the South.

In any event, the North Korean economy was effectively stuck with three different but very costly war machines—the nuclear weapons system, the underground fortress self-defence army and a panzer Blitzkrieg force. The economic strain was immense, but the North Koreans seemed unable to agree on a way to cut back the 'second economy'. No one could rationalize it, possibly because without prices, it was impossible to know what any part of it cost, what part of it was an effective use of resources, and what the returns might be if it was reformed. Defence spending, which consumed half the economy, was lost in a statistical fog.

The country needs to transfer most of the farms, factories and transport facilities owned by the military and return them to the service of the civilian economy. And it needs to demobilize many of the troops working in its factories or farms. By the time Kim Jong Il had taken over the reins of power, China was reaping the benefits of doing just that. Deng Xiaoping slashed China's military budget, cancelled most of the procurement projects, demobilized its troops and started moving factories back into urban areas. He cut foreign aid to countries like North Korea and demanded that the DPRK implement Chinese-style reforms.

It is hard to demonstrate the destructive effect of living in an economy without prices on the psychology of the North Koreans. The priority of any North Korean is to loyally obey the commands of the leadership no matter what. Yet the harm done is evident in a number of failed policy initiatives. In the 1960s, North Korea borrowed money from the Soviet Union and East European governments to build dozens of factories. Pyongyang never repaid the debts because whatever goods it exported proved to be so poor that they were worthless. In the 1970s, North Korea took out more loans, totalling $1.2 billion, this time from Sweden, West Germany, Japan and Italy under a plan to build factories producing cotton towels, garments, beer and other consumer goods. Again, it was unable to produce any goods on time that met basic standards. The debts were never repaid.[3]

The malinvestment of the ten great domestic projects of the 1980s launched by Kim Jong Il proved ruinous too. After the famine ended with fresh foreign aid, North Korea tried to lure in more foreign investment to restore coal and iron mines or to operate hotels in tourist resorts and many other ventures. Those Chinese or South Korean businessmen who took up the challenge came back defeated by the lack of understanding of basic business concepts of profit and loss. In fact, the whole of North Korea is littered with disastrous examples of ruinous ill-conceived investment projects gone wrong.

The scale of this economic folly is so great it's obvious to any visitor. On one visit to Pyongyang in the late 1980s, we were shown giant modern stadiums that would never be used, huge new hotels untouched by any guests and a motorway to the DMZ completely deserted apart from a handful of people pushing brooms. To be sure, the entire colossal military defence budget is best understood in this light. It is unrestrained, irrational spending that bears no proportionate relation to any strategic rewards or benefits. It could surely be cut in half and achieve the same aims. The cost of this economic folly is borne by the deprivation of its stunted, malnourished population, and partly by foreign governments who have squandered money investing in or aiding North Korea.

Yet beneath the surface, market forces have re-asserted themselves despite all the government efforts to supress them. It's hard to know if a shadow economy existed before the great famine of the early 1990s, but one can only surmise that it did since we now know the black market certainly flourished out of sight in the USSR and in China during the 1970s. Although one suspects that the black market played a smaller role in North Korea than elsewhere, it was still large enough for the state to order currency reforms in 1947, 1949, 1959, 1978 and 1992.[4]

The state took the same actions again and again. To deal a sudden blow against the black market, the state would require citizens to trade in their banknotes for new ones. Only a small amount of cash could be switched and always at an unfavourable rate. This sort of currency reform (which also took place in the USSR in 1947, 1961 and 1992) confiscated profits by wiping out savings. It also kept inflationary forces in check when there was too much cash chasing too few goods. It was similar to the actions of medieval monarchs when they called in gold and silver coins to the royal mint in order to clip them and debase their value.

All this shows how the DPRK is no exception to the theories of Mises. When the state rationing system broke down completely in the early 1990s, North Koreans faced a life and death struggle to survive. It forced millions to turn to the market to survive, and the state could do little to stop it. People began growing their own food wherever they could, sometimes in hidden plots in the hills out of the sight of the authorities. Others stole equipment like old machinery and traded the metal for scrap. Some traded in timber, fish, minerals, mushrooms, ginseng and anything else they could lay their hands on, including emergency food supplies shipped in by the World Food Programme. They first conducted barter exchanges, but soon semi-official marketplaces sprang up where goods were bought and sold for cash.

After tens of thousands, maybe hundreds of thousands, sneaked or bribed their way across the border to China to find refuge or to work, they returned with pockets full of Chinese renminbi, as well as dollars. With this influx of a trusted means of exchange, a secondary market in state housing sprang up, and it became possible to re-invest the cash into property. Above all, people sought to acquire foreign currencies as the only real store of value.

With the profits came savings, and as traders accumulated capital they could bring in more goods and hire others to work for them. This breached a fundamental socialist taboo. With a shadow market came dual pricing so officials could divert scarce goods from the state economy and resell them for a big mark up in the marketplace. Soon everyone was depending on the market to meet their basic needs, and the famine abated. Then something even more remarkable happened.

After half a century, the North Korean state had a chance to embrace the market and escape its poverty. Unwillingly or not, the state took it. It lifted official food prices, aligning them with market prices and simultaneously adjusted the exchange rate to match the real black market rate. In July 2002, the official price went up fifty times from 0.8 (North Korean) won per kilo to 44 won. Bus tickets in Pyongyang went up of from 2 to 20 won. Overall, prices of everything were hiked up ten- or twentyfold.[5]

For decades, the official exchange rate had been set at 2.16 North Korean won to the dollar, an entirely arbitrary rate fixed by decree in order to commemorate Kim Jong Il's birthday which is also a national holiday. Now it was fixed at 150 won to the dollar. The official foreign exchange coupons were abandoned. These were bits of paper that enabled visitors to pay for goods in hard currency shops. Another set of these coupons could be used by locals to buy things in hard currency shops. Each used a different exchange rate.[6]

Inevitably, the price rise had to be accompanied by drastic increases in pay so that people could afford to buy either from the state or the market. The wage of an average North Korean worker, previously 100 to 150 won a month, was also lifted to 2,000 won. Soldiers did even better, but not as well as miners who now got 6,000 won a month.[7]

The partial lifting of price controls quickly boosted the availability of food, and the famine began to ease. People stopped dying in huge numbers. If it had continued, the economy could actually grow, but like reforms in all communist countries, things had to get worse, a lot worse, before they got better. The price reforms were always going to be a J curve with hyperinflationary price rises until supply and demand stabilized prices and incomes.

Any government that took this road needed determination and popular support to carry it off. Yet whether such support existed in North Korea is questionable to say the least. The starving populace reeled from several shocks. The drastic devaluation instantly wiped out everybody's savings. Further, North Koreans began to grasp just how much poorer they were than those in the South. The average North Korean monthly salary was now just 11 dollars compared to over 600 dollars in South Korea. (Of course, this was not the whole story, as life in the two systems was quite different.) Even though the government tried to keep its people ignorant of life in South Korea, a difference so startlingly large could never be kept secret.

There was another destabilizing factor. Although it appeared that the population relied on the market to survive on a day-to-day basis, the authorities did not recognize any private property rights. Traders faced constant harassment, and their goods or cash could be confiscated at any time. Some were sent to jail. Others were beaten and shot in public. Bribery became commonplace, but it brought no security or safety. Nobody could trust anyone else, not even relatives.

The actions of the international community largely hindered North Korea's shift to a market-based economy. The South Koreans shipped in half a billion dollars' worth of food. Various international private aid organizations led by the World Food Programme delivered aid worth over $1.6 billion. Once the goods arrived at the handful of ports still operating, North Korean soldiers loaded them into trucks and drove off. No one could tell for sure where the cargo went or who it benefitted. UN inspectors authorized to check on the work of the public distribution system in allocating rations were easily bamboozled. They had to give a week's notice before turning up anywhere. It was easy to play the same tricks that had worked so well when inspectors came to check up on grain harvests.

It is quite likely, although hard to prove, that the food aid was given to the North Korean elite, the military and security services in order to guarantee their loyalty. It was the lower ranks of the *Songbun* (those considered disloyal or wavering) who were forced to scavenge or flee in search of food. No one can tell for sure how many perished during the famine years—it could be as many as 3 million—but a core of the regime remained loyal. The unintended consequence of the food aid is that it sheltered the elite from pressure to change.

It's significant that in the worst years of the famine the Chinese government drastically cut grain shipments to its neighbour in the hope of forcing it to reform. The famine did bring change but only temporarily.[8] The pattern of events soon took a turn similar to that seen in Russia in the early 1920s and China in the early 1960s. Like the NEP in Russia, famine and emergency heralded a short period of market liberalization, followed by a crackdown, a return to communist orthodoxy and a persistent shadow economy.

In North Korea, seven years passed before the crackdown took place. In September 2003, Kim Jong Il opened the official Tong Il marketplace in Pyongyang, where goods were sold at market prices. Similar markets opened around the country until there were at least 480 in 2018. From then on, official prices began to track market prices.[9]

Yet at 11:00 a.m. on 30 November 2009, Korean officials suddenly heard that a currency reform would take place that very afternoon. Everyone was given seven days to trade their old notes for new ones at a rate of 100:1, and no more than 100,000 per person (under $40 at unofficial rates) could be converted. After protests, the limit was raised to 150,000 won in cash and 300,000 held in bank accounts.[10]

Three weeks later, Pyongyang ordered that foreign currency could no longer be used in domestic transactions and that all foreign notes must be exchanged at the wildly unrealistic official rate. Businesses had to deposit their foreign currencies in banks and could only withdraw it with official permission.

These measures were designed to smash the private trading system, but as the economy staggered in shock, public anger threatened to boil over into an uprising. The state started to backpedal. The government tried to appease the public by having the official responsible, seventy-seven-year old Pak Nam-gi, shot by a public firing squad. He was 'a son of a bourgeois conspiring to infiltrate the ranks of revolutionaries to destroy the national economy', the Yonhap news agency reported.[11]

As the state made room for the private sector, the economy began to grow, albeit slowly. North Korea watcher Professor Andrei Lankov believes that perhaps 75 per cent of North Korean household income may come from private business—growing food on private plots, running food stalls, making clothes and footwear in unofficial workshops and so on. 'This private economy is massive', he observed. State cadres became de-facto entrepreneurs by switching whatever capital, land or equipment they controlled in order to make goods and services to sell on the market.[12]

The revalued won did not hold its value against the dollar since people realized that only foreign currencies or gold offered any safety from runaway inflation and anti-market crackdowns. The official rate, pegged at 900 won to the dollar, remained arbitrary since the real value, revealed by black market rates, rose to around 8,000 new won.

Using free market prices and the black market exchange rates, a sketchy picture of the economy can be gleaned. The growing private economy is delivering a measure of new prosperity, and fears of another famine have receded. Yet an economy distorted by massive military spending and the related external economic sanctions can never really prosper. Barriers to foreign trade stop a proper balancing of external and internal prices and therefore a more rational allocation of resources.

In the end, the market won—no pun intended—even in North Korea. It took seventy-five years, but the state had to abandon price controls, even though it did not admit defeat. Private sector activities continue to be illegal at the time of writing, so private property could be seized at any time. The drift of economic policy seems to be to try to give room to market prices but ultimately to keep as much as possible under state ownership by favouring state enterprises over the private sector, much as China has pioneered.

AFTERWORD

When the Russians abandoned communism in 1991, it was a revolution. Yet unlike the October Revolution of 1917, there was little bloodshed, no terror, no executions or arrests. There was no retribution against Communist Party members. Almost no one was put on trial or shot. Instead, what you saw all over Moscow were people standing on street corners, or gathering in a field or park higgling and haggling. The power of the market had won, but were the losers held to account?

Many East and Central European countries, notably Poland, Hungary and the Czech Republic, passed a lustration law—a special public employment law governing the process of examining whether a person holding certain higher public positions had worked or collaborated with the repressive apparatus of a communist regime. Only one country attempted to put communist leaders on trial, and that was Cambodia. Even so, by the time verdicts were reached the leaders of the Khmer Rouge were either dead or so elderly that the verdicts were just symbolic.

In Western Europe, there was no kind of lustration or decommunization campaign similar to the denazification campaign that took place in Germany after 1945. No one lost their job. A long-time leader of the Italian Communist Party, which was very much under Moscow's control, Giorgio Napolitano, was even appointed Italy's president. Olaf Scholz, in the 1980s an ardent Marxist who openly sided with Moscow and East Germany, became German

Chancellor. In Britain, leaders like Jeremy Corbyn can attack the market economy as destructive and maintain that socialism is necessary to combat the evils of capitalism. Few individuals, even if they were known to have actively collaborated with the USSR, or East Germany, or Mao's China, met with any official sanctions.

The general perception that socialists were good people with good intentions, with their hearts in the right place, remains largely unchallenged. Socialists are therefore considered to be quite unlike the Nazis who were defeated and put on trial or put through a process of denazification. This interpretation of history allows contemporary socialist leaders to be absolved of any moral responsibility.

Socialism has maintained or even strengthened its grip on the minds of the Western intelligentsia. Who could have imagined that thirty years after the Soviet Union dissolved, aged and unrepentant old school socialist politicians—like Bernie Saunders and Corbyn—would win electoral triumphs in Britain and America? In academia, enthusiasm for socialism is growing. Surveys of both academics and university administrators in British and American universities indicate that the majority identify as left wing and that more identify as left wing than ever before.-

We have whitewashed the moral stigma that should stain those who actively supported or defended communist states and who gullibly embraced nonsense about central planning, five-year plans, communist-led modernization and state ownership. Those responsible for decades of poor scholarship and faulty intelligence work have been absolved, and the many Western political leaders who embraced socialism throughout their careers have been exonerated from their moral and intellectual failings.

Instead of trying to understand the lessons of the collapse of communism across the world, students are made to digest and regurgitate a confusing succession of wars, crises, summits and treaties. China's modern history too is transformed into a series of unfortunate events, a confusing kaleidoscope of purges, wars and campaigns in which the Chinese Communist Party's own propaganda talking points are thrown about as a legitimate explanation for what was going on. The real explanation—that Mao's policies were a huge and predictable failure—is omitted altogether.

The idea that Mao understood the peasants and had their best interests at heart persists. In reality those in the 'red areas' that had been ruled by the communists in the 1930s suffered greatly. Generally, rural living standards had been rising thanks to innovations like kerosene lamps, electricity, bicycles, cinemas, cheap books, rubber boots, cheaper machine-made textiles, better seeds and fertilizers, modern communications and transport, and a great deal more. It is quite hard to imagine why any peasant or farmer would have supported any of Mao's policies.

Grain production most certainly did not rise during the 1950s. Instead, the closure of the markets and credit systems, the government's compulsory purchase of grain at prices below market costs, and its purchasing monopoly helped destroy the rural economy. The grain shortages and mass starvation started well before the 1958 Great Leap Forward.

Industry fared no better. Shanghai's large and modern cotton-spinning industry went into decline and did not reach pre-war levels for another twenty years. No new railway lines were built for twenty-five years, and not much new housing either. The social reforms that are cited to justify Mao's policies, such as the improvement in women's rights, were not a communist policy but a result of the 1911 revolution and the gradual Westernization of society that followed in the succeeding years. And it makes no sense to claim that Mao introduced nurseries so that women could go to work when in fact they were compelled to march to work in military-style labour gangs for twelve hours a day. No one in China enjoyed any basic human freedoms or claimed any legal protection from the state, let alone women's rights. To cite voting rights for women as a noteworthy benefit of the revolution is absurd, since this totalitarian dictatorship has not held any meaningful elections for over seventy years. The claims of the Chinese (or Russian, Vietnamese) communists that they are simply nationalists opposed to foreign interference in their countries and idealists driven to help the poorest classes in society, redistribute land and promote egalitarianism do not stand up to scrutiny.

If the utter failure of Mao's economic policies and the reasons for it are not made explicit, then the rest of China's story becomes very hard to understand. It explains why Mao had so many enemies and opponents at every level of society and why he had to destroy them in repeated political campaigns, why his policies were overturned after his death, why there was a national rebellion in 1989, and why the current government continues to censor all books, literature, film and comment about the past.

Mao was always committed to reproducing Stalin's collectivization and industrialization policies, and he carried them out as quickly as he could. This meant stripping the peasants of both their land and grain in order to finance his military–industrial programme. He never intended to allow them to keep their land or sell their products at market prices, and he certainly expected them to resist and surely knew that, as in Russia, there would be large-scale famines. The closure of the markets and credit systems, the government's compulsory purchase of grain at prices below market costs and its purchasing monopoly helped destroy the rural economy.

Nowhere in school or university courses are students taught that communist economies were never able to feed themselves or why they suffered from huge man-made famines. Socialist policies led to famines in many countries—Russia, China, Cambodia, Ethiopia, Mozambique, Zimbabwe, Vietnam, Syria—and persistent food shortages and malnutrition in dozens of others all over the world. In these countries, the state treated small farmers as outright enemies, suspected criminals or as a group opposed to modernization who had to be compelled to change.

Communist leaders like Mao, Stalin and Pol Pot all believed that peasants wanting to grow extra potatoes or tomatoes in their cottage garden to sell in a market were criminals because they were re-introducing 'the roots of capitalism'. A notion embraced first by Lenin and Stalin and then by Mao was that there existed huge numbers of 'rich peasants'. Anyone who lived in China during the 1930s or 1940s would have laughed at the very notion of such a thing as a rich peasant.

The claim made in the introduction to the A-Level textbook (Oxford AQA) that 'Mao was determined to pursue a specifically

Chinese route to socialism' is odd. He may have said that, but it is not supported by anything he actually did. He stuck rigidly to Stalin's template, and when this led to a catastrophe, he militantly refused to change or heed those advocating a Bukharin-style mixed economy. While the Chinese communists were certainly skilful at propaganda work, their policies were largely indistinguishable from those of Russia. Indeed, what exactly is Maoism? Is there really such a thing as 'Chinese socialism' or 'Jewish socialism' or 'Burmese socialism' or 'Vietnamese socialism' or indeed 'National Socialism'?

Mises' theory explains that they are all the same. It explains why the Soviet Union, despite possessing vast resources of people and territory, was never able to produce enough grain and other basic goods. Instead, it endured three major famines that had to be alleviated by foreign aid and rationing. Mises' theory explains why the rulers of such states, despite the despotic power they commanded, were unable to see the extent of this economic planning failure. Sometimes, the consequences of malinvestment took a long time to manifest. Even if the data was not being deliberately manipulated or falsified, leaders would still have no ability to make rational decisions. There was no way to replace the constant and helpful feedback that markets offer.

Many people found Mises' reasoning hard to accept and they still do. Everyone in a market economy witnesses daily why markets are frequently compared to casinos—everyone is dancing to the music of an erratic boom and bust cycle. Large firms suddenly going bust, shedding steady jobs. Others make sudden fortunes. Housing prices careen up and down; everything is in constant flux.

In a socialist economy, nothing seems to change. No enterprises ever go bankrupt. There is no unemployment. Prices are stable and fixed by the state. Everything seems secure and predictable as the population marches in step towards a brighter future. This future is planned and organized by the state, led by great leaders advised by experts and professionals following respected scientific theories.

After the Berlin Wall came crashing down in 1989, followed by the sudden disintegration of the Soviet Union, the fallacy of central planning was revealed. It was as if the stage lights came on and the audience finally saw what had been going on backstage all these years. After 1989, Mises began to get the recognition he deserved.

Even his biggest detractors admitted that he had been right all along. By this time, he was long dead, yet his most important vindication was still to come. In 1920 Mises could see what would go wrong with a collective economy and also how to restore it.

After 1989, many Western economists opposed immediate price liberalization and recommended gradual change. If Mises was right, though, the invisible hand of the market could quickly bring an end to the shortages. This is what happened. Within two years, food shortages in Poland had ended, and prices of daily goods began to stabilize. A country that had been plagued by rationing and bread riots became a food exporter, and by 2021 Poland exported agricultural goods worth 37 billion euros, a net surplus of 13 billion euros.

Other countries like neighbouring Ukraine, which opted for gradual reforms in the interests of social stability, fared far worse. They lurched from one economic and political crisis to another with slow growth and poor investment. China and Russia chose staggered price reforms, often delaying the lifting of price controls over products considered vital to state interests. They became corrupt oligarchies because a few made easy fortunes by buying at local state-controlled prices and then reselling at market prices. Even so, it is astonishing to note the degree to which agriculture in both Ukraine and Russia have been transformed. Russian wheat production had doubled to 60 million tons by 2010 and hit a record 85 million tons in 2020. It doubled the acreage for many of the grain crops such as wheat and sunflower seed. In Ukraine, agricultural output tripled in the thirty years following the breakup of the Soviet Union. Together, Russia and Ukraine accounted for nearly a third of global wheat exports in 2021, an incredible turnaround when one recalls that the Soviet Union had to import grain to feed itself and collapsed when it could not afford to pay for the imports.

The most eye-catching benefit of applying Mises' thinking on pricing can therefore be seen in the reduction of world hunger. Communist agricultural policies were the major cause of famine in the twentieth century. Liberalizing agricultural prices has been far more transformative than the trillions spent on international aid, debt relief and the work of international aid organizations and

NGOs. After 1945, governments in newly independent developing countries, inspired by the apparent success of Stalin's policies, introduced state purchasing monopolies, low procurement prices and collective farming. After 1980, when communist countries started liberalizing state controls over agriculture and freeing prices, all these countries quickly became food exporters. In the twenty-five years since the Berlin Wall came down, the UN Food and Agriculture Organization says that the percentage of hungry people fell from 23.3 per cent to 12.9 per cent, a reduction of around 700 million despite the world's population growing by 2 billion, from 4.5 billion to 6.5 billion.

Ethiopia, where most of the population live off the land, is another striking example. It suffered grave famines under Emperor Haile Selassie, until in 1974 the Ethiopian Revolution brought a communist government into power. It introduced price controls, state monopolies and collective farms. These controls were inevitably followed by famines, notably in 1984 and 1985. Then in 1990 a new government liberalized price controls over agricultural products. What followed was an immediate and astonishing recovery. In the first year, agricultural production surged by 3 per cent. Over the next twenty years, Ethiopian household farmers quadrupled cereal production. Farming so turbo-charged the economy that it grew twice as fast as nearly any other African economy, and Ethiopia developed into a major coffee exporter. In 2015, the International Monetary Fund ranked Ethiopia, a rural country, as one of the five fastest growing economies in the world. At the same time, between 1990 and 2014, the population almost doubled, expanding from 48 to 94 million, and yet the proportion of malnourished fell from 75 per cent to 35 per cent. Ethiopia still suffers from droughts, but there have been no more dramatic famines.

In East Asia, the same pattern of events took place. Over 30 million died of hunger not long after Chairman Mao took power in 1949. Right after Mao died in 1976, Chinese peasants spontaneously began dividing up the state fields into private plots and trading grain and other food stuffs. Then the state lifted grain procurement prices and permitted peasants to contract only part of the harvest to the state, leaving them to sell the rest at market prices. The state lifted all price controls over non-essential food stuffs like fish, fruit, chickens, eggs and all market garden produce.

By 1984, grain production had shot up, and there was enough to eat for the first time in thirty-five years. China's grain harvest doubled between 1977 and 1996, when so much was produced that the state ran out of places to store it. China saw 600 million, perhaps a billion people, lifted out of hunger. Once known as the land of famine, China hasn't had a famine since 1980. On the contrary, it has an obesity problem.

Vietnam lifted price controls in 1989 and similarly went swiftly from shortage to surplus. Despite the population increasing by 25 million to 93 million, it exported around 7 million tons of rice in 2013. It also emerged as one of the world's largest coffee exporters. The only East Asian country to suffer famines and continual food shortages is North Korea. In Latin America and the Caribbean, the lifting of price controls has had the same effect—the percentage of people rated as hungry dropped over twenty-five years from 14.7 per cent to 5.5 per cent.[1]

It is far easier to see the impact of free prices and market trading on the lives of small farmers than to understand how irrational pricing leads to malinvestment in industry; given the right incentives, a small farmer can quickly double egg sales or milk production. In industry, the product cycle is much longer, and so many price decisions must be considered that cause and effect are easily obscured. It can take years before the cost of malinvestment becomes apparent and more years to undo the damage.

This is the case with China, which despite its economic successes is also a victim of massive malinvestment into unproductive infrastructure projects, and above all housing. With a third of the economy tied up in empty and overpriced housing, it is at risk of a massive crash, perhaps the biggest in history. Huge amounts of debts are tied to house prices. A sudden crash could plunge many sectors like steel or cement into bankruptcy.

Mises' contribution to history and economic theory should be better known. A common sense theory about accounting and statistics is never going to be as exciting as promising a new utopia of free healthcare, free education, free housing and so on. But this book is not just about how accounting—fraudulent or otherwise—brought down a mighty empire; it is also a warning about the dangers of groupthink, and an appreciation of an individual who proved to be right in the face of contempt and derision from his peers.

NOTES

INTRODUCTION

1. Robert S. Norris and Hans M. Kristensen, 'Global Nuclear Weapons Inventories, 1945–2010', *Bulletin of the Atomic Scientists* 66(4) (2010), pp. 77–83, https://journals.sagepub.com/doi/full/10.2968/066004008
2. Daniel Patrick Moynihan, 'Do We Still Need the C.I.A.?', *New York Times*, 19 May 1991.
3. Choh-Ming Li, *The Statistical System of Communist China*, Berkeley: University of California Press, 2021.
4. Kathleen Elkins, 'Most Young Americans Prefer Socialism to Capitalism, New Report Finds', CNBC, 14 August 2018, https://www.cnbc.com/2018/08/14/fewer-than-half-of-young-americans-are-positive-about-capitalism.html; Flora Laven-Morris, 'Groupthink Rife in British Academia: New Asi Report', Adam Smith Institute, https://www.adamsmith.org/news/groupthink-rife-in-british-academia-new-asi-report
5. 'Battle of Shanghai', Wikipedia, last edited 23 May 2022, https://en.wikipedia.org/wiki/Battle_of_Shanghai
6. The USSR could not have defeated Germany in the Second World War if it had not become one of the world's great industrial powers by 1941. See Chris Corin and Terry Fiehn, *AQA A-level History: Tsarist and Communist Russia 1855–1964*, Kindle edn, London: Hodder Education, 2015.
7. Melanie Vance, *My Revision Notes: AQA AS/A-Level History; The Cold War, c.1945–1991*, London: Hodder Education, 2017.
8. Seumas Milne, 'Communism May Be Dead, But Clearly Not Dead Enough', *The Guardian*, 16 February 2006.

9. Ludmila Stern, *Western Intellectuals and the Soviet Union, 1920–40: From Red Square to the Left Bank*, Kindle edn, London: Routledge, 2007, loc. 277. 'I was shocked to discover that Western writers had conducted orchestrated campaigns against fellow intellectuals who criticised the USSR.'

10. A joint statement by twenty-five countries addressed to the United Nations on the seventieth anniversary of the Holodomor estimated the death toll at between 7 and 10 million.

11. Walter Duranty, *Duranty Reports Russia*, New York: Viking Press, 1934, p. 318.

12. 'Economy of East Germany', Wikipedia, last edited 7 June 2022, https://en.wikipedia.org/wiki/Economy_of_East_Germany

13. Bo Yang, *The Ugly Chinaman: And the Crisis of Chinese Culture*, ed. and trans. Don J. Cohn and Jing Qing, Sydney: Allen & Unwin, 1992.

1. VIENNA 1914

1. The topic is explored in detail in Tony Judt's book *Past Imperfect: French Intellectuals 1944–1956*, Berkeley: University of California Press, 1992. Paul R. Gregory, *Politics, Murder, and Love in Stalin's Kremlin: The Story of Nikolai Bukharin and Anna Larina*, Kindle edn, Stanford: Hoover Institution Press, 2013, loc. 201.

2. Stephen F. Cohen, *Bukharin and the Bolshevik Revolution: A Political Biography, 1888–1938*, Oxford: Oxford University Press, 1980, p. 19.

3. Eugen von Böhm-Bawerk, *Capital and Interest*, Grove City, PA: Libertarian Press, 1959 [1889].

4. 'Cincinnati Time Store', Wikipedia, last edited 13 January 2021, https://en.wikipedia.org/wiki/Cincinnati_Time_Store

5. Friedrich Engels, *Anti-Dühring: Herr Eugen Dühring's Revolution in Science*, trans. Emile Burns, Leipzig, 1878, p. 228, https://www.marxists.org/archive/marx/works/1877/anti-duhring/index.htm

6. Ibid.

7. Friedrich Engels, *The Principles of Communism*, in *Selected Works*, vol. 1, Moscow: Progress Publishers, 1969, pp. 81–97, paragraph 20, https://www.marxists.org/archive/marx/works/1847/11/princom.htm

8. Lenin, *State and Revolution*, in *Collected Works*, vol. 25, Chapter 5, pp. 381–492, see p. 71, https://www.marxists.org/archive/lenin/works/1917/staterev/index.htm

9. Nikolai Bukharin, *Programme of the World Revolution* (May 1918),

Glasgow: Socialist Labour Press, 1920, https://www.marxists.org/archive/bukharin/works/1918/worldrev/index.html

10. Nikolai Ivanovich Bukharin and Evgenii Preobrazhensky, *The ABC of Communism*, Ann Arbor: University of Michigan Press, 1966.

2. VIENNA AND THE SOCIALIST CALCULATION PROBLEM

1. Stefan Zweig, 'Going Home to Austria', in *The World of Yesterday*, Kindle edn, New York: Pushkin Press, 2009, loc. 4095.

2. Ibid., loc. 4207.

3. Ludwig von Mises, *Notes and Recollections*, Spring Mills, PA: Libertarian Press, 1978, p. 77.

4. Margaret Somers and Fred Block, 'The Return of Karl Polanyi', *Dissent* (Spring 2014), https://www.dissentmagazine.org/article/the-return-of-karl-polanyi

5. Zweig, *World of Yesterday*, loc. 4251.

6. Ibid., loc. 4261.

7. Ibid., loc. 4546.

8. Many others fled abroad too, including some from the Hungarian film studios and theatres, which were all nationalized. Among these exiles were some who became Hollywood giants: film directors Mihály Kertész, later known as Michael Curtiz, who directed *Casablanca*; Sándor (later Sir Alexander) Korda; and Béla Blaskó, who, under the name of Bela Lugosi, was to become famous for playing Dracula.

9. Ibid., loc. 4237.

10. Ibid., loc. 4216.

11. Anna Eisenmenger, *Blockade: The Diary of an Austrian Middle-Class Woman, 1914–1924*, London: Constable, 1932, cited in Adam Ferguson, *When Money Dies: The Nightmare of the Weimar Collapse*, London: William Kimber, 1975, p. 11.

12. In *Notes and Recollections*, he wrote that in 1908 he had joined the Central Association for Housing Reform: 'It was an association of all those who sought to improve the unsatisfactory housing conditions in Austria. I was appointed a reviewer of the pending reform of real-estate taxation … The undesirable housing conditions in Austria were caused by the fact that taxation prevented large capital and entrepreneurship from entering the field of housing.'

13. Zweig, *World of Yesterday*, loc. 4246.

14. 'Karl-Marx-Hof', Wikipedia, last edited 30 December 2021, https://en.wikipedia.org/wiki/Karl-Marx-Hof

15. 'Red Vienna', Wikipedia, last edited 20 December 2021, https://en.wikipedia.org/wiki/Red_Vienna

16. Jörg Guido Hülsmann, *Mises: The Last Knight of Liberalism*, Auburn, AL: Ludwig von Mises Institute, 2007, p. 401.

17. Ibid., p. 376.

18. Ludwig von Mises, *Economic Calculation in the Socialist Commonwealth*, trans. S. Alder with corrections by H. Anderson in 'Die Wirtschaftsrechnung im sozialistischen Gemeinwesen', *Archiv für Sozialwissenschaft und Sozialpolitik* 47(1) (1920), pp. 86–121.

19. Ludwig von Mises, *Socialism: An Economic and Sociological Analysis*, New Haven: Yale University Press, 1951, Chapter 9, 'The Position of the Individual under Socialism'.

3. WHY LENIN'S PROGRAMME FAILED AND THE EXCUSE OF WAR COMMUNISM

1. Stéphane Courtois et al., *The Black Book of Communism*, ed. Mark Kramer, Cambridge, MA: Harvard University Press, 1999, p. 89.

2. 'Lenin Confesses Economic Defeat', *New York Times*, 19 October 1921: 'The real meaning of the new economic policy is that we have met a great defeat in our plans and that we are now making a strategic retreat', said Lenin. Lenin also said: 'In the beginning of 1918, we made this mistake that we decided to effect a direct transition to communist production and distribution. We had decided that the peasants would give us in the way of *razverstka* (requisitioning of surpluses) the amount of grain we needed and we would then apportion this among the factories and we would have communist production and distribution.'

3. This was the line pushed by British historian E. H. Carr.

4. Nikolai Bukharin, *The Path to Socialism in Russia*, New York: Omicron Books, 1967, p. 178.

5. Norman Stone, *Europe Transformed, 1878–1919*, Oxford: Blackwell, 1999, p. 143.

6. Sean McMeekin, *History's Greatest Heist: The Looting of Russia by the Bolsheviks*, Kindle edn, New Haven: Yale University Press, 2009, loc. 391.

7. On 17 October 1921, Lenin gave a speech to The Second All-Russia Congress Of Political Education Departments in which he said that they had wrongly tried to go straight to the lower stage of communism and 'bypass the period of socialist accounting and control...' He declared that: 'In substance, our New Economic Policy signifies that, having

sustained severe defeat on this point, we have started a strategical retreat. ...In attempting to go over straight to communism we, in the spring of 1921, sustained a more serious defeat on the economic front than any defeat inflicted upon us by Kolchak, Denikin or Pilsudski. This defeat was much more serious, significant and dangerous. It was expressed in the isolation of the higher administrators of our economic policy from the lower and their failure to produce that development of the productive forces which the Programme of our Party regards as vital and urgent.' Lenin's Collected Works, 2nd English Edition, Progress Publishers, Moscow, 1965, Vol. 33, pp. 60–79, https://www.marxists.org/archive/lenin/works/1921/oct/17.htm

8. F. O. Lindley, 'Report on Recent Events in Russia', 25 November 1917, in PRO, FO 371/3.

9. Christopher Andrew and Vasili Mitrokhin, *The Sword and the Shield: The Mitrokhin Archive and the Secret History of the KGB*, New York: Basic Books, 1999; 'Cheka', Wikipedia, last edited 19 May 2022, https://en.wikipedia.org/wiki/Cheka

10. Andrew and Mitrokhin, *Sword and the Shield*, p. 28.

11. Lancelot Lawton, *An Economic History of Soviet Russia*, vol. 1, London: Macmillan, 1932, p. 15.

12. Courtois et al., *Black Book of Communism*, p. 109.

13. McMeekin, *History's Greatest Heist*, loc. 3376–7.

14. Colonel Ryan's observations, as reported by Robert E. Olds, American Red Cross commissioner to Europe, in a 15 April 1920 letter to Dr Livingston Farrand, Red Cross chairman in Washington, in RSU, HP 494, p. 2.

15. Courtois et al., *Black Book of Communism*, p. 86.

16. Ibid., p. 88.

17. Ibid., p. 107.

18. Ibid., pp. 110–11

19. Ibid., p. 133.

20. See 'Report of the Commissar of Finance, Gukovsky, to the Central Committee Executive Committee, 15 April 1918'.

21. Stella Zoe Whishaw Meyendorff, *Through Terror to Freedom: The Dramatic Story of an English Woman's Life and Adventures in Russia before, during and after the Revolution*, London: Hutchinson & Co., 1929.

22. Courtois et al., *Black Book of Communism*, p. 117.

23. Ibid., p. 118.

24. Cited in Courtois et al., *Black Book of Communism*, p. 120.

25. 'Polish–Soviet War', Wikipedia, last edited 2 May 2022, https://en.wikipedia.org/wiki/Polish%E2%80%93Soviet_War

26. L. Kritsman, *The Heroic Period in the Great October Revolution* (1926) p. 166. 'Russian Civil War', Wikipedia, last edited 21 May 2022, https://en.wikipedia.org/wiki/Russian_Civil_War

4.   HOW A GOLD-BACKED CURRENCY BROUGHT PROSPERITY TO MANY COUNTRIES IN THE 1920S

1.   Adam Fergusson, *When Money Dies: The Nightmare of the Weimar Hyper-Inflation*, London: Old Street Publishing, 2010, p. 1.
2.   S. S. Katzenellenbaum, *Russian Currency and Banking*, London: P. S. King & Son, 1925, p. 59.
3.   Lawton, *Economic History of Soviet Russia*, vol. 1, p. 151.
4.   Richard Pipes, *The Russian Revolution 1899–1919*, London: Collins Harvill, 1990, pp. 686–7. McMeekin, *History's Greatest Heist*, loc. 741–2.
5.   Pipes, *Russian Revolution*, p. 687.
6.   Fergusson, *When Money Dies*, pp. 18, 98.
7.   Ibid., p. 7.
8.   McMeekin, *History's Greatest Heist*, loc. 768.
9.   Ibid., Chapter 8, 'London'.
10. Ibid., Chapter 4, 'The Church'.
11. Ibid., loc. 2547.
12. Ibid., loc. 2436.
13. 'Soviet Gold Production, Reserves and Exports through 1954', CIA, 17 October 1955, https://www.cia.gov/readingroom/docs/DOC_0000496246.pdf
14. 'Russian Famine of 1921–1922', Wikipedia, last edited 13 March 2022, https://en.wikipedia.org/wiki/Russian_famine_of_1921%E2%80%931922

5.   HOW BUKHARIN LOST HIS LIFE BUT SAVED MILLIONS OF LIVES IN CHINA

1.   Cohen, *Bukharin and the Bolshevik Revolution*, pp. 105, 150–2.
2.   Bukharin, *Path to Socialism in Russia*, p. 178.
3.   *Pravda*, 3 December 1932.
4.   'On the New Economic Policy and Our Tasks', 17 April 1925; N. I. Bukharin, *Izbrannye proizvedeniya*, Moscow: Izdatel'stvo politicheskoy literatury, 1988, pp. 195–6, 197.
5.   Gregory, *Politics, Murder, and Love in Stalin's Kremlin*, loc. 310.

6. Leon Trotsky, *The Revolution Betrayed*, Garden City, NY: Doubleday, Doran & Company, 1937, pp. 50–5.

7. Cohen, *Bukharin and the Bolshevik Revolution*, pp. 161–9.

8. 'Soviet Famine of 1930–1933', Wikipedia, last edited 18 May 2022, https://en.wikipedia.org/wiki/Soviet_famine_of_1930%E2%80%931933; Sheila Fitzpatrick, *Everyday Stalinism: Ordinary Life in Extraordinary Times; Soviet Russia in the 1930s*, Kindle edn, Oxford: Oxford University Press, 1999, loc. 168.

9. Gregory, *Politics, Murder, and Love in Stalin's Kremlin*, loc. 410.

10. The writer Arthur Koestler based his novel *Darkness at Noon* on Bukharin, except that the confession of the fictional hero, Rubasov, is presented as a final act of loyal service to the Party. The reality was very different.

11. Ibid., loc. 476.

6.   WHY WESTERN INTELLECTUALS WERE FOOLED BY SOVIET STATISTICS

1. Walter Duranty, 'Soviet Fixes Opinion by Widest Control', *New York Times*, 22 June 1931, https://www.garethjones.org/soviet_articles/duranty_1931_6.htm

2. Stern, *Western Intellectuals and the Soviet Union*, loc. 258–65. All members of the Society of Friends of the New Russia.

3. Ibid., loc. 377.

4. Jean-Richard and Marguerite Bloch, 'Journal du voyage en URSS', cited in Stern, *Western Intellectuals and the Soviet Union*.

5. Ilya Ehrenburg, *Selections from People, Years, My Life*, vol. 2, New York: Pergamon Press, 1972, p. 208.

6. Lion Feuchtwanger, *Moscow 1937: My Visit Described for My Friends*, trans. Irene Josephy, New York: Viking Press, 1937.

7. Yueh Sheng, *Sun Yat-sen University in Moscow and the Chinese Revolution: A Personal Account*, Lawrence, KS: University of Kansas, 1971.

8. Bernard Shaw, *The Rationalisation of Russia*, ed. Harry M. Geduld, London: Bloomington, 1961.

9. 'Harry Dexter White', Wikipedia, last edited 14 May 2022, https://en.wikipedia.org/wiki/Harry_Dexter_White

10. Kevin Morgan, *The Webbs and Soviet Communism: Bolshevism and the British Left Part II*, London: Lawrence & Wishart, 2005, p. 8.

11. Andrew J. Williams, *Labour and Russia: The Attitude of the Labour Party to the USSR, 1924–34*, Manchester: Manchester University Press, 1989.

12. Sidney and Beatrice Webb, *Soviet Communism: A New Civilisation*, London: Longmans, Green, 1944, p. 938.

13. In his autobiography *Chronicles of Wasted Time*, vol. 1, *The Green Stick* (London: Collins, 1972), Muggeridge wrote: 'Wise old Shaw, high-minded old Barbusse, the venerable Webbs, Gide the pure in heart and Picasso the impure, down to poor little teachers, crazed clergymen and millionaires, drivelling dons and very special correspondents like Duranty, all resolved, come what might, to believe anything, however preposterous, to overlook anything, however villainous, to approve anything, however obscurantist and brutally authoritarian, in order to be able to preserve intact the confident expectation that one of the most thorough-going, ruthless and bloody tyrannies ever to exist on earth could be relied on to champion human freedom, the brotherhood of man, and all the other good liberal causes to which they had dedicated their lives. ALL RESOLVED, in other words, TO ABOLISH THEMSELVES AND THEIR WORLD, THE REST OF US WITH IT. Nor have I from that time ever had the faintest expectation that, in earthly terms, anything could be salvaged; that any earthly battle could be won, or earthly solution found. It has all just been sleep-walking to the end of the night.'

14. Webbs, *Soviet Communism*, pp. 559–61; Robert Conquest, *Harvest of Sorrow: Soviet Collectivization and the Terror-Famine*, New York: Oxford University Press, 1986, pp. 317–18. The Webbs' postscript to the second edition of *Soviet Communism* defends the Moscow show trials and confirms the Webbs' enthusiasm for collectivized agriculture. See pp. 919ff.

15. R. Davies, 'Carr's Changing Views of the Soviet Union', in *E. H. Carr: A Critical Appraisal*, ed. Michael Cox, London: Palgrave, 2000, pp. 91–108, here p. 98.

16. Stephen G. Wheatcroft, 'More Light on the Scale of Repression and Excess Mortality in the Soviet Union in the 1930s', in *Stalinist Terror*, ed. John Arch Getty and Roberta Thompson Manning, Cambridge: Cambridge University Press, 2009, pp. 282–9, cited in Fitzpatrick, *Everyday Stalinism*, loc. 2051.

17. Fitzpatrick, *Everyday Stalinism*, loc. 1052–3.

18. Ibid., loc. 232–7.

19. Ibid., loc. 1137.

20. Ibid., loc. 1160.

21. Ibid., loc. 1177–8.

22. David Caute, *The Fellow Travellers: Intellectual Friends of Communism*, New Haven: Yale University Press, 1988, p. 70.

23. Webbs, *Soviet Communism*, pp. 548–54.
24. Stalin, report to the Seventeenth Party Congress on the Work of the Central Committee, 26 January 1934, in *Works*, vol. 13, *1930–January 1934*, Moscow: Foreign Languages Publishing House, 1954.
25. Trotsky, *Revolution Betrayed*, p. 53.
26. Naum Jasny, *Soviet Industrialisation 1928–1952*, Chicago: University of Chicago Press, 1961, pp. 168–72.
27. Anne Applebaum, *The Gulag: A History*, New York: Doubleday, 2003.

7.　WHY EVEN THE CIA BELIEVED SOVIET STATISTICS

1. 'Abram Bergson: Memorial Minute', *Harvard Gazette*, 8 January 2004, https://news.harvard.edu/gazette/story/2004/01/abram-bergson. Roger E. Backhouse, 'Scientific Welfare Analysis: The Origins of Bergson–Samuelson Welfare Economics, 1936–1947', University of Birmingham, February 2013.
2. Abram Bergson, 'Recollections and Reflections of a Comparativist', *American Economist* 31(1) (Spring 1987), pp. 3–8.
3. '*The Structure of Soviet Wages* by Abram Bergson', *Harvard Economic Studies* 76 (1944), pp. 390–3.
4. 'Abram Bergson, 89, Theorist Who Studied Soviet Economy', *New York Times*, 25 April 2003.
5. Padma Desai, 'Abram Bergson: A Tribute', Proceedings of the American Philosophical Society, https://warwick.ac.uk/fac/soc/economics/staff/mharrison/archive/noticeboard/bergson/desai.pdf
6. Abram Bergson, 'Socialist Economics', in *A Survey of Contemporary Economics*, ed. Howard S. Ellis, Philadelphia, PA: Blakiston Company for the American Economic Association, 1948, p. 447.
7. Ibid.
8. Von Mises, *Notes and Recollections*.
9. Hülsmann, *Mises*, pp. 480–4.
10. Oskar Lange, 'On the Economic Theory of Socialism', *Review of Economic Studies* 4(1) (October 1936), pp. 53–71.
11. Lionel Robbins, *The Great Depression*, New York: Macmillan, 1934, p. 151.
12. Friedrich A. Hayek, 'The Present State of the Debate', in *Collectivist Economic Planning*, ed. Friedrich A. Hayek, London: Routledge, 1935, p. 212.
13. Oskar Lange, 'The Computer and the Market', in *Socialist Economics*, ed. Alec Nove and D. Nuti, London: Penguin Books, 1972, pp. 401–2.

14. *Tâtonnement*, a concept introduced by French economist Leon Walras (1834–1910), is a trial-and-error process by which equilibrium prices and stability are reached in competitive markets.

15. Ludwig von Mises, 'Economic Calculation in the Socialist Commonwealth', in Hayek, *Collectivist Economic Planning*, pp. 87–130.

16. Ibid.

17. J. K. Galbraith in *The New York Times Book Review*, 22 April 1973, cited in John Toland, *Adolf Hitler*, New York: Doubleday, 1976, p. 403 (note).

18. Llewellyn H. Rockwell, 'The Meaning of the Mises Papers', *Free Market* 15(4) (April 1997), https://mises.org/library/meaning-mises-papers

19. Margit von Mises, *My Years with Ludwig von Mises*, 2nd edn, Cedar Falls, IA: Center for Futures Education, 1978, p. 45.

20. Joseph Schumpeter, *Capitalism, Socialism and Democracy*, London: G. Allen & Unwin, 1943, prologue to part 2.

21. 'Oskar R. Lange', Wikipedia, last edited 21 March 2022, https://en.wikipedia.org/wiki/Oskar_R._Lange

8. HOW THE CIA CREATED PHANTOM SOVIET GNP STATISTICS

1. 'Soviet Famine of 1946–1947', Wikipedia, last edited 21 March 2022, https://en.wikipedia.org/wiki/Soviet_famine_of_1946%E2%80%931947

2. 'GDP: One of the Great Inventions of the 20th Century', Bureau of Economic Analysis, US Department of Commerce, https://apps.bea.gov/scb/account_articles/general/0100od/maintext.htm

3. Bergson, 'Socialist Economics', p. 14.

4. Abram Bergson and Simon Kuznets, *Economic Trends in the Soviet Union*, Cambridge, MA: Harvard University Press, 1963, p. 23; Steven Rosefielde, ed., *Economic Welfare and Economics of Soviet Socialism: Essays in Honor of Abram Bergson*, Cambridge: Cambridge University Press, 1981, pp. 8–10. Jasny, *Soviet Industrialisation*, p. 162.

5. Bergson and Kuznets, *Economic Trends in the Soviet Union*, pp. 14, 31.

6. 'Wassily Leontief', Wikipedia, last edited 7 April 2022, https://en.wikipedia.org/wiki/Wassily_Leontief; 'Simon Kuznets', Wikipedia, last edited 7 May 2022, https://en.wikipedia.org/wiki/Simon_Kuznets

7. Alexander Gerschenkron, 'Soviet Heavy Industry: A Dollar Index of Output, 1927/28–1937', *Review of Economics and Statistics* 37(2) (May 1955), pp. 120–30.

9.   NO ONE WAS ALLOWED TO CHALLENGE ABRAM BERGSON

1. Abram. Bergson, 'Soviet National Income and Product in 1937', *Quarterly Journal of Economics* 64(2) (1950), pp. 208–41.
2. Taken from Strobe Talbott, ed. and trans., *Khrushchev Remembers*, Boson: Little, Brown and Co., 1970, p. 139.
3. 'Jasny, Naum', https://www.encyclopedia.com/religion/encyclopedias-almanacs-transcripts-and-maps/jasny-naum; author interview with Jasny's son, Tom Artin, in 2014.
4. Jasny, *Soviet Industrialisation*, p. 153.
5. Ibid.
6. Ibid., p. 5.
7. Ibid., pp. 11–21.
8. Joseph S. Berliner, *Factory and Manager in the U.S.S.R.*, Cambridge, MA: Harvard University Press, 1957, pp. 58–63.
9. Paul Gregory, *The Political Economy of Stalinism*, Cambridge: Cambridge University Press, 2004, pp. 111–19
10. Ibid.
11. Ibid.

10.   WHY AMERICAN ECONOMIC TEXTBOOKS WERE WRONG

1. Paul Samuelson. 16 December 2011. Nasar, 1995 C1.
2. *New Yorker*, 3 September 1984.
3. 'Statement of Aims', Mont Pelerin Society, https://www.montpelerin.org/statement-of-aims
4. Paul Samuelson, *Economics: An Introductory Analysis*, New York: McGraw-Hill, 1948, p. 20.
5. Ibid., p. 831.
6. Ibid. (1985 edn).
7. William Nordhaus in Samuelson, *Economics*, 12th edn (1989), p. 776. Mark Skousen, 'The Perseverance of Paul Samuelson's Economics', *Journal of Economic Perspectives* 11(2) (Spring 1997), pp. 137–52.
8. Campbell McConnell, *Economics: Principles, Problems and Policies*, New York: McGraw-Hill, 1963, p. 750.
9. George Leland Bach, *Economics: An Introduction to Analysis and Policy*, Englewood Cliffs, NJ: Prentice-Hall, 1954, p. 698.
10. Robert L. Heilbroner, *The Economic Problem*, Englewood Cliffs, NJ: Prentice Hall, 1968, pp. 629–30.

11. WHY THE GULAG ECONOMY WAS ABANDONED

1. Courtois et al., *Black Book of Communism*, p. 242. Aleksei Tikhonov, 'The End of the Gulag', in *The Economics of Forced Labor: The Soviet Gulag*, ed. Paul R. Gregory and V. V. Lazarev, Stanford: Hoover Institution Press, 2003, p. 2.
2. See Amy Knight, *Beria: Stalin's First Lieutenant*, Princeton: Princeton: University Press, 2020.
3. Gregory and Lazarev, *Economics of Forced Labor*, p. 196.
4. Oleg Khlevnyuk, 'The Economy of the OGPU, NKVD, and MVD of the USSR, 1930–1953: The Scale, Structure, and Trends of Development', in Gregory and Lazarev, *Economics of Forced Labor*, p. 65.
5. In her book on the Gulag, Applebaum says that 18 million passed through the system and another 6 million were sent into exile or deported between 1929 and 1953. But this excludes those killed and imprisoned from 1917 to 1928 and those shot and arrested in jails inside and outside the USSR. More recent Russian research puts the total death toll at 25 million.
6. In his book on Kolyma, Robert Conquest states that the death toll was 3 million (*Kolyma: The Arctic Death Camps*, New York: Viking Press, 1978, pp. 228–9).
7. Schumpeter, *Capitalism, Socialism and Democracy*, p. 26.
8. Friedrich Engels, *The Collected Works of Friedrich Engels*, Kindle edn, n.p.: Halcyon Classics, 2009, loc. 246–52.
9. Galina Mikhailovna Ivanova, *Labor Camp Socialism: The Gulag in the Soviet Totalitarian System*, trans. Carol A. Flath, ed. Donald J. Raleigh, Armonk, NY: M. E. Sharpe, 2000, p. 107. Routledge, 17 July 2015.
10. Khlevnyuk, 'Economy of the OGPU, NKVD, and MVD', p. 65.
11. Ibid., p. 62.
12. Courtois et al., *Black Book of Communism*, loc. 5987–99, 5999–6001, 5988.
13. Circulation letter of the chief of the Gulag, Dobrynin, to local administrators of camps and colonies (4 May 1947). Report by Minister of Interior Kruglov including a similar proposal, written in 1948.
14. Tikhonov, 'End of the Gulag', pp. 1–7.
15. Khlevnyuk, 'Economy of the OGPU, NKVD, and MVD', p. 63.

12. MOSCOW'S FAILED GLOBAL BARTER SYSTEM

1. 'Inadequate Barter System in International Trade', UIA, 4 October 2020, http://encyclopedia.uia.org/en/problem/149677

2. Zbigniew Brzezinski, *The Soviet Bloc: Unity and Conflict*, Cambridge, MA: Harvard University Press, 1967, p. 348.

3. Randall Stone, *Satellites and Commissars: Strategy and Conflict in the Politics of Soviet-Bloc Trade*, Princeton: Princeton University Press, 1996, p. 5.

4. Khrushchev repeatedly predicted that by around 1970 the USSR would overtake the United States in per capita production, and in 1961 the goal of surpassing America by the end of the decade was even included in the official party programme.

5. Fursenko, A.A., ED. Prezidium TsK KPSS 1954–65. *Chernovye protokol'nye zapici zasedanii*, Moscow: ROSPEN, 2003, p. 722.

6. Oscar Sanchez-Sibony, *Red Globalisation: The Political Economy of the Soviet Cold War from Stalin to Khruschev*, New York: Cambridge University Press, 2014, p. 15, citing Soviet archives GARF, f. 5446, op. 97, d. 1382, II. 63–4.

7. Ibid., p. 173. Even the oil exported proved to be of a poor quality.

8. Stone, *Satellites and Commissars*, pp. 36, 208.

9. Ibid., p. 239.

10. Ibid., pp. 116–21.

11. Ibid., pp. 121–3.

12. Byung-Yeon Kim, 'Causes of Repressed Inflation in the Soviet Consumer Market, 1965–1989: Retail Price Subsidies, the Siphoning Effect, and the Budget Deficit', *Economic History Review* 55(1) (2002), pp. 105–27.

13. FAKE STATISTICS AND SOVIET DEFENCE SPENDING

1. 'Soviet Famine of 1946', Wikipedia, last edited 2 July 2022, https://en.wikipedia.org/wiki/Soviet_famine_of_1946%E2%80%931947#:~:text=The%20Soviet%20famine%20of%201946,900%2C000%20perished%20during%20the%20famine

2. Marc Trachtenberg, 'Assessing Soviet Economic Performance during the Cold War: A Failure of Intelligence?', *Texas National Security Review* 1(2) (February 2018), p. 15.

3. Daniel Patrick Moynihan, *Secrecy: The American Experience*, New Haven: Yale University Press, 1998, pp. 190–3.

4. 'Missile Gap', Wikipedia, last edited 13 May 2022, https://en.wikipedia.org/wiki/Missile_gap

5. 'Harmel Report', NATO, 1 July 2022, https://www.nato.int/cps/en/natohq/topics_67927.htm

6. David Arbel and Ran Edelist, *Western Intelligence and the Collapse of the*

Soviet Union, 1980–1990: Ten Years That Did Not Shake the World, Kindle edn, Hoboken: Taylor & Francis, 2004, loc. 3632, 3662, 3672.

7. Mark Harrison and R. W. Davies, 'The Soviet Military-Economic Effort during the Second Five-Year Plan 1933–1937', *Europe-Asia Studies* 49(3) (1997), pp. 369–406.

8. Noel E. Firth and James H. Noren, *Soviet Defence Spending: A History of CIA Estimates 1950–1990*, College Station: Texas A&M University Press, 1998, pp. 57–8.

9. Ibid., p. 49.

10. Ibid., pp. 65, 257.

11. Arbel and Edelist, *Western Intelligence and the Collapse of the Soviet Union*, loc. 3507b.

12. David R. Jardini, *Thinking Through the Cold War: RAND, National Security and Domestic Policy, 1945–1975*, Santa Monica, CA: RAND, 2013.

13. Henry Rowen and Charles Wolf Jr, eds, *The Impoverished Superpower: Perestroika and the Soviet Military Burden*, San Francisco: Institute for Contemporary Studies Press, 1990, p. 22.

14. Interview with Dina Birman. Interview with Birman's widow, Albina Birman, December 2015.

15. Igor Birman, 'Limits of Economic Measurements', *Slavic Review* 39(4) (1980), pp. 603–7.

16. Birman's autobiography, pp. 302–3, supplied to the author by Albina Birman.

17. Louise Shelley, *Igor Birman: Biography*, New York: American Jewish Committee, Oral History Library, 1980.

18. Igor Birman, 'The Imbalance of the Soviet Economy', *Soviet Studies* 40(2) (1988), pp. 210–21.

19. Igor Birman. *Personal Consumption in the USSR and USA*, New York: St. Martin's Press, 1989.

20. Igor Birman, *Secret Incomes of the Soviet State Budget*, The Hague: Martinus Nijhoff, 1981.

21. Birman, *Personal Consumption in the USSR and USA*.

22. Igor Birman, 'The Way to Slow the Arms Race', *Washington Post*, 27 October 1980, p. A15.

23. Interview with Dina Birman and Birman's widow, Albina Birman, December 2015.

24. 'Outside View: Winning the Cold War; Part 1', UPI, 11 June 2004, https://www.upi.com/Defense-News/2004/06/11/Outside-View-Winning-the-Cold-War-Part-1/44791086934200

25. Birman, 'Way to Slow the Arms Race'; Igor Birman, 'The Soviet

Economy: Alternative Views', *Survey* 29(2) (Summer 1985), p. 113.

26. T. Rees Shapiro, 'Igor Birman; Forecast Fall of Soviet Economy; at 82', *Washington Post*, 23 April 2011; Birman, *Personal Consumption in the USSR and USA*.

27. Arbel and Edelist, *Western Intelligence and the Collapse of the Soviet Union*, loc. 4915.

28. Shapiro, 'Igor Birman; Forecast Fall of Soviet Economy; at 82'.

29. *Commanding Heights: The Battle for the World Economy*, PBS, n.d., https://www.pbs.org/wgbh/commandingheights

30. Noel and Noren, *Soviet Defence Spending*, pp. 190–4. Arbel and Edelist, *Western Intelligence and the Collapse of the Soviet Union*, loc. 3507.

31. Geir Lundestad, *The Rise and Decline of the American 'Empire': Power and Its Limits in Comparative Perspective*, Oxford: Oxford University Press, 2012, p. 137.

14. HOW AMERICAN EXPERTS MISUNDERSTOOD MAO'S CHINA

1. 'People's Volunteer Army', Wikipedia, last edited 19 Mary 2022, https://en.wikipedia.org/wiki/People%27s_Volunteer_Army

2. National Intelligence Estimate (NIE) no. 13-6-14 April 1961. NIE 13-5-66.

3. In this letter in the *New York Review of Books*, CIA officer Wes Pedersen writes: 'Jasper Becker's *Hungry Ghosts: Mao's Secret Famine* is yet another indictment of United States Intelligence as it operated in the 1950s and 60s. As Nicholas Eberstadt notes in his review (Feb. 16): "One of the most amazing aspects of the great Chinese famine was Beijing's success in concealing it from the outside world. The Chinese Government was aided in its shameful task by a procession of witless or willing Westerners." Both the Central Intelligence Agency and the State Department ignored evidence that was crystal clear to (again quoting Mr. Eberstadt) "some Western academics, journalists and politicians".

   'In 1961, as a Foreign Service officer with the United States Information Agency in Hong Kong, I prepared a report, "Famine: Grim Specter Over China", for distribution to Foreign Service posts around the world. The report was canceled by the USIA, acting on advice from the CIA and the State Department. There was, I was instructed by Washington, "no famine in China". Meanwhile, refugees continued to flood into Hong Kong with tales of widespread, massive food shortages.

   'This was very much part of a pattern of faulty American

intelligence in that period—intelligence that insisted, in January 1953, that Stalin could not possibly be seriously ill (he died two months later) and that insisted, up to the day of Nikita Khrushchev's purge of Georgi Malenkov, that there was no power struggle in the Kremlin.'

4. NIE 13-5-66, 1976 NIE 13-76, NIE 1961, NIE 13-4-62, NIE 13-2 59.

5. Angus Maddison, 'Measuring the Performance of a Command Economy: An Assessment of the CIA Estimates for the USSR', *Review of Income and Wealth* 44(3) (September 1998), pp. 5, 6: 'For China, the CIA had much less information than for the USSR because of the collapse of the Chinese statistical system from 1960 to the mid 1970s. Their industrial index was first presented in 1967 with only 11 indicators. In 1975 the number of indicators more than doubled, but for 7 of the 11 sectors it contained, performance was measured by output of a single commodity. The index was last presented in 1982, for the years 1949–80. By then its coverage was widened, but it was based on indicators for only 45 commodities. The sector weights were wage bills, with gross output weights for handicrafts …

'For China, the CIA made no serious effort to compare levels of performance with the USA. In JEC (1972), pp. 42–3, they cited dollar estimates for China without attribution, which were drawn from crude estimates for 1955 by Hollister (1958), pp. 146–7. JEC (1975), p. 23, gives dollar estimates for Chinese GNP, with no indication of how they were made. JEC (1978), p. 208, also provided dollar estimates, and on p. 230 explained that they were an update of the 1955 benchmark. Their last effort in 1982 gave dollar estimates with no source indication.'

6. John Frankenstein and Bates Gill, 'Current and Future Challenges Facing Chinese Defence Industries', *China Quarterly* 146 (June 1996), p. 403.

7. 'Five-Year Plans of China', Wikipedia, last edited 10 May 2022, https://en.wikipedia.org/wiki/Five-year_plans_of_China

8. Frank Dikötter, *The Tragedy of Liberation: A History of the Chinese Revolution 1945–1957*, Kindle edn, London: Bloomsbury, 2013, loc. 3222–4.

9. See John Lossing Buck, *Food and Agriculture in Communist China*, New York: Praeger for the Hoover Institution on War, Revolution, and Peace, Stanford University, 1966.

10. John K. Fairbank, *China Perceived*, New York: Knopf, 1974.

11. Dwight H. Perkins, *Agricultural Development in China 1368–1969*, Chicago: Aldine, 1969.

12. Jasper Becker, *Hungry Ghosts: Mao's Secret Famine*, London: John Murray, 1996, pp. 108–10.

13. Edward Friedman, Paul G. Pickowicz and Mark Selden, *Chinese Village, Socialist State*, New Haven: Yale University Press, 1991.

14. Pan Fusheng speech, 'Socialist High Tide', as reported by *Henan Daily*, 23 September 1957.

15. 'Thirty Years in the Countryside: True Records of Economic and Social Development in the Fengyang Agricultural Region', Research Center for Rural Development.

16. Dikötter, *Tragedy of Liberation*, p. 237.

17. Friedman, Pickowicz and Selden, *Chinese Village, Socialist State*, p. 217. *People's Daily*, 13 October 1958.

18. 'Thirty Years in the Countryside'.

19. Mao's speech at a meeting of the Party Central Committee in Chengdu on 22 March 1958. Mao Zedong, *Collected Works*, vol. 7, Springfield, VA: National Technical Information Service, 1978, p. 371.

20. Frankenstein and Gill, 'Current and Future Challenges'.

15. CHINA'S GREAT FAMINE AND THE SOCIALIST CALCULATION PROBLEM

1. See Ding Shu's book *Ren Huo*, Hong Kong: Nineties Magazine, 1993.

2. Quoted in Roderick Mcfarquhar, *The Origins of the Cultural Revolution*, Oxford: Oxford University Press, 1983.

3. Wang Lixin, *Agricultural Reforms of Anhui: A True Record*, Beijing: Unity Publishing House, 1983.

4. 'Thirty Years in the Countryside'.

5. Author interview with retired Anhui official.

6. 'Thirty Years in the Countryside'.

7. Ibid.

8. Ding Shu, *Ren Huo*.

9. Hu wrote a report, 'My Witness: Traveling through the Countryside [of Hunan Province] in Twenty-Five Days, Covering 1,800 Kilometers', 1 October 1961, but though he was shocked by what he saw, he did not tell Mao the truth, according to an internal speech that circulated twenty years later.

10. 'The Red Flag Canal', Ministry of Water Resources, People's Republic of China, 11 January 2022, http://www.mwr.gov.cn/english/MagnificentAchievements/202201/t20220112_1559412.html

11. 'Thirty Years in the Countryside'.

12. Jung Chang and Jon Halliday, *Mao: The Unknown Story*, New York: Knopf, 2005, p. 398.

13. Frankenstein and Gill, 'Current and Future Challenges', p. 403.

14. 'China's GDP Is "Man-Made", Unreliable: Top Leader', Reuters, 6 December 2010.

16. THE EAST GERMAN ECONOMIC MIRACLE THAT NEVER WAS

1. 'Allied Plans for German Industry after World War II', Wikipedia, 25 May 2022, https://en.wikipedia.org/wiki/Allied_plans_for_German_industry_after_World_War_II
2. Daniel Yergin and Joseph Stanislaw, *Commanding Heights: The Battle between Government and the Marketplace That Is Remaking the Modern World*, New York: Simon & Schuster, 1999.
3. Hülsmann, *Last Knight*, p. 877.
4. *CIA World Factbook*, 1986. The 1980 *World Factbook* put the East German per capita GNP at $8,082 and West Germany's at a mere $3,530.
5. *CIA World Factbook*, 1980.

17. FAKE STATISTICS LED TO DÉTENTE

1. Timothy Garton Ash, *In Europe's Name: Germany and the Divided Continent*, New York: Vintage, 1994, pp. 65–6.
2. Arbel and Edelist, *Western Intelligence and the Collapse of the Soviet Union*, loc. 2886–94, 2873–83.
3. Ibid., 2810–20, 2772–84.
4. Ibid., loc. 3008–15.
5. Ibid., loc. 2907–11.
6. M. E. Sarotte, *Dealing with the Devil: East Germany, Detente, and Ostpolitik 1969–1973*, Chapel Hill, NC: University of North Carolina Press, 2001, pp. 148–53.
7. Ash, *In Europe's Name*, p. 144.
8. Ibid., p. 146.
9. Heiner Timmermann, ed., *Die DDR zwischen Mauerbau und Mauerfall*, Münster: LIT Verlag, 2012, pp. 101–4.
10. Ash, *In Europe's Name*.
11. Vienna Institute for Comparative Economic Studies, *Comecon Data 1990*, London: MacMillan, 1991.
12. Gaidar. *Cost of Grain*, p. 126.
13. Ibid., p. 84.
14. Ibid., p. 75.
15. Ibid., pp. 95–103.
16. Michael Myer, *The Year That Changed the World: The Untold Story of the Fall of the Berlin Wall*, New York: Simon & Schuster, 2009.

18. HOW MISES' IDEAS CHANGED EASTERN EUROPE AND RUSSIA

1. Anatoly Chernyaev, *My Six Years with Gorbachev*, University Park, PA: Pennsylvania State University Press, 2000.
2. Leszek Balcerowicz, *Socialism, Capitalism, Transformation*, Budapest: Central University Press, 1995.
3. Anders Åslund, *The Great Rebirth: Lessons from the Victory of Capitalism over Communism*, Kindle edn, Washington, DC: Peterson Institute for International Economics, 2014, loc. 652.
4. Ibid., loc. 969.
5. Václav Klaus, 'Conclusion: The Hayek Difference', in *F. A. Hayek and the Modern Economy: Economic Organization and Activity*, ed. Sandra Peart and David Levy, Houndmills, Basingstoke: Palgrave MacMillan, 2013, p. 230.
6. Åslund, *Great Rebirth*.
7. Ibid., p. 69.
8. Ibid., loc. 2168.
9. 'SPIEGEL Interview with Anatoly Chubais: "40 Million Russians Are Convinced I'm a Scoundrel"', *Der Spiegel*, 25 September 2007, https://www.spiegel.de/international/business/spiegel-interview-with-anatoly-chubais-40-million-russians-are-convinced-i-m-a-scoundrel-a-507834.html
10. Åslund, *Great Rebirth*, loc. 2140.
11. 'SPIEGEL Interview with Anatoly Chubais'. https://www.spiegel.de/international/business/spiegel-interview-with-anatoly-chubais-40-million-russians-are-convinced-i-m-a-scoundrel-a-507834.html
12. Roy Aleksandrovich Medvedev, *Post-Soviet Russia: A Journey through the Yeltsin Era*, New York: Columbia University Press, 2000, pp. 92–3.
13. 'SPIEGEL Interview with Anatoly Chubais'.
14. Anders Åslund, *Russia's Capitalist Revolution: Why Market Reform Succeeded and Democracy Failed*, Washington, DC: Peterson Institute for International Economics, 2007, pp. 160–2.
15. 'GDP Per Capita (Current US$): Poland, Ukraine, Vietnam', World Bank, https://data.worldbank.org/indicator/NY.GDP.PCAP.CD?locations=PL-UA-VN
16. Central Government Debt, Total (% of GDP): China', World Bank, https://data.worldbank.org/indicator/GC.DOD.TOTL.GD.ZS?locations=CN
17. 'China's Special Economic Zones: Experience Gained', World Bank, n.d., https://www.worldbank.org/content/dam/Worldbank/

Event/Africa/Investing%20in%20Africa%20Forum/2015/ investing-in-africa-forum-chinas-special-economic-zone.pdf

18. Chinese inflation data is unreliable given the nature of the economy, with many products still rationed and considerable regional variations, but 30 per cent inflation is probably too low a figure.

19. Zhao's meeting with Friedman is recounted in an appendix to Friedman's autobiography, *Two Lucky People: Memoirs*, Chicago: University of Chicago Press, 1998, pp. 607–16.

20. Like all Chinese unemployment statistics, the 70 million figure is hard to verify. Many kept their jobs even though their enterprises had ceased all activity. State-owned enterprises probably shed half their workforce—some say 30 million, others 50 million, but I think the larger figure is more likely.

21. China tried voucher privatization in Shenyang in the late 1980s and again in the 1990s in Jiangsu.

22. Daniel Altman, 'Abram Bergson, 89, Theorist Who Studied Soviet Economy', *New York Times*, 25 April 2003.

23. Ibid.

24. Paul A. Samuelson, 'Abram Bergson, Economist, April 21, 1914–April 23, 2003', *Economic Journal*, 115(501) (February 2005), pp. F130–F133.

25. Robert Heilbroner, 'After Communism', *New Yorker*, 16 September 1990, p. 90.

26. 'CIA's Analysis of the Soviet Union, 1947–1991', CIA, n.d., https:// www.cia.gov/static/c0fa3ca632f62a88b79e8ebc038ec36c/CIAs-Analysis-Soviet-Union.pdf

27. Ludwig von Mises, *Human Action: A Treatise on Economics*, New Haven: Yale University Press, 1949, p. 879.

28. Interview with Dina Birman and Birman's widow, Albina Birman, December 2015.

19. CHINA AND THE ROAD LESS TRAVELLED

1. David Shambaugh explores this in detail in *China's Communist Party: Atrophy and Adaptation*, Washington, DC: Woodrow Wilson Center Press, 2008.

2. 'Chinese Leaders Repeat Warning on Farm Payments', UPI, 19 March 1993, https://www.upi.com/Archives/1993/03/19/Chinese-leaders-repeat-warning-on-farm-payments/2444732517200

3. Official website of Beijing, http://english.beijing.gov.cn

4. 'Residents in Beijing "Support Relocation"', *Times of Malta*, 15 August 2007, https://timesofmalta.com/articles/view/residents-in-beijing-support-relocation.7886; 'Paying the Price: Worker Unrest in Northeast China', Human Rights Watch, 22 December 2008, https://www.hrw.org/report/2008/12/22/paying-price

5. Edward S. Steinfeld, *Forging Reform in China: The Fate of State-Owned Industry*, Cambridge: Cambridge University Press, 1998, p. 114.

6. John King Fairbank and Merle Goldman, *China: A New History*, 2nd enlarged edn, Cambridge, MA: Harvard University Press, 1998, p. 416.

7. William James Hurst, *The Chinese Worker after Socialism*, Cambridge: Cambridge University Press, 2009, p. 53.

8. 'Migration in China', Wikipedia, last edited 5 July 2022, https://en.wikipedia.org/wiki/Migration_in_China; 'Polish Diaspora', Wikipedia, last edited 6 July 2022, https://en.wikipedia.org/wiki/Polish_diaspora#:~:text=About%202%20million%20primarily%20young,as%20part%20of%20Catholic%20missions

9. Elise Donovan, 'Knowing on Which Side the BVI's Bread Is Buttered: A Case for Economic Diplomacy', British Virgin Islands, 23 June 2018, https://bvi.gov.vg/media-centre/knowing-which-side-bvi-s-bread-buttered

10. 'China: Government Exceeds Target of 11 Million New Jobs in 2019 Despite Slower Economic Growth', Staffing Industry Analysts, 10 December 2019, https://www2.staffingindustry.com/row/Editorial/Daily-News/China-Government-exceeds-target-of-11-million-new-jobs-in-2019-despite-slower-economic-growth-China.org.cn-52171

11. David Ren, 'Beijing to End Price Controls on Most Products', *South China Morning Post*, 8 May 2015.

12. 'Price Reform in China', World Bank Report no. 10414.CHA, 28 May 1992, Office of the Director China and Mongolia Department East Asia and Pacific Regional Office, https://documents.worldbank.org/en/publication/documents-reports/documentdetail/582991468015853321/price-reform-in-chinareport%20no.%2010414.cha

13. 'Anbang', Wikipedia, last edited 18 December 2021, https://en.wikipedia.org/wiki/Anbang

14. Yap Chuin-Wei, 'State Support Helped Fuel Huawei's Global Rise', *Wall Street Journal*, 24 December 2019, https://www.wsj.com/articles/state-support-helped-fuel-huaweis-global-rise-11577280736

15. Ben Heubl, 'Night Light Images Paint Accurate Picture of China GDP', Nikkei Asian Review, 24 March 2018, https://asia.nikkei.

com/Spotlight/Datawatch/Night-light-images-paint-accurate-picture-of-China-GDP

20. HOW NORTH KOREA TRIED TO DEFY THE MARKET

1. 'Kim Il Sung "Plant Beans Instead of Potatoes"', Daily NK, 19 November 2007, https://www.dailynk.com/english/kim-il-sung-plant-beans-instead-o

2. Thomas B. Cochran and Matthew G. McKinzie, 'Insights into the DPRK Military Threat Gained from Commercial Satellite Imagery', paper presented at the fifty-fourth Pugwash Conference on Science and World Affairs, Seoul, Republic of Korea, 4–9 October 2004, https://nuke.fas.org/cochran/nuc_04100401a_237.pdf

3. 'Economy of North Korea', Wikipedia, last edited 25 May 2022, https://en.wikipedia.org/wiki/Economy_of_North_Korea

4. 'The 1992 Currency Reform "Trick"', Daily NK, 12 February 2009, https://www.dailynk.com/english/the-1992-currency-reform-trick

5. Shin Hyon-Hee, 'Failed 2002 Reform Sowed Seeds of Change in N.K.', Korea Herald, 4 July 2012, http://www.koreaherald.com/view.php?ud=20120704001383; 'Stitch by Stitch to a Different World', Economist, 25 July 2002, https://www.economist.com/special-report/2002/07/25/stitch-by-stitch-to-a-different-world

6. 'North Korean Won', Wikipedia, last edited 13 May 2022, https://en.wikipedia.org/wiki/North_Korean_won

7. Doug Struck, 'A Taste of Capitalism in N. Korea', Washington Post, 13 September 2022.

8. Marcus Noland, Sherman Robinson and Tao Wang, 'Famine in North Korea: Causes and Cures', Economic Development and Cultural Change 49(4) (July 2001), pp. 741–67.

9. Lee Sang Yong, 'North Korean Authorities Using Market Prices for Policy', North Korean Economy Watch, 16 November 2016, http://www.nkeconwatch.com/2015/11/16/north-korean-authorities-using-market-prices-for-policy

10. 'DPRK Revalues Currency', North Korea Economy Watch, https://www.nkeconwatch.com/2009/12/04/dprk-renominates-currency

11. 'S. Korea Investigates Media Reports of N. Korean Execution over Currency Reform', VOA News, 17 March 2010, https://www.voanews.com/a/s-korea-investigates-media-reports-of-n-korean-execution-over-currency-reform-88422902/165486.html

12. Andrei Lankov, 'N Korea and the Myth of Starvation', Al Jazeera, 27 March 2014, https://www.aljazeera.com/opinions/2014/3/27/n-korea-and-the-myth-of-starvation

AFTERWORD
1. 'Latin America Hunger Facts', World Hunger, Hunger Notes, n.d., https://www.worldhunger.org/lac-hunger-and-nutrition-facts

BIBLIOGRAPHY

Aldred, John and A. Mamaux. *The Cold War c.1945–1991*. Oxford AQA History for A-Level. Oxford: Oxford University Press, 2015.

Andrew, Christopher and Vasili Mitrokhin. *The Sword and the Shield: The Mitrokhin Archive and the Secret History of the KGB*. New York: Basic Books, 1999.

Arbel, David and Ran Edelist. *Western Intelligence and the Collapse of the Soviet Union, 1980–1990: Ten Years That Did Not Shake the World*. Kindle edn. London: Taylor & Francis, 2004.

Ash, Timothy Garton. *In Europe's Name: Germany and the Divided Continent*. New York: Vintage, 1994.

Åslund, Anders. *The Great Rebirth: Lessons from the Victory of Capitalism over Communism*. Kindle edn. Washington, DC: Peterson Institute for International Economics, 2014.

—— *Russia's Capitalist Revolution: Why Market Reform Succeeded and Democracy Failed*. Washington, DC: Peterson Institute for International Economics, 2007.

Bach, George L. *Economics: An Introduction to Analysis and Policy*. 1st edn. Englewood Cliffs, NJ: Prentice-Hall, 1968.

Becker, Abraham S. *Sitting on Bayonets? The Soviet Defense Burden and Moscow's Economic Dilemma*. Santa Monica: RAND, 1983.

Bergson, Abram. 'Reliability and Usability of Soviet Statistics: A Summary Appraisal'. *American Statistician* 7(5) (1953), pp. 13–16.

—— *Socialist Economics*. Edited by Howard Ellis. Survey of Contemporary Economics. Philadelphia, PA: Blakiston Company for the American Economic Association, 1948.

Bergson, Abram and Simon Kuznets. *Economic Trends in the Soviet Union*. Cambridge, MA: Harvard University Press, 1963.

Berliner, Joseph S. *Factory and Manager in the USSR*. Cambridge, MA: Harvard University Press, 1957.

Birman, Igor Yakovlevich. 'The Imbalance of the Soviet Economy'. *Soviet Studies* 40(2) (1988), pp. 210–21.

—— 'Limits of Economic Measurements'. *Slavic Review* 39(4) (1980), pp. 603–7.

—— *Personal Consumption in the USSR and USA*. New York: St. Martin's Press, 1989.

—— *Secret Incomes of the Soviet State Budget*. The Hague: Martinus Nijhoff, 1981.

—— 'The Soviet Economy: Alternative Views'. *Russia* 12 (1986), pp. 69–71.

—— 'The Way to Slow the Arms Race'. *Washington Post*, 27 October 1980, p. A15.

Böhm-Bawerk, Eugen von. *Karl Marx and the Close of His System*. N.p.: n.p., 1896.

—— *Positive Theory of Capital*. Innsbruck: Verlag der Wagner'schen Universitäts-Buchhandlung, 1889.

Brzezinski, Zbigniew. *The Soviet Bloc: Unity and Conflict*. Cambridge, MA: Harvard University Press, 1967.

Bukharin, Nikolai Ivanovich. *Economic Theory of the Leisure Class*. New York: Monthly Review Press, 1972 [1917].

—— *The Economics of the Transition Period*. New York: Bergman, 1971.

—— *Historical Materialism*. New York: International Publishers, 1915.

—— *Imperialism and World Economy*. London: Martin Lawrence, 1915.

—— *Programme of the World Revolution*. Glasgow: Socialist Labour Press, 1920.

—— *Put'k sotsializmu v Rossii*. 1st edn. New York: Omicron Books, 1967.

Bukharin, Nikolai Ivanovich and Evgenii Preobrazhensky. *The ABC of Communism*. Ann Arbor: University of Michigan Press, 1966.

Cahn, Anne Hessing. *Killing Détente: The Right Attacks the CIA*. University Park, PA: Pennsylvania State University Press, 1998.

Caute, David. *The Fellow-Travellers: Intellectual Friends of Communism*. New Haven: Yale University Press, 1988.

Chernyaev, Anatoly C. *My Six Years with Gorbachev*. University Park, PA: Pennsylvania State University Press, 2000.

Cohen, Stephen F. *Bukharin and the Bolshevik Revolution: A Political Biography, 1888–1938*. Oxford: Oxford University Press, 1980.

The Commanding Heights. PBS Documentary. Broadcast 11 December 2002.

Corin, Chris and Terry Fiehn. *Tsarist and Communist Russia 1855–1964*. AQA A-Level History. Kindle edn. Hodder Education, 2015.

Courtois, Stéphane, Nicolas Werth, Jean-Louis Panné, Andrzej Paczkowski, Karel Bartošek and Jean-Louis Margolin. *The Black Book of Communism*. Edited by Mark Kramer. Cambridge, MA: Harvard University Press, 1999.

Damon, Fred. '*Barter, Exchange and Value: An Anthropological Approach*. Caroline Humphrey and Stephen Hugh-Jones'. *American Anthropologist* 96(1) (1994), pp. 199–200.

Davies, R. W. 'Carr's Changing Views of the Soviet Union'. In *E. H. Carr: A Critical Appraisal*, edited by Michael Cox, pp. 91–108. London: Palgrave, 2000.

Dikötter, Frank. *The Tragedy of Liberation: A History of the Chinese Revolution 1945–1957*. Kindle edn. London: Bloomsbury, 2013.

Dobbs, Michael. *Down with Big Brother: The Fall of the Soviet Empire*. New York: Alfred A. Knopf, 1997.

Duranty, Walter. *Russia Reported*. London: Victor Gollancz, 1934.

Engels, Friedrich. *The Collected Works of Friedrich Engels (Unexpurgated Edition)*. Kindle edn. N.p.: Halcyon Classics, 2009.

—— *The Origin of the Family, Private Property and the State*. Chicago: C. H. Kerr & Co., 1902.

—— *Principles of Communism*. Moscow: Progress Publishers, 1969.

Fairbank, John K. *China Perceived*. New York: Knopf, 1974.

Fergusson, Adam. *When Money Dies: The Nightmare of the Weimar Hyper-Inflation*. London: Old Street Publishing, 2010.

Firth, Noel E. and James H. Noren. *Soviet Defense Spending: A History of CIA Estimates 1950–1990*. College Station, TX: Texas A&M University Press, 1998.

Fitzpatrick, Sheila. *Everyday Stalinism: Ordinary Life in Extraordinary Times; Soviet Russia in the 1930s*. Oxford: Oxford University Press, 1999.

Friedman, Milton and Rose D. Friedman. *Two Lucky People: Memoirs*. Chicago: University of Chicago Press, 1998.

Gaidar, Yegor. *The Collapse of an Empire: Lessons for Modern Russia*. Washington, DC: Brookings Institution Press, 2007.

Galbraith, J. K. *A China Passage*. London: André Deutsch, 1973.

Gregory, Paul. *The Political Economy of Stalinism*. Cambridge: Cambridge University Press, 2004.

—— *Politics, Murder, and Love in Stalin's Kremlin: The Story of Nikolai Bukharin and Anna Larina*. Stanford: Hoover Institution Press, 2010.

Gregory, Paul R. and V. V. Lazarev. *The Economics of Forced Labour: The Soviet Gulag*. Stanford: Hoover Institution Press, 2003.

Hanhimäki, Jussi M. *The Rise and Fall of Détente*. Issues in the History of American Foreign Relations. Kindle edn. Dulles, VA: Potomac Books, 2012.

Hayek, Friedrich von. *Collectivist Economic Planning*. London: Routledge, 1935.

—— *The Road to Serfdom*. Chicago: University of Chicago Press, 1944.

Heilbronner, Robert. *The Worldly Philosophers: The Lives, Times and Ideas of the Great Economic Thinkers*. London: Penguin, 2000.

Hollander, Paul. *The End of Commitment: Intellectuals, Revolutionaries, and Political Morality in the Twentieth Century*. Chicago: Ivan R. Dee, 2006.

—— *Political Pilgrims: Travels of Western Intellectuals to the Soviet Union, China and Cuba, 1928–1978*. New York: Oxford University Press, 1981.

Hülsmann, Jörg Guido. *Mises: The Last Knight of Liberalism*. Auburn, AL: Ludwig von Mises Institute, 2007.

Humphrey, Caroline and Stephen Hugh-Jones. *Barter, Exchange, and Value*. Cambridge: Cambridge University Press, 1992.

Jardini, David R. *Thinking Through the Cold War: RAND, National Security and Domestic Policy, 1945–1975*. Meadowlands, PA: Smashwords, 2013.

Jasny, Naum. *The Socialized Agriculture of the USSR; Soviet Industrialization 1928–1952*. Chicago: University of Chicago Press, 1961.

Kessler, Ronald. *Inside the CIA*. New York: Simon & Schuster, 1992.

Khlevnyuk, Oleg. 'The Economy of the OGPU, NKVD and MVD of the USSR, 1930–1953; The Scale, Structure and Trends of Development'. In *The Economics of Forced Labour: The Soviet Gulag*, edited by Paul R. Gregory and V. V. Lazarev, pp. 43–66. Stanford: Hoover Institution Press, 2003.

—— *The History of the GULAG; From Collectivization to the Great Terror*. Annals of Communism Series. New Haven: Yale University Press, 2004.

Khrushchev, Nikita Sergeevich. *Khrushchev Remembers: The Last Testament*. Translated and edited by Strobe Talbott. London: André Deutsch, 1974.

Kim, Byung-Yeon. 'Causes of Repressed Inflation in the Soviet Consumer Market, 1965–1989: Retail Price Subsidies, the Siphoning Effect, and the Budget Deficit'. *Economic History Review* 55(1) (2002), pp. 105–27.

Klaus, Václav. 'Hayek, the End of Communism, and Me'. CATO Institute Policy Report, September–October 2013.

Knight, Amy. *Beria: Stalin's First Lieutenant*. Princeton: Princeton University Press, 1995.

Kornai, János. *Economics of Shortage*. Amsterdam: North-Holland Pub. Co., 1980.

Kuznicki, Jason. *The Socialist Calculation Debate*. Washington, DC: Cato Institute Press. Washington, 2014.

Lange, Oscar. 'On the Economic Theory of Socialism, Part One'. *Review of Economic Studies* 4(1) (1936), pp. 53–71.

—— 'On the Economic Theory of Socialism, Part Two'. *Review of Economic Studies* 4(2) (1937), pp. 123–42.

Larina, Anna. *This I Cannot Forget: The Memoirs of Nikolai Bukharin's Widow*. New York: W. W. Norton, 1994.

Lavoie, Don. 'A Critique of the Standard Account of the Socialist Calculation Debate'. *Journal of Libertarian Studies* 5(1) (1981), pp. 41–87.

Lawton, Lancelot. *An Economic History of Soviet Russia: Volume 1*. London: Macmillan, 1932.

Lenin, Vladimir Ilyich. *The State and Revolution*. London: Penguin Books. London, 1992 [1917].

Levy, David M. and Sandra J. Peart. 'Soviet Growth & American Textbooks'. *Journal of Economic Behavior and Organization* 76 (2011), pp. 110–25.

Lippe, Peter von der. 'The Political Role of Official Statistics in the Former GDR (East Germany)'. *Historical Social Research* 24(4) (1999), pp. 3–28.

MacKenzie, D. W. 'Were the Socialists Really Wrong about Calculation?' https://citeseerx.ist.psu.edu/viewdoc/download?doi=10.1.1.192.6909&rep=rep1&type=pdf. Accessed 14 March 2022.

Marx, Karl. *Critique of the Gotha Programme*. Moscow: Progress Publishers, 1971.

—— *Das Kapital*. Moscow: Progress Publishers, 1887 [1867].

Marx, Karl and Friedrich Engels. *Communist Manifesto*. Harmondsworth: Penguin, 1967.

—— *The German Ideology*. London: Lawrence & Wishart, 1965.

McConnell, Campbell. *Economics: Principles, Problems and Policies*. New York: McGraw-Hill, 1996.

McMeekin, Sean. *History's Greatest Heist: The Looting of Russia by the Bolsheviks*. New Haven: Yale University Press, 2009.

Menger, Carl. *On the Origins of Money*. Auburn, AL: Ludwig von Mises Institute, 2009.

—— *Principles of Economics*. Auburn, AL: Ludwig von Mises Institute, 2004.

Mises, Ludwig von. *The Anti-Capitalistic Mentality*. Auburn, AL: Ludwig von Mises Institute, 2008.

—— *Human Action: A Treatise on Economics*. New Haven: Yale University Press, 1949.

—— *Socialism: An Economic and Sociological Analysis*. New Haven: Yale University Press, 1951.

—— *The Theory of Money and Credit*. New Haven: Yale University Press, 1953.

—— 'Die Wirtschaftsrechnung im sozialistischen Gemeinwesen' [Economic calculation in the socialist commonwealth]. *Archiv fuer Socialwissenschaften* (1920).

Mises, Ludwig von, with Margit von Mises. *Notes & Recollections*. Spring Mills, PA: Libertarian Press, 1976,

Morgan, Lewis Henry. *Ancient Society*. New York: Henry Holt & Co., 1877.

―――― *Houses and House Life of the American Aborigines: Contributions to North American Ethnology, Volume IV*. Washington, DC: United States Geological Survey, 1881.

Moynihan, Daniel Patrick. *Secrecy: The American Experience*. New Haven: Yale University Press, 1998.

Muller, Jerzy, Z. *The Mind and the Market: Capitalism, and Western Thought*. New York: Anchor Books, 2002.

Nasar, Sylvia. *Grand Pursuit: The Story of Economic Genius*. London: Fourth Estate, 2011.

Peebles, Gavin. *Money in the People's Republic of China*. Sydney: Allen & Unwin, 1991.

―――― *A Short History of Socialist Money*. Sydney: Allen & Unwin, 1991.

Perkins, Dwight H. *Agricultural Development in China 1368–1969*. Chicago: Aldine, 1969.

Plokhy, Serhii. *The Last Empire*. Kindle edn. New York: Oneworld Publications, 2014.

Radford, R. A. 'The Economic Organisation of a P.O.W. Camp'. *Economica* 12(48) (November 1945), pp. 189–201.

Robbins, Lionel. *The Great Depression*. London: MacMillan & Co., 1934.

Rosefielde, Steven, ed. *Economic Welfare and the Economics of Soviet Socialism: Essays in Honor of Abram Bergson*. Cambridge: Cambridge University Press, 1981.

―――― 'Tea Leaves and Productivity: Bergsonian Norms for Gauging the Soviet Future'. Paper prepared for Bergsonian Memorial Conference, Harvard, 2004.

―――― 'Thirty years in the Countryside: True Records of Economic and Social Development in the Fengyang Agricultural Region'. Research Centre for Rural Development, China, 1989.

Samuelson, Paul. *Abram Bergson: A Biographical Memoir*. Washington, DC: National Academies Press, 2004.

―――― *Economics: An Introductory Analysis*. New York: McGraw-Hill, New York, 1964.

Sahlins, Marshall. *Stone Age Economics*. Chicago: Aldine-Atherton, 1974.

Sanchez-Sibony, Oscar. 'Red Globalization: The Political Economy of Soviet Foreign Relations in the 1950s and 60s'. PhD diss., University of Chicago, 2009.

Sarotte, Mary E. *Dealing with the Devil: East Germany, Détente and Ostpolitik 1969–1973*. Chapel Hill, NC: University of North Carolina Press, 2001.

Schumpeter, Joseph A. *Capitalism, Socialism and Democracy*. New York: Harper, 1950.

Short, Philip. *Pol Pot:The History of a Nightmare*. London: John Murray, 2004.

Simmel, Georg. *Philosophie des Geldes* [The philosophy of money]. Leipzig: Duncker & Humblot, 1900.

Simmons, Michael. *The Unloved Country: A Portrait of East Germany Today*. London: Abacus, 1989.

Smith, Adam. *The Wealth of Nations*. London: Wordsworth, 2012 [1776].

Stern, Ludmila. *Western Intellectuals and the Soviet Union, 1920–40: From Red Square to the Left Bank*. London: Routledge, 2007.

Stone, Randall W. *Satellites and Commissars: Strategy and Conflict in the Politics of the Soviet-Bloc Trade*. Princeton Studies in International History and Politics. Princeton: Princeton University Press, 1996.

Trachtenberg, Marc. 'Assessing Soviet Economic Performance during the Cold War: A Failure of Intelligence?' Paper published by Department of Political Science, University of California at Los Angeles, 2014.

Trotsky, Leon. *The Revolution Betrayed*. Garden City, NY: Doubleday, Doran & Company, 1937.

Vance, Melanie. *My Revision Notes: AQA AS/A-Level History: The Cold War, c.1945–1991*. London: Hodder Education, 2017.

Walsh, Ben. *GCSE Modern World History*. London: Hodder Education, 2001.

Webb, Beatrice and Sidney Webb. *Soviet Communism: A New Civilisation*. London: Longmans, Green & Co., 1944.

Whitfield, Robert. *Oxford AQA History for A-Level:The Transformation of China 1936–1997*. Kindle edn. Oxford: Oxford University Press, 2015.

Wilhelm, John. 'The Failure of the American Sovietological Economics Profession'. *Europe-Asia Studies* 55(1) (2003), pp. 59–74.

Yueh Sheng. 'SunYat-sen University in Moscow and the Chinese Revolution: A Personal Account'. International Studies, East Asian Series Research Publication 7, Center for East Asian Studies, University of Kansas, 1971.

INDEX

Note: Page numbers followed by '*n*' refer to notes.